**Studia Fennica**
Ethnologica 8

The Finnish Literature Society was founded in 1831 and has from the very beginning engaged in publishing. It nowadays publishes literature in the fields of ethnology and folkloristics, linguistics, literary research and cultural history.

The first volume of Studia Fennica series appeared in 1933.

Since 1992 the series has been divided into three thematic subseries: Ethnologica, Folkloristica and Linguistica. Two additional subseries were formed in 2002, Historica and Litteraria.

In additional to its publishing activities the Finnish Literature Society maintains a folklore archive, a literature archive and a library.

# Memories of My Town

## The Identities of Town Dwellers and Their Places in Three Finnish Towns

Edited by
Anna-Maria Åström, Pirjo Korkiakangas & Pia Olsson

Finnish Literature Society • Helsinki

ISBN 951-746-433-9
ISSN 1235-1954

www.finlit.fi

Tammer-Paino Oy
Tampere 2004

# Contents

Discourses of Space – Planning Practices

Everyday Knowledge and Remembrances
– The Town Dwellers' Views

# Introduction

The articles in this book are part of the results of a research project financed by the Finnish Academy and entitled "Town dwellers and their places". The title refers to the relation between urban ways of life and the urban environment, and this is discussed from different viewpoints. It should be pointed out that the urban environment is not seen merely as the geographical location of, or background for, human activities and daily life, but as a complex structure consisting of time-stratified meaningful experiences. The urban environment may be seen as a conglomeration of places whose meaning is derived from human experience and individual interpretations. As a concept 'urban environment' is unambiguously defined, and in fact, the words seem to contradict each another. The paradox is that 'urban' is used for the built environment, whereas 'environment', in Finland, is often understood to mean the natural environment; urban equivalents could then be parks, esplanades, marketplaces.

Thus, in the relations of townspeople to places, and in their experiences, both the built environment and the elements of nature play a role. Contextually, the urban environment may also be thought to refer to the full network of social and economic relations, the local community and its material items, which make up life in towns and which provide it with meaning. But urban culture is in itself the focus of our investigations, through the experiences of the town dwellers.

As people in urban milieus relate themselves to the environment, this takes place on many levels, where especially the time level becomes problematic. Time is of course layered also in the environments themselves for instance as buildings from different times. The built environment can in itself be looked upon as a kind of collective history. Thus, the environments are carriers or witnesses of times past. But environments can only reflect this history through intermediation. The buildings speak only to those who can recognize what they tell and it is only the individuals, the town dwellers that experience urban time itself, the time they live in but through their memory also times passed. In this past some elements take symbolically dense expressions. Through reliving or narrating their experiences, these symbolically important factors in the narrations will be outlined for investigations. This is the kernel of this book. Our intention is to explore how the

7

memories of town dwellers keep the histories of their town alive and how the memories function as cornerstones for the individual orientations in urban environments. Personally experienced time is the missing point in many town planning strategies (Lehtonen 1997, 14–17). Contrary to the focusing on the immediate present our intention is to explore urban identity processes that take the "wanderers in times" to the past of their towns for the sake of their present orientations. The flaneurs of big cities have been considered to be explorers of change and beholder of historical memory (Frisby in Tester 1994, 95); our contributions concerning also smaller towns in Finland will show that this is line with what urban dwellers are also in environments of smaller size with nature luring behind the corner.

Experiencing time through the memories give stability to the conception of urban space. The great memories of pioneer times in areas of suburbia might thus be due to the fact that there is no history before the new inhabitants shaping of it. In these areas "history started" with the inhabitants. On the contrary more central urban areas might have their social practices that the newcomer or tourist experiences as a stabilizing factor in itself. It is however seldom reckoned that such practices have a history of their own that have undergone considerable changes not the least in the second half of the 20th century.

Thus, the urgent need to recapitulate former stages becomes understandable. Those who have experienced former urban stages cannot ignore them; on the contrary they are part of their individual identity and unless the memories get no affirmation, the feeling of loss becomes even more inevitable and immediate. When radical changes then take place in such environments the constructions of new buildings themselves can be seen as a way of ignoring the identity of the place as felt by those who know its history. Hence the often very emotional defense of certain threatened areas by new constructions can be more understandable.

## Urban places and roots

Urban culture, the urban way of life, exists in different milieus. The different authors of this book illustrate this fact through their choice of three different towns for the study: Helsinki, the capital, Jyväskylä, a medium-sized town in central Finland, and finally Vyborg, a town in ceded Karelia. While these towns are different cultural environments, their histories also present different mosaics that the townspeople have to relate to. The history of each town runs parallel with the history of its townspeople. Here, then, lies the tension that we want to analyse. How have the townspeople experienced the changes in their towns, what are their reactions to the disappearance and changing character of places? What does the memory of these places mean when they are thought of today?

The articles all set out from a dialectical relation between the towns and their inhabitants, so that the towns, and living in them, are seen to affect the life courses of the residents, but also in such a manner that their ideas and memories of the towns are, in the present, projected back on to the remembered towns and the various places.

In ethnological research, the spatial identity of the individual, and his or her different ways of mastering space, are considered to be focal. The relations between townspeople are also seen as reflecting the development of urban culture. For example, different parts of a town and different places obtain a cultural character of their own. The present articles look for the spatial patterns of the townspeople, in memory and today, and for the differing conceptions of urban space that are articulated in interviews and in the townspeople's own narratives of their town.

Another of the main themes of this book is that the inherently heterogeneous social and spatial urban patterns are transposed into 'images' of the towns, of the districts and places, to which people have different attitudes. The fact that these images exist, and that it is possible to place oneself into them, gives both stability and freedom to the experience of urban space. It can also be maintained that the social differences which always exist in towns are toned down by means of common everyday techniques, so that daily life becomes free from friction. Such mechanisms do in fact come out in the narratives and remembrances on which the articles are based.

At the same time, it is striking how the places described, and towards which the narrators have deep feelings, in themselves offer experiences which require no intermediaries or catalysts. This, too, has to do with the memories which are in continual existence in people's relations to space. The informants themselves make comparisons between lost milieus and present ones, as well as giving their opinions on future or planned milieus.

The issues comprise both entire milieus and single elements. The concept of 'loss' gains importance through the nostalgia which sometimes accompanies the memories of the townspeople. For their local identities, some places hold more symbolic value than others, and such cases are also analysed in the texts.

Since the time span covered in the book is several decades, the history and the cultural history of each town provides a background which also permeates the reports. The urban history which gives the book its structure rests on the idea that during the 20th century, the towns have run through a series of development where different types follow one another: beginning with a wooden, grid plan or a stone built town in square blocks or traditional town, going through the stage of a functional town, that took place in Finland especially in the 1960's and 1970's, and ending up in a post-modern town, where functions have again been dispersed. At the post-modern stage, a new meaning is attached to urban culture and historical surface. Our historical perspective has been achieved as we present Vyborg as a long-lost grid plan town, the central parts of Helsinki as a similarly constructed town in development, and also coloured by post-modern features and additionally through a newly built district, whereas Jyväskylä is both a wooden town, a modern town, and the finishing point of the industrial era, but with various cultural streaks which make it a receptacle of numerous memories.

Some of the articles focus on the memories of the townspeople and descriptions of these stages. In his spatial theory Henri Lefebvre talks about *the level of lived space*, which refers to the level of social practices as a space governed by the senses, including imagination, symbols and utopias (Lefebvre 1991). He emphasizes the significance of images by observing that building take place on the basis of papers and plans, but urban activity is modified according to visual stimulation. Thus the force of imagination must be taken into account also concerning memories that town dwellers hold of their towns.

The concept 'townspeople' has subtle nuances. Insofar as our ethnological material consists of different voices, we want to stress the polyphonic character of the texts. Here, the 'common' or 'ordinary' townsman's voice is heard; but the persons speaking are always individuals with life histories of their own. Therefore, the tension between the *individual* and the *collective* becomes another pervading theme in the discussion of memories, values, and urban customs and norms, as expressed in the narratives. Also how the signification processes take place are then important and how they continue over a lifespan.

There are two ambivalent dichotomies which embrace the urban reality of today, and which constitute eternal poles in urban discourse, in town planning and in the consciousness of the townspeople. We are referring to the tension between *anonymity* and *sociability*, and to the tension between *change* and *constancy*, today perhaps in the shape of the prevailing *consumption ideology* and the *longing for roots*, sometimes in the form of the past, sometimes in the form of less complicated circumstances. Within this field of tensions, the townspeople adapt their patterns into a daily urban practice. We have also tried to locate these life patterns with their autobiographical depths, which means that certain places have been experiences in a long life span, that embraces also the changes that the places have undergone.

The voices on the past through the dwellers of different towns thus belong to a historical restoring and affirming process that lie parallel to but is not so often appreciated by official history as more than a certain flavor. As will be shown in the studies the existence of the memories nevertheless constitute the memories of the towns in a manner similar to reminiscences for individuals. An example of this is the nickname for Helsinki, Stadi that symbolizes the former traditional way of life in the capital. The notion of it can be found in all sorts of circumstances signalising that there was a life here before this hectic present, a life with its own peculiarities that also the newcomer might gain to know and is invited to explore. At the same time this name hold in it all aspects of time, the past, the present and even the future in a more subtle way than the official name Helsinki.

The memories and ideas from 'previous times' often underscore a multi-functionality of the towns and urban environments as well as and urban ready made fabric that the young generation socialised into. The kind of 'traditional urbanity' that comes out from our examples from pre-functionalist times is one that is nowadays also sought for, for instance when pondering of planning practices (Radović 1997). The outcome of all sorts of mixtures of old and new urban forms ultimately depend on if the economic and logistic systems support them or not. In our cases we want to move in different historical times as to show both the complexity of urban areas in the past and today and the importance of the notion of space as the key factor for producing a multi-functional urban culture. In all articles the appropriation of space is narrated as happened at a minimum of moving around over large distances. Thus time and memories are concentrated to certain culturally dense milieus.

## Remembrance and reminiscence

It is essential, in individual and collective memories, that the individual or individuals can appropriate the past and thus strengthen their individual or collective identities. In general, remembrances comprise small episodes or events, and in remembering them, the informant builds up a logical entity which may, for example, consist of his or her individual life story. These recollections are illustrated with the contents and experiencing of events, im-ages which are part of the informant's personal history, and which are vital parts of his or her personality and identity. When recalled into memory, the events are re-lived, and the reminiscence is accompanied by a strong sense that what is remembered is true and corresponds in detail with what really took place. In recalling things to memory, the informant attaches the events to a specific time and place, although the formulation of that time and place requires interactive association between numerous loose details. The sphere of life of the informant, and the resultant identification with a place, where both individual and collective images and memories characterise the place, ties these memories to a given time and place; the images and memories of the place are in fact also a localisation of the informant's self.

Memories tend to be individual and based on personal experience, that is, largely autobiographical. Nevertheless, autobiographical memories may be supplemented, or transformed, with features of collective memory: in remem-brances and reminiscences, the private and the collective meet and cross in relation to one another. The collective or social character of remembrances is based on the fact that as individuals, our community influences our memories: the community in which we live and act will determine the guidelines for what is worth remembering or what we are supposed to remember. In fact, our identification with a community and its events is so close that we may actually 'remember' things we have never personally experienced, and our experiences may be tinted by issues which, at the outset, had no connection at all with the actual experience.

The opposite of remembering is forgetting, and the identification and study of forgetfulness is connected with remembrances. Nostalgia, as a way of remembering, has its own dichotomy: it holds both remembering and forgetting. As a matter of fact, anything from the past may evoke nostalgic feelings, as long as it can be recalled as something positive or pleasant. What is remembered may not, at the time of experience, have been thought worth longing for, but nevertheless, it may, in the course of remembering, achieve a nostalgic tenor. This type of nostalgia often comes up in situations of change, especially if those changes have not fulfilled expectations. However, all memories do not contain a nostalgic element, but nostalgic memories are often accompanied by a feeling of something lost and by some degree of longing to have the past back. Nostalgia has, in fact, been compared with homesickness, a wish to return to a state which is felt to be safe and which can be mastered. Nostalgia is always accompanied by an emotional load, and the remembrances are expressly coloured by details which evoke a nostalgic feeling. Experiencing times gone without a nostalgic touch is thus rear. Nevertheless the remembrances together constitute a collective history of each town explored, that fills the gap between official history and individual narratives. Thus a new dimension to the history of each town will be given.

## The towns

The attraction of the capital, Helsinki, comes out in the continuous population increase. The only breaks in this trend come in the war years of the 20th century and in the periods of serious economic stagnation. In 1966, the

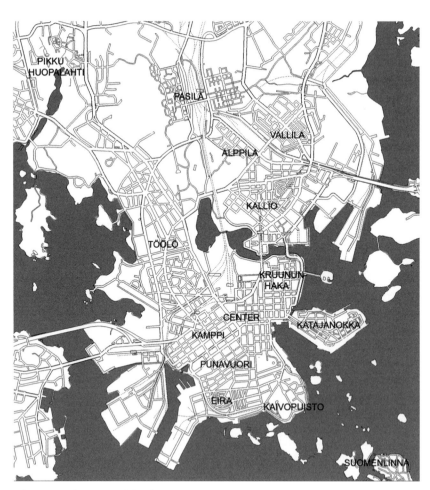

*The research area in Helsinki.*

population figure surpassed half a million for the first time, and in the period from 1946 to 1989, the overall population increase was about 44 %. Nevertheless, in the 1920's, 1960's and the 1980's, strong suburban growth and a population increase in adjacent regions also detracted from further growth in the central districts of the town. The polarisation between different districts, that is, the specialisation into districts for specific groups, continued after the Second World War, strengthening the symbolic significance of the different residential areas. There was almost no major change in the structure of livelihoods until the 1950's, and the majority of the working population, about 25%, then still worked in industry. Towards the end of the 1950's, the importance of industrial employment gave way, while service occupations began to proliferate, and new residential areas began to be built. The era of 1960's also meant a new opening to international influences. The fact that Helsinki forms the capital of Finland means that since the 19th century major national institutions and sites of cultural life has been situated here, a trend that is still continuing. Again, in the last decades of the 20th century, the new technology made its home in the town.

The youngest of the towns included in the project is Jyväskylä, which was founded in a nearly uninhabited area in 1837, primarily to serve commercial interests in central Finland. The atmosphere of the town has been deeply coloured by the fact that the first Finnish-language secondary school was set up there in 1858, and a similarly Finnish-language teacher training institute in 1863. The latter was converted into Jyväskylä University in the 1960's. In the early 20th century, industry began with wood refining and, later, with metal industry. The industrial development profited from the location and the good communication lines. In the 1970's, absolute industrial employment figures went down, and the structure of business and industry changed. In the early 1990's, nearly one-fourth of all employment was in production. During the last few years, the fastest increase in the town is in the number of

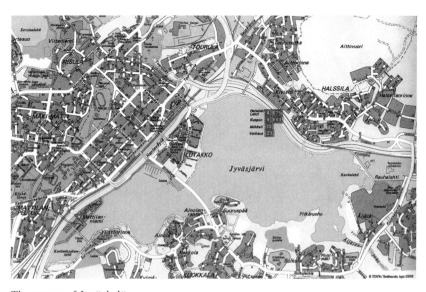

*The centre of Jyväskylä.*

13

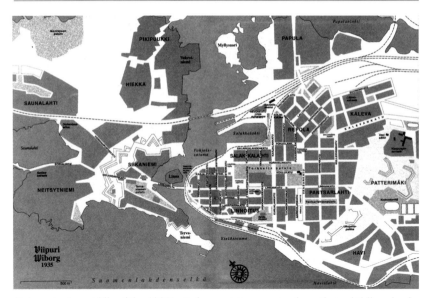

*Vyborg in the middle of the 1930's. Informants' memories from their childhood refer mainly to these streets and quarters. The map is from the book "Wiborg – en stad i sten" by C. J. Gardberg & P. O. Welin (Helsingfors 1996).*

people having taken a university degree. In the 1990's, the population figure exceeded 80 000. Jyväskylä has for quite some time been the tenth biggest town in Finland, by population figures.

In the context of this work, Vyborg, Finland's medieval town in match only with Turku, again, represents a lost town. In the early 20th century, Vyborg was the third biggest town in Finland after Helsinki and Turku, and in the 1930's its population numbered over 72 000. Before the war, one-third of the population earned their livelihood in industry and handicrafts. There were also garrisons placed in the town. In the Moscow Peace Treaty in 1940, Vyborg was part of the area ceded to the Soviet Union and again, after its reoccupation in the following war years the Finnish civilian population again had to leave the town in 1944, when it once more became a war arena. In the Paris Peace Treaty of 1948 Karelia and Vyborg where stabilised as Soviet ground, a situation that continues until today. After 1958, Finns have had the possibility of visiting Vyborg, but these visits only gained impetus in the 1980's and 1990's.

## Notes on the background material

In 1996, the Tyrgils museum in Helsinki, specialising in the cultural history of Vyborg, initiated a project focussing on life and destinies in Vyborg (Wiborgsliv och Wiborgaröden). Interviews were made with 34 Swedish-speaking former residents of Vyborg, 18 of whom were female and 16 male, with an average age of 82 years. Socially, they belonged to the upper middle class. The interview questions were ranged on a time axle, from childhood, youth and young adulthood, to the evacuation of Vyborg and to the settling in a new place. A precondition was that the respondents had lived in Vyborg for over or at least for nearly twenty years, that is, in the 1920's and 1930's.

The interviews ran through almost the whole life spans of the respondents, and the collection of material followed the life-history method. A few of those interviewed refused to talk about or remember the evacuation or their experiences of it. This is why some of the interviews ended in the year 1939, when the interviewee left Vyborg for the first time. Only very few would narrate anything about the years 1941–1944. This material has been annotated and is kept by the Society for Swedish Literature in Finland, in the Folk Culture Archives' collection SLS 1881.

The articles on Helsinki are based on a vast collection of responses to a series of inquiries, collected towards the end of the 20th century. The collection was made in order to record memories of after-war Helsinki. The respondents were asked to describe various aspects of life, particularly in relation to their own living environment. They were offered individualised questions as a support for writing, but it was also possible to send in individually formulated responses. The themes of the inquiries, made in 1996–1997, and the numbers of answers were as follows: Helsinki as a living environment (182 answers); The Helsinki of my generation (90 answers); The capital – my city (96 answers); and What does Helsinki mean to me? (128 answers).

The result is autobiographical responses, where the events of the respondents' private lives are intertwined with the changes occurring in the town. The most popular periods to describe were the decades after the war, when the respondents were children. This was also the stage when the urban environment was experienced as very near and idyllic, before future changes, which were often seen in a negative light. The centre of the city was often described through the eyes of a youngster or a young adult. Remembering the home town turned out to be a valuable experience for the respondents. All in all, 496 answers were received. The material reflected the heterogeneous social composition of the population, and all classes of society may be said to be represented among the respondents, although workers and middle-class people sent in most of the answers. They deal with experiences of time and space, the decades in after-war Helsinki, what happened and who did what, and the importance accorded to the town by the townspeople themselves. This material will in the future be kept in the Helsinki City Archives.

A special inquiry was made in 2000 of the residents of the Pikku Huopalahti district, to find out how people had adapted to this very recently built part of the town. The respondents were asked to describe the area and to expound on its image in the press and other media. The inquiry also focussed on the activities and movements of the residents in the area and outside it, and on the social relations. It turned out that the residents use numerous approaches to study, assess, organise and use their residential area, and the study aimed at pinpointing these approaches.

The articles on Jyväskylä are based on a variety of material. The most important of this material is the collection of autobiographical interviews, 60 in all, with male and female residents of different ages in different parts of the town, namely, Kuokkala, Kortepohja, Kangaslampi, Huhtasuo, Halssila,

15

Yläkaupunki and Seminaarinmäki. Besides this, eight residents have written down their remembrances, narrated their lives and indicated places that have been important to them. And, finally, five town planning specialists have been interviewed.

Another group of material from Jyväskylä consists of the townspeople's comments on and feedback relating to two planning projects: the renovation plan for the Kirkkopuisto area (102 comments) and the building plan for the Jyväskylä University Teacher Training Elementary School (Jyväskylän normaalikoulun ala-aste) (some 60 comments). Both plans have also been commented on by the public in the newspapers. In addition, newspaper writings and articles on town planning and the plans and strategy papers pertaining to the development of the town have been used as background material for the articles.

This introduction has been translated by Elwa Sandbacka. All the articles, except "Steps to the Past" by Pirjo Korkiakangas translated by Anna Rouhento, have been translated by Heidi Granqvist with Sarah Bannock as her language reviser. We thank them all.

*Anna-Maria Åström*                    *Pirjo Korkiakangas*

## BIBLIOGRAPHY

Hoffman, Kai 1997. Elinkeinot. [Means of livelihood]. *Helsingin historia vuodesta 1945. Väestö, Kaupunkisuunnittelu ja asuminen, Elinkeinot*. [The history of Helsinki from the year 1945. Population, Town planning and living, Means of livelihood]. Helsinki: Helsingin kaupunki.

Lefebvre, Henri 1991. *The Production of Space*. Oxford & Cambridge: Blackwell.

Lehtonen Hilkka 1997. Aika, arkkitehtuuri ja sen kuvat. [Time, architecture and its images]. In Liisa Knuuti (ed.) *Aika ja kaupunki*. [Time and town]. Yhdyskuntasuunnittelun täydennyskoulutuskeskus. C 44. Espoo: Teknillinen korkeakoulu.

Nummela, Ilkka 1997. *Jyväskylän kirja. Katsauksia kaupunkielämän vaiheisiin 1940-luvulta 1990-luvulle*. [The book of Jyväskylä. Studies of urban life from the 1940's to the 1990's]. Jyväskylä: Jyväskylän kaupunki.

Paavolainen, Jaakko 1978. Väestöstä ja sen asuinoloista. [About population and housing conditions]. In *Viipurin kaupungin historia. Osa V. Vuodet 1917-1944*. [The history of Vyborg, V. The years 1917-1944]. Helsinki: Torkkelin säätiö.

Radović, Ranko 1997. Urban time is people – not money. In Liisa Knuuti (ed.): *Aika ja kaupunki*. [Time and town]. Yhdyskuntasuunnittelun täydennyskoulutuskeskus. C 44. Espoo: Teknillinen korkeakoulu.

Schulman, Harry 2000. Helsingin suunnittelu ja rakentuminen. [Planning and construction of Helsinki]. In *Helsingin historia vuodesta 1945. 2. Suunnittelu ja rakentuminen, Sosiaaliset ongelmat, Urheilu*. [The history of Helsinki from the year 1945. 2. Planning and construction, Social problems, Sport]. Helsinki: Helsingin kaupunki.

Tester, Keith (ed.) 1994. *The Flaneur*. London: Routledge.

Tommila, Päiviö 1972. *Jyväskylän kaupungin historia 1837-1965*. I. [The History of the town of Jyväskylä 1837-1965]. Jyväskylä: Jyväskylän kaupunki.

Turpeinen, Oiva 1997. Väestö. [Population]. In *Helsingin historia vuodesta 1945. 1. Väestö, Kaupunkisuunnittelu ja asuminen, Elinkeinot*. [The history of Helsinki from the year 1945. Population, Town planning and living, Means of livelihood]. Helsinki: Helsingin kaupunki.

# Identity Constructions in the Capital of Helsinki

ANNA-MARIA ÅSTRÖM

# The City as Living Room
## Changing Meanings of the Centre of Helsinki

Since the mid 1970's, the significance of the centre in large cities in Europe and the USA has intensified as it has become part of the urban mosaic created by the culture of these large cities. In Scandinavia the heightened and elevated meanings of the centre emerge, on the one hand, as a reaction against the suburban process that has mostly taken place here after the Second World War and particularly in the 1960's when, coincidentally, the expression 'concrete ghetto' was coined. On the other hand, and in connection with this, a re-evaluation of the more complex life that is seen as typical of the concentration of commerce, culture and entertainment at the centre has taken place since the end of the 1970's. In addition, a conscious investment in activity at the centre, starting in the 1980's, forms part of a process where various cities compete in creating profiles for themselves, using culture as a driving force and a guarantee for financial success. Thus, the increased significance of the centre is not a return to the old city as it was originally built, in systems of blocks, but in fact the continuation of a process which restructures urban society according to the principles of the global market economy.

This article explores various old and new ways of perceiving the centre of Helsinki. It concludes with a description of Helsinki's centre today, which is a city centre that has gradually been developed according to a number of emphases and with more or less intensive creations of space during the various decades. Today, the centre above all forms an urban space which is to be immersed in, to move through, but also a place in which to stroll, linger and socialise. Past decades have left their marks as traces in the buildings, while the 'movements' and activities that were present in earlier times at the centre have completely disappeared. First, I will discuss two different nostalgic urban trends that have appeared in Helsinki at least in the last few years. I am partly thinking of the phenomenon of reminiscing about one's city, which old city dwellers are engaged in, and partly of the phenomenon of highlighting the old-fashioned in those characteristically dichotomised post-modern attitudes to the modern and the old which are manifested in the tendency of emphasizing the historical surface. Research also provides its own historical view of the centre.

19

The variety of ways in which city dwellers continuously appropriate the centre and respond to the rapid increase in choices offered by the city is, using a term as defined by Michel de Certeau, a question of *tactics*, while the mental *re-creation* of one's city is a variation of what Henri Lefebvre terms producing one's city through personal representations. The object is the *lived space* which is portrayed, for example, in writing (de Certeau 1988; Lefebvre 1998 [1991]). In my work, lived space is presented in the form of various responses to four questionnaires consulting respondents' experiences of the urban space of Helsinki since World War II.[1] The material thus consists of the city dwellers' own stories of their past and present experiences of the city of Helsinki.

Contrary to free narratives containing their own emphases, these stories are more like one side of "written interviews" where the initial questions are formulated and presented by the researcher. Since the researcher poses the questions and chooses the subjects to be discussed, his or her intentions and frames of reference should be included in the interpretation of the responses to the questionnaire. In my case this is relatively simple: I am myself a native of Helsinki and have memories of the city similar to those presented by the respondents, but for the questions I have also used aspects from theories on urban development in general. In formulating the questions, I have also "imagined the past times of the city".

The fact that my questions were of a general character is reflected in the polyphony of voices to be heard in the answers: persons from varying social, linguistic and cultural environments have submitted their responses (Questionnaire answers I, II, III and IV). The experiences of the centre are therefore described in a number of different ways, but the descriptions are nevertheless similar on one level, in that certain common features are emphasized. This might, after all, reflect the fact that the "reality" that they are based on contains features that can be traced back to specific decades. However, our perception of the urban existence also has its own genres, which are governed by other narratives surrounding us (Finnegan 1998, 4–9). The history of the city exists in parallel with personal experiences and life stories; this relation is one of the themes of this article. The fact that the centre has largely been regarded as "common property" is reflected in the narratives as descriptions of the way the narrator has appropriated the centre.

Until the beginning of the 1960's, 250 000 of Helsinki's 350 000 inhabitants lived in the inner city, or what later came to be spoken of as the city centre. In the present of the narratives, the mid-1990's, only some 100 000 inhabitants live in these same areas of the city, while the total population of Helsinki has grown to over half a million (and that of the whole Helsinki region to almost one million). It is clear that the centre has gradually changed from something 'that was close by' to something that one primarily 'visits' for various purposes. However, the perception of what constitutes the absolute city centre has not changed much: indeed, the centre is defined as approximately the same areas – with varying emphases nevertheless – during the entire latter half of the 20th century.

*The Esplanade towards the harbour; at the end of the street lies the Market Place. Photo: Kari Hakli 1973, Helsinki City Museum, Helsinki.*

The significance ascribed to the centre in light of the memories one has of the area is one of the main themes of this article. In this, personal tactics are important. What happens as a result of a global process where the centre is given new meanings in that it is marketed using new means, is, in turn, a version of what de Certeau calls *strategies* (de Certeau 1988). The concrete changes in attitudes become important. The strategies, here primarily in the field of architecture and city planning, can be innovative as well as preserving and conserving. They may be expressed in new architectural solutions, such as tunnels; post-modern culture and administrative buildings, or in reconstructions, rebuildings, changes of façade, roofing and function, and they may result in galleries, passages, new inner yards and, as a particular example, brick castles in a place that was previously occupied by a factory built in brick. These strategies aim at channelling human actions and movements. Tactics can be seen as a response to the strategies. The central spaces in Helsinki are largely the same as fifty years ago, but, nevertheless, they are also completely different. The tension arising out of this fact is also discussed here.

## The many faces of nostalgia; or, administering the cultural heritage

Nostalgia is never merely a longing for the past, but also a response to circumstances in the present. In his book *The Heritage Industry*, Robert Hewison claims that a nostalgic attitude is often present in times of dissatisfaction,

21

unrest and disappointment, but that the times we are nostalgic about have often themselves been times of unrest, or periods of stress (Hewison 1987).

When I called for descriptions of Helsinki in 1997, Finland was still in a phase of deep financial depression – but what people, to my surprise, wanted to describe was the local environment in the Helsinki of the 1940's and 1950's with its aura of a post-war era characterised by cramped housing and the very limited everyday lives that the inhabitants then experienced. The individual nostalgia that casts its light over the Helsinki of the 1950's possibly constitutes an attempt to recreate an urban world which from the present perspective feels different and which seemed to be significant for people's self-esteem in times of radical change (see Hewison 1987). This urban heritage had not in the mid-1990's yet received the kind of interest it was later to attract (Åström 1999, see Olsson p. 49 in this book). Many narrators ended their texts with gratitude for the opportunity they had been offered to re-enter the Helsinki of the past.

It has also been claimed that a nostalgic recapitulation takes place against the backdrop not only of dissatisfaction with the present, but also because the present is experienced as unclear, with no definition, no tension; as empty and with no future. The fact that the informants enthusiastically return to the former urban life defined by blocks of streets, can thus be thrown into sharp relief against the background of the present as it was experienced in 1995–97.

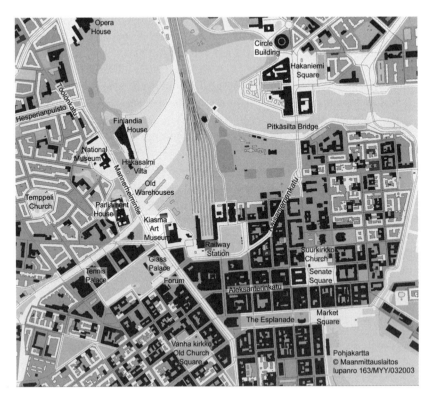

*The centre of Helsinki with some main spots.*

However, particularly when development seems to take large strides forward, a nostalgic attitude functions as a counter-force, a security and point of reference from which to view the present (Hewison 1987). On the other hand, a retrospective attitude need not at all be nostalgic in the sense of denying the present. When considering that memories can hardly exist without being attached to certain places, the character and ontology of the place becomes important. Michel de Certeau puts this as follows:

> A memory is only a Prince Charming who stays long enough to awaken the Sleeping Beauties of our wordless stories. "*Here*, there used to be a bakery." "*That's* where old lady Dupuis used to live." It is striking here that the places people live in are like the presences of diverse absences. What can be seen marks what is no longer there: you *see*, here there used to be…", but it can no longer be seen. Demonstratives indicate the invisible identities of the visible: it is the very definition of a place, in fact, that it is composed by these series of displacements and effects among the fragmented strata that form it and that it plays on these moving layers. (de Certeau 1988, 108.) *But some places (Robertson School, St Cat') can still be seen, but are not the same – not a school any more,*

It is in this light that I wanted to observe the recreation of childhood environments and experiences at the centre that my writers' descriptions of Helsinki constitute. That is to say, these are descriptions of place where accumulated time can be unfolded, although the places themselves at the same time remain in an enigmatic position, as symbols of what "the body" has experienced (de Certeau 1988, 108). And it is important against the background of the restructuring that, in fact, has taken place in the spatial practices and even in the physical space at the centre to compare the old city dwellers' internal image of the cityscape and the urban culture that is even now changing before their very eyes. Memories are personal and, in a way, uninteresting for anybody else, but these time layers give places their character, even in retrospect, claims de Certeau (ibid.). One can imagine places *maybe* as living *containers* of memories; if they offer nostalgic pleasure, this can be a result of the fragmentary, simultaneously clear and ungraspable, character of memories and places.

The questions in the questionnaires expressly sought to conjure up various urban places as such. Individuals and events are surrounded by places and this is something which is stored in the memory. When the process of reminiscence is actively started, experiences are attached to those environments of Helsinki that are topicalised by the questionnaires (see Ilmonen 1999, 91–92, 102).

However, at the same time we must be aware of this same place in the present. What is interesting is also how the urban environment and the heritage of the built environment is administered, and what the average city dweller thinks of the changes in the cityscape. This is thus also a question of what image of the past is publicly preferred, and how this relates to the individual recollection, that is, which urban history is given preference. This is a question that I will return to in the second part of this article.

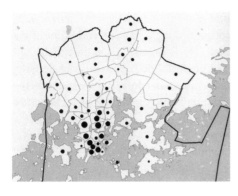

*The population of Helsinki in diffe-
rent areas of the city in 1950 and
1998.*

*30 000 to 35 400 inhabitants*
*20 000 to 30 000    "*
*10 000 to 20 000    "*
*5 000  to 10 000    "*
*1 000  to  5 000    "*
*100    to  1 000    "*

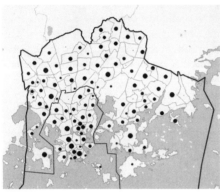

*The map above shows the popu-
lation of Helsinki in 1950 after the
incorporation of new areas in 1946,
and the one below the population
in 1998. In 1950, the population
in the city amounted to 370 000
and in 1998 to 540 000. The dense
housing and living in 1950 and the
urban culture this resulted in, can be
compared with the present situation
with large suburban areas and
sparse housing in the centre.*

*Memories of the centre*

In the writers' memories from the 1940's to the 1960's, the local environment
– the nearest blocks to one's home block in the stone city – played absolutely
the most central role. Here, everyday life took place with the inhabitants of
the same block of flats as the nearest social network, with the yard as the
children's playground and the shops on the block as the most important
points of reference.

Nevertheless, the answers to the questions explicitly concerning the experience of the centre show that locations in the centre were not unimportant,
either. A picture emerges where clothes are bought in department stores,
cafés in the centre are visited together with classmates and going to the cinemas which are scattered over the inner city is a recurring entertainment, and
where, finally, the representative buildings of the city take a natural place
(Åström, Olsson & Kivistö 1998). The symbolically important buildings of
the city (e.g. the Parliament House, the cathedral, the railway station) are
often presented in long lists as if to prove that one was aware of them, knew
their meaning and in retrospect values them:

*Quote*

*given as Senate Square on map p.22*

When we turned toward the Aleksanterinkatu street, a new world opened
up for me. The history of the Senaatintori square gave the whole place a
new kind of life. This is still the most beautiful and most fascinating place
in Helsinki. Several decades later I still stroll here. I walk up towards the
Snellmaninkatu street, look at the renovated Estates House, I walk past
the Bank of Finland, where I often as a young girl took the day's cash and
so got to see the building from the inside. I walk to the University Library,
whose interior still stuns me. I sit down for a while on the steps to the
Suurkirkko church, as I've done hundreds of times before. I walk along
the Aleksanterinkatu street and look up at the walls, windows, decorations
and roofs of the buildings. I turn back along the Esplanade towards the
Market Square. Nowadays there are a lot of tourists, but there's still a
distinctive atmosphere here. I sit down at a coffee stall and look out over
the sea. The ferry to Suomenlinna is docked at the quay and it represents
many memories. The large ferries going to Sweden have continued to
dominate the view for several decades. If I can manage it, I go up the hill
to Observatorionmäki. From there, I can see all of my Helsinki all the
way to Suomenlinna. (Waitress, b. in Vyborg 1930, IV:37, 1–2.)

*(female) worker*

*The hectic area at the Railway Station (to the right, by architect Eliel Saarinen
1919) in the 1960's. To the left, the Sokos department store, which was finished in
1952, and next to it the Main Post Office built in 1937. Photo: Helsinki City Museum,
Helsinki.*

The writer describes the ambiguity in the experience of the urban space; the fictive present and the past are enfolded into one single experience, which is actually formed only the moment it is written. There is a feeling that she in fact is describing a "reminiscence walk", which is possibly something she sometimes actually undertakes.

*[Comment on the quote]*

As with the image of the home blocks, which is sketched in fairly similar terms regardless of district, the image of the centre is often presented both in a naturally personal way, and at the same time in a somewhat stereotypical way. The city has left a similar mark on the minds and memories of the Helsinki dwellers. The writers seldom use a picturesque language. The everyday life of the residential blocks is noted with reference to routines, spaces, their utilitarian aspects and to the people one met. The centre is described by means of mentioning various places one visited, how visits to and from relatives were possible – e.g. by walking or taking the tram to various parts of the city – and how the visits to the centre were defined according to routes taken along shopping streets, across markets squares and to some observation point. Sentimental images also occur, as one here is invoked by a woman who grew up right in the middle of the centre, in a flat in the inner yard of the Ateneum art museum:

> My memories of the centre of Helsinki in winter are surrounded by a nostalgic, dim yellow light; and accompanied by the bells of the Aleksi street Christmas decorations chime. The snow falls slowly, there is just a little traffic. Perhaps there is a tingling feeling of expectation as before a visit to the Swedish Theatre, to see *The Pearl of Truth* by Topelius, for example. A special kind of pastel-coloured, twisted candy bar from Wickholms is also part of these memories. Or the wonderful smell in the Karjakunta butcher's at the corner of Aleksanterinkatu and Kluuvikatu, where business was lively and the atmosphere friendly, I particularly remember one kind of Karjakunta sausage. (Psychoanalyst, b. 1945, *Att bo i stan* 1998, 79.)

*[female professional]*

In her memories, the light, the sounds, the feeling, the smells and the taste and even the anticipation of an art experience, take on very clear elements of depth, which give the child's experience of urbanity a concentration, and, in this case, a nostalgic shimmer, which the writer is fully aware of. This centre was her local environment.

On the whole, the neighbourhoods were places where people had their most vivid memories, and thus real roots. Some urban phenomena also clearly indicate powerful emotions by appearing regularly. One such is the existence of small food shops in every block, others are cafés and milk bars for young people, the most prominent of these situated in the inner city areas:

> Rita's and my passion was ice cream. After school and during weekends we would go to one of the Valio cafés for ices. One was in Forum and another big one was in the Marski house. We would have milk shake or a banana split. Somewhat later we would start visiting the "Upper Primula" (later Old Bakers), a café which also had the nickname "Pimppis". The café obtained a licence to serve alcoholic beverages at the start of the

1960's and it stayed my favourite place until I was grown up. (Librarian, III:10, 2.)

I spent my first salary cheque on a tracksuit, a Yankee bag and a swimsuit. I began paying one third of those which followed to my parents. On pay days I would go with the girls to a Valio or Colombia café to indulge: ice cream with crushed pineapple, whipped cream and biscuits was the flavour of the month. Alternatively we would go to Ekberg's or Hildén's to have a rice pastry or a cup of coffee and a Tosca cake. We let the meat pies at the station alone: we had to think of our figures, too. Compared with today's cafés, those in the 1950's were modest and boring; even in those days Ekberg and Fazer were the elite. A wealthy aunt once invited me to Fazer and it really was impressive. (Unemployed secretary, b. 1940, III:16, 2.)

The somewhat specific places are significant in an obvious way as part of the process of becoming an adult. They are scenes of breaks and recurrent openings in everyday life, which are often remembered. Even green spaces would do as this kind of place:

During lunch breaks we used to sit on the grass at the Vanhakirkko church park and have our lunch, or whatever food we had bought in nearby shops. Kappeli was my favourite café, along with the Ursula café on the shore in Kaivopuisto park. There you had to stand in a long queue to wait for your coffee and bun. But then you could enjoy sitting for a long time in the sunshine facing the sea. Usually you met many acquaintances there. (Accountant, unemployed, III:64, 11.)

Visiting the cinema was one way in which one enlarged one's knowledge of the city. There are minute descriptions of what movies the writer had seen and where – cinemas could be found everywhere. Helsinki as a commercial city has not been neglected, either. Amongst the reminiscences, there are descriptions of department stores and busy streets where the narrators used to buy their clothes. Some shops feature in several recollections. The low-budget department store Tempo seems to have been irreplaceable and other lost environments are also mentioned repeatedly:

From my way to school I must also mention Tempo opposite Rake in the beginning of the Mannerheimintie street. It was a discount shop, the like of which no longer exists in the city, even if there are budget shops everywhere. Time passed Tempo. On the whole, shops were more personal and original before commerce turned into supply and demand, efficiency and large units. Modern shops come and go without leaving much of an impression… Our family bought all its clothes at the Pukeva Coat Centre. There we bought clothes by hire-purchase. During my studies I didn't buy that much in the way of clothing, perhaps only buying things in the autumn with money from my summer job. When I was young, Ajanmies was a fashionable place, I bought stylish things there. (Economist, b. 1935, III:45, 4.)

27

Kaisaniemenkatu remained a shopping street until the Forum building was erected, which was in the autumn of 1985. When I was young, I used to go to Teinitalo (the Teenagers' House) to buy my clothes, I even had an account there. The shop Seppälä opened in 1970 and I used to go there with my friends. In the years between 1967 and 69, my friend and I used to spend our day off from school wandering about in the shops that imitated fashion shops in London. We only fingered the clothes and looked at the prices, we hardly ever tried anything on, and we never bought anything. These shops were called Pihaputiikki (the Backyard Boutique) and Carnaby Street. (Author, b. 1954, III:21, 6.)

Besides Stockmann we frequented the Elanto department store at the Aleksi street, Minkki at the corner of Kaisaniemenkatu and Mikonkatu, and the Pukeva department store a bit further up along Kaisaniemenkatu. At Teinitalo you could find nice clothes made especially for teenagers. You could get bras in a shop at Erottaja, Triumph and Figura were good brands. The saleswoman helped you in the fitting rooms even if you didn't want her to. You could buy your shoes in the same block, in the Bensow house. (Accountant, unemployed, b. 1947, III:64, 5.)

Social life is described as an ongoing process through which people widen their spheres. The city shops were also places of initiation into a more adult life and provided an arena for the expression of an urban life, where one could manifest one's longing for fashionable cities.

There lay a certain aura around the centre and its various places, the writers note. Often the centre is also described as having a hectic atmosphere to it, the centre is remembered as representing the only international feature there was in the whole city. At the same time, there is a feeling of intimate familiarity with the environments in most of the descriptions – and a longing for that which is lost.

It is **repeated actions** that seem to give memories their luminousness and not isolated events. The descriptions are made up of accounts of personal relations to places couched in terms such as "I used to go", "my mother and I often were", "my friends and I used to sit there". In the main, the various ways of appropriating the centre form an experience of it which, in the memory of the narrators, has been transformed into a kind of network, where the nodes, the places are replaceable, but the whole remains constant.

## The centre as an area – the centre as a parade

Thus, it is also interesting to see how the centre was perceived as an area, that is, how the centre is described as a place in itself. Did the centre form a mental map or was it seen as a place through which certain specific routes were made? I will quote excerpts from some of the different narrators' descriptions:

Mentally, the city was divided into two parts: the working class districts north of the Pitkäsilta bridge and the districts of the better off in the rest of the city. Going to the centre was always an event, which had to be carefully prepared for. You made detailed plans of which places to visit… I learnt to know the centre in 1955 when I got my first job. It was at the SOK co-op, at their head office at the Vilhonkatu street, as a cycle courier. I learnt to know all the short-cuts since couriers had to be quick. So I moved quite a lot around the centre, first as a courier and then working in restaurants, home and back. I think of the railway station, the main post office, Hankkija, the bus station, Makkaratalo (the "Sausage house"), the Aleksi street, the Kaivohuone restaurant and the night life of the city. The image of the city is created by the buildings, movements, streets and people. (Unemployed waiter, b. 1941, IV:14, 7; III, 4–1.)

I would say that before the new buildings (the 'Metal Building', the 'Circle Building'), people did not move in either direction to go shopping on the other side of the Pitkäsilta bridge. People liked to make their purchases locally. The working class districts Hakaniemi and Kallio were quite self-sufficient. In the 1950's there was a new rush southwards, when the Kaisaniemenkatu street became popular because of its fashion shops. The Pukeva department store inaugurated a new era when you could buy clothes and shoes on credit… Kaisaniemenkatu became an area for many fashion stores, such as Simola, Halonen, Valioasu, Vestio, Minkki and later Seppälä, so it was worth while to go there for shopping. At Christmas a fantastic light curtain was switched on and the luminous neon sign of Pukeva was visible from afar. (Secretary, b. 1934, III:22, 5.)

In both the above cases, the centre is limited and concentrated to certain, intensively used places. The centre is an area for moving through, with various focal points, important buildings that function as landmarks or buildings that the narrator visits. The writer above also makes a fantasy walk in Helsinki of the 1950's:

We turn into Mikonkatu towards Aleksi street. In the building on the corner, there is the Osuuspankki bank and in the yard a beauty salon and a hairdresser's. In the same building, there is Paavo Nurmi's menswear shop. The runner king does not himself serve customers, but occasionally you might glimpse him in a gentleman's outfit. Then comes a goldsmith's and then the large cinema REA. If we turn into the Hallituskatu, there is the sports shop Raul Hellberg, a company owned by the famous cyclist. In the corner of the Vuorikatu, there is another cinema, Aloha, if I remember correctly. Opposite is Hotel Helsinki, the second floor of which is a fine lunch restaurant, frequented by freemasons and members of the Lions Club.

The description continues with a minute wealth of details about shops and other establishments. It is also a personal account, as this flaneur is familiar with what he describes. He not only knows the various places, but also who owns them and what kinds of customer a restaurant might attract. This is knowledge gained through his own and others' experiences. At the same time, the centre here has a focal point in the approach from the working class districts, thus the experience of the centre is also given a social emphasis: the centre is different depending on where one comes from. Another walk, from

29

*The Erottaja Crossing, with the Swedish Theatre and the Wulff and Stockmann department stores to the right. In the distant background along the same street, Mannerheimintie, the Parliament House and the National Museum can be seen. The low building to the left housed the low-budget shop Tempo, an unforgettable shopping spot for children of the 1950's and 1960's. Photo: C. Grünberg in the 1960's. Helsinki City Museum, Helsinki.*

another direction, that is, from the middle-class district Töölö, is described in the present tense; the reader is invited to walk with the narrator through these historical landscapes:

> In the winter, it was sometimes fun to take a little walk from Temppelikatu in the evening… Having passed the Hankkija building I'm already at the Lasipalatsi (the Glass Palace). The neon sign of the Rex cinema glimmers on the roof; this is one of the landmarks of Helsinki. Should I go in and see a film? The ice cream bar is far too childish for me. So, I walk on past the Post Office towards the Railway Station. As usual, I buy a paper. Since I get both Helsingin Sanomat and Hufvudstadsbladet delivered, I choose Uusi Suomi supplemented by Schweitzer Illustrierte… From the station, I walk on across Kaivokatu, but this time I don't go through the City Passage, but turn towards Keskuskatu at the Skoha corner. In front of me to the right, in the low building, is the Central restaurant, which later moved to Pietarinkatu. To the right, there is the house of the Voluntary

Fire Brigade, where the typically Finnish restaurant Kestikartano serves its tempting lunch buffet. I turn into Aleksi street towards Senaatintori Square. The Colombia café has already closed, but I could go for a cup of cocoa to Fazer on Kluuvikatu. There is some Swedish comedy on at the Maxim cinema, but I turn into the Esplanade towards the Erottaja crossing. (b. 1932, *Att bo i stan* 1998, 34–35.)

In this reminiscence, certain buildings are listed that were central in the then modern Helsinki, the Post Office and the Lasipalatsi, but also buildings that have disappeared and recur in accounts of other writers – these include Skoha, a shop for sports equipments and the Kestikartano and Central restaurants. Other central, traditional places such as the Fazer café and the cinema Maxim are also included. In memory, different places have different meanings, as places for shopping, as attractive or less attractive places to drop into. Here too, the city expert appears: the writer knows which types of films were shown where. The places function as markers, they were there, and I, who remember them, am part of this city. As a complement to these stories by then young men, there is a narrative by a housewife who often moved in the centre. She approached the centre from a third direction, from the Kruunuhaka district:

Both sides of the Esplanade have, for as long as I remember, been the ultimate place to be seen in the centre. When the sun's warmth began to come through in early spring, the inhabitants of Helsinki found their way there again… If, in the 1950's, you started your stroll at the Edlund corner, you came across the Scala cinema in the first block. Left of that was Sjöblom's corset shop and soon after that you could drop into C. A. Gustavsson's spacious colonial shop where you could be sure you would be served in Swedish. After crossing Fabianinkatu you soon came to the Grönqvist house, where the Wasenius book shop was. Mattlin's clothes shop specialised in overalls and aprons was situated in the same building, as was Bögelund's photography shop. (Pensioner, b. 1923, *Att bo i stan* 1998, 38–39.)

In this account, too, knowledge of the distribution of products and services in various places and shops comes through. The central shops are those that a housewife needed and the linguistic aspect also proves to be of importance. At the same time, also this description has a certain old-fashioned tinge: the corset shop, the colonial shop and the book shop are kinds of shop associated particularly with a certain era, which ended approximately with the 1960's. After that, they turn, more or less, into mere memories, or change character altogether.

The recollections also take as their starting point the desire that Henri Lefebvre ascribes to the urban lifestyle: the play, the bodily actions such as sports, the creative activities such as art and knowledge. Of these, the first two are often dealt with in connection with the living environment, while art and knowledge are placed in the cultural institutions and schools in the centre. The narrators give a great deal of attention to their schools and visits to concerts and theatres in their youth in the 1950's and 1960's.

I think we went to the theatre and the cinema quite often. There weren't that many theatres but we almost always went to the National Theatre, that was an impressive building. Sometimes we would sit on the top balcony, sometimes in the stalls… In Liisankatu there was the Aula cinema, which showed Tarzan films in the daytime, I saw quite a few of those. The Umbrellas in Cherbourg was a wonderful film that I saw together with my cousin, my mother and my friend… But my absolute favourite was Sound of Music, which I saw seven times… The age limit for many films was 16 years, so there wasn't that much of a selection. With hindsight, an exceptional experience was the Beatles film in BioBio in about 1964. The audience mostly consisted of teenage girls who shouted and shrieked as if in a trance like at a live concert. I was too young to be totally in love, but I was absolutely convinced of my future marriage to George… Concerts were not a customary leisure pursuit in my family, but I wanted to go to Danny's concerts with my friends. (Nurse, b. 1954, III:56.)

In the stories, which are here exemplified by quotations slightly out of context, the centre emerges in the form of coherent mental maps, where every place has its function, its atmosphere and a specific significance for the nar-

*Every spring the stairs of the Cathedral attract people to greet the sun, the forerunner of summer in Helsinki. This picture is from the 1950's. Photo: Helsinki City Museum, Helsinki.*

32

rating self. At the same time, however, the centre is seen in the light of the way the various places appeared from different angles and as the site for certain activities.

The centre is consciously frozen to certain epochs, but the writers move in and out of these with ease. They are also able to perceive changes: the dissolving of the division of the city into two distinct areas, the opening of the centre by the new route along Kaisaniemi street, the intense era of this route and also its decline, the heyday of the ice-cream bars, department stores such as Stockmann, Elanto and Sokos, and the composition of the city's cultural supply. The changes in consumption patterns are also noted. As to the present of the time of writing, a recurring element is the observation of how a new café culture has emerged to replace the one that disappeared in the 1980's.

However, a far too one-sided concentration on various kinds of urban practice does not permit a description of how the city dwellers have perceived changes. Some seem to have got stuck in a certain decade, others travel more freely in time, seeing the present from the perspective of yesterday, while still others appreciate and primarily describe the present. At the same time, the image of the process of change is fragmentary:

> A note in the hand of the doorman and in you came. Such restaurants were König on Mikonkatu, Canjon on Hämeenkatu. If we found ourselves on the Esplanade, we went to Catani. The drink of choice was whisky and soda: that was supposed to be so American. There were plenty of classy cafés: the Colombia cafés all over town and Kestikartano on Keskuskatu was a favourite place for a cup of coffee… For the First of May you had to buy new clothes. A jacket, trousers and a light trench coat. The winds of change blew over Helsinki, but I will never forget the best days, the 1950's. (Lift installer, b. 1938, III:43.) *male*

> While writing this I have noticed that I have so many favourite places. I stand in the Senate Square. I turn around. Beautiful, peaceful, and pure lines. I walk across the square and feel like I'm living as many generations of women before me. When evening turns to night in Pohjoisranta in November, the big passenger ships, the shores, the islands and the sea are full of light. The Great Church (the Cathedral) rises against the sky. This was the city I came to when I moved from Tampere. (Graphic artist, b. 1924, III:36.) *female*

> When I want to have something special, I go to the city centre, to the small boutiques on Korkeavuorenkatu, Tehtaankatu or Fredrikinkatu and Uudenmaankatu: there are marvellous shops there. Sometimes I stick to just looking, because of the prices, and then go back to my Itäkeskus shopping centre… The make up department in the Sokos department store was better arranged and even cheaper in the old days. I get lost in this new department… We have started to use the tunnel between the metro and the department stores Stockmann, Forum and Sokos instead of crossing Mannerheimintie with its noise – how pleased we are with this innovation. (Secretary, b. 1934, III:22.) *female*

In the urban space, memories are woven into today's practices. As containers of memories, the buildings, both in terms of their exterior and interior,

*The Esplanade of the 1950's, built for promenades, but still housing ordinary food shops with none of today's trendiness. Photo: Museum of Finnish Architecture, Helsinki.*

appear as places for atmospheres and eras which pass review in the imagination. The streets take form through the function that they were first built for. Certain places, which have not changed very much, such as the Senate Square, function as amplifiers of a feeling of continuity, while others that have changed or disappeared function as indicators of general trends of change. The elevated centre of power (the Senate Square), the restaurants and cafés for leisure, and the points for consumption appear for the flaneurs as separate spheres with their own respective atmospheres, connected by the space of the street. The familiar characteristics of a city built in blocks are no longer so apparent: the overlapping of activities of living, working life and leisure has become more fluid.

Lefebvre talks about an urban network that gradually spread during the post-war era and that lead to a crisis in urbanity (Lefebvre 1982, 96–112). He emphasizes the continually quickening pace of urban life: speedy communication (including the car), the television, the dances and music of urban leisure, the style of dressing, the quick changes of fashion, and the modern principle of safety and prediction of the future, the urban rationality. Youths are particularly sensitive in terms of experiencing the spirit of the time, and they actively contribute to the assimilation of the city's objects and notions

(Lefebvre 1982, 20). The city dwellers' memories support the idea that they have embraced these characteristics of urbanity and also its crisis.

Lefebvre also claimed that the history of the city at its various nodes supports the memory of the urban sociality, which was threatened during the 1970's. However, monuments, churches, public buildings and the experience of the diversity of the streets and squares gave, according to him, constant promises of new appropriations of time and space. Despite the changes and the growth of the cities, ordinary people experienced and still experience the city as a specific living space which defines their everyday life. When our city dwellers remember their daily life of yesterday, they compare it to the current situation. And as they welcome the new changes, they affirm the revitalisation that took place during the mid-1990's.

Particularly in final comments not quoted in this article, the narrators have reacted against the over-rationality of contemporary urban life and emphasized the urban lifestyle as such, which needs diversity (Cf. Ronneberger 1990, 30). It was also important for these city dwellers to re-establish the polarity between centre and periphery in order for the centrality to be restored (Lefebvre 1982, 25; Ronneberger 1990, 29–30). Those who had moved to the suburbs still often visited the city centre.

According to Lefebvre, the city is both a mediating space and a creation – that is, an arena for social conditions and their manifestation, but simultaneously also a result of all the activities that the city dwellers carry out, and also of where these activities are placed. The narrators of the material used here also seem to have been aware of their active role in the creation of the city during the past decades and eager to follow its development.

## The centre in the present

During the years of intense activity that centred on the student revolt, its leading theoretician, Henri Lefebvre, wrote his book *The City as a Right. He described the situation at that time thus:*

> The centres resist and are transformed. They remain centres for intensive urban life. The aesthetic qualities of the old centres become an important factor in their preservation. They not only contain monuments and institutional buildings, but also spaces suitable for festivities, parades, walks, entertainment. Thus, the city centres become a high quality commodity for foreigners, tourists, people coming from the outskirts, suburban dwellers. They owe their survival to this dual role of being both a place for consumption and of consumption… They become centres of commodification. (Lefebvre 1982, 21.)

At this time of change, the centre became emphatically a place of decision-making, and power, but also leisure pursuits demanded their space there, while activities of production fled to the outskirts. In moving from a consideration of memories of Helsinki during the 1950's and 1960's to a period four or five decades further on, we find that the centre and the image of the centre

see p 36

35

have changed. What has taken place regarding the urban development as a whole, is, partly, a de-industrialisation of Helsinki, where large areas close to the centre have lost their former activities aimed at production. Partly, the most central spaces have increasingly been aimed at consumption and leisure, whereas the main offices of many firms have moved out of the center proper since the 1970s.

see p 35

From the 1980's onwards, an additional change has taken place within city planning, in that the extremely modernist, rationalistic view of planning has given way to a "softer" approach, where concepts such as "culture, community, quality of life and street life" are also given consideration in the allocation of space (Cantell 1999; cf. Ronneberger 1990 on Frankfurt). Under the pressure of globalisation it has here – as in other cities – become important to emphasize the uniqueness of the city of Helsinki, that is, to produce an individual, positive image of it.

Certain radical groups within the arts have, according to the Finnish sociologist Timo Cantell, been able to agree with the city's planning and cultural sector on starting processes that have been labelled "revitalisation", "re-imagination", "re-enchantment" and "urban renaissance" (Cantell 1999). It is not totally far-fetched to mention Henri Lefebvre as one of the first advocates of this merger of arts and planning, even if he doubted that such plans could be realised in a society oriented towards consumption.

What has happened in Helsinki is, according to Cantell, that a hard and a soft line have been able to meet within the planning sector. As a result, an innovative, late modern architecture has been given more space, while, at the same time, there has been an effort in the older environments to meet the needs of leisure and art, which, when satisfied and realised, in an external sense also have been able to profile Helsinki as a city of culture (Cantell 1999). The planners would speak of an image that could join culture and technology in Helsinki, while Lefebvre talked about the city dwellers' right to the city as a creation, as a work of art, and their right to appropriate the urban space (Lefebvre 1982, 176).

As Lefebvre also claims, city planning emerges more clearly when the city is in a crisis: it tries to solve some problematic situation. As a result of a rapid decrease of the number of inhabitants in the centre of Helsinki during the 1970's and 1980's, the city centre was faced with the threat of urban stagnation: of, amongst other things, being entirely converted into office space. On a traditional basis, some attempts at preventing this development and reinvigorating activities at the centre were made: conversions into offices were stopped, one of the city's historic events, the traditional fish market, was revitalised at the end of the 1970's and the Market Square was allowed to open during the evenings in 1982. However, a more fundamental renewal did not yet happen, even if it was foreshadowed by the building of a new consumption complex, Forum, opened in 1985 on the central street Mannerheimintie, and by the establishment of the carnival known as the Night of the Arts in 1989 (Åström 1993; Cantell 1997).

A new merger between various creative institutions in the 1990's had a greater impact and rapidly led to several far reaching consequences. I will

*A spot in Helsinki that has seen radical changes since this picture of the late 1960's. At the statue of Marshal Mannerheim, the Kiasma Museum for Contemporary Art was erected just before the turn of the millennium and on the other side of the street, the Glass Palace was restored to a media house. The Parliament House will get an annex and a huge shopping area is under construction behind the Glass Palace. This solemn but busy place to commemorate the independence of Finland is being transformed into a junction of late modern city life with cultural and other forms of consumption as its core. Photo: Helsinki City Museum, Helsinki.*

list some in order for certain place shifts and changes in the centre to clearly emerge: the old functionalist-style building Lasipalatsi (the Glass Palace) next to Forum had a protection order placed upon it and it has been restored to its original 1930's form, now functioning as media centre incorporating TV studios, IT services, cafés and a restaurant. A museum for contemporary art, Kiasma, has, despite protests, been built next to the nationally important statue of Marshal Mannerheim (icon of the "first and second republic" in Finland). This museum, too, has both a café and a restaurant, as well as various rooms for films and lectures, and is expressly promoted as a "living room" (see Linko 1999). The main national newspaper, *Helsingin Sanomat*, has built an even larger glass palace – perhaps with the idea of being seen as a challenge to the Parliament House. This building is also planned with the function of a living room in mind, with a passage all along it on the ground floor which houses boutiques and cafés. However, this plan seems to have not born fruit; the public has not been drawn into this space. The site next to the railway station has also been renovated as a square, Elielinaukio, and underground tunnels connect the city's three largest department stores Stockmann, Forum and Sokos. Further, the old Tennis Palace (built as a car palace but from its early days used for sports and later as a training hall during the Olympic Games in 1952) has been renovated to its 1940's style and become a culture palace with eleven cinemas and large museum space, partly for the "Museum of Cultures", that is, the ethnographic collections of the National Museum, and partly for the city's collections of modern art. This building, too, teems with hamburger bars and cafés. Two cinema concentrations are situated near Kaisaniemenkatu. All these restructurings mean that the centre has shifted: leisure has new focal points at the centre, which lie slightly away from the spaces which were more intensively used earlier and which were situated by the Old Students' Union House and the central streets of Aleksanterinkatu and the Esplanades.

But, in the same spirit, during the late 1990's, the façades at the old centre of Helsinki have been externally cleaned, and inner yards and parks have also been subjects of renovation. This process has taken historical aspects of the sites into consideration, but with the planners' own interpretation of these aspects. The Esplanade Park has acquired new old-fashioned streetlamps and benches, both Esplanades have been provided with closely spaced rows of lights and the neo-renaissance façades have been furnished with spotlights that illuminate them in the winter darkness. The light from the lamps in the building where Marimekko's shop emerges at street level, has, since then, been pink during the Christmas season. On the site of the venerable former Hotel Kämp now stands a pastiche, which on the inside has been renovated as a five star hotel, with hotel porters wearing livery and an elegant terrace. The interior of the whole block is a similarly elegant shopping centre, housing, among others, Hennes & Mauritz in the main office of the former national bank KOP. The Wrede Passage, one of the former passages from the turn of the 19th century on Aleksanterinkatu, has experienced a revitalisation in that it functions during the summer months as a space for live music and a stylish drinks terrace for nearby restaurants. On the northern side of Aleksanterinkatu, there are another three inner yards that function as smaller galleries and restaurants with glass-covered yards and passages.

During the summer, a large part of the street space is occupied by various restaurant terraces. In this huge living room, both façades and the inner yard walls take on an architectural role of providing historically interesting, elegant or picturesque surfaces in which to reflect the present. The houses at the centre are not only houses, but also beautiful walls. The fascination of late modernism with the historical, which is expressed both as preservation and as "polishing", is carefully documented (Harvey 1989; Ziehe 1993; Zukin 1995), and has, according to this model, expressed itself in Helsinki, too.

These processes for the remodelling of the centre were completed only at the very end of the 1990's and had not therefore been carried out when the questionnaire material was collected. Most answers revealed a great interest in the buildings that were then being built or renovated – both Kiasma and the Lasipalatsi. The continentally inspired cafés that had appeared at the centre – in the middle of a recession – were also welcomed.

## Reactions and analyses

Many of the new creations in Helsinki in the 1990's were aimed to be finished

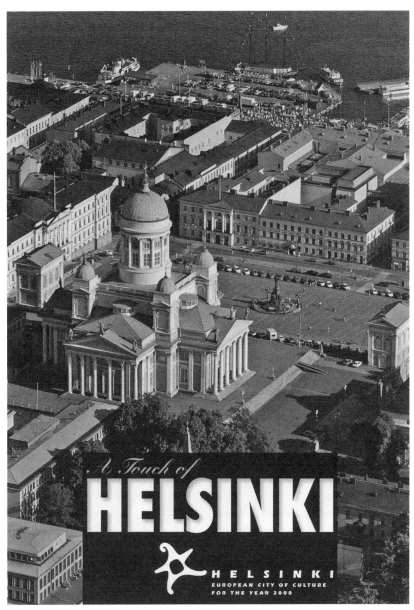

*The Senate Square in Helsinki with the Cathedral in the foreground and the Market Place and the sea in the background. This was chosen the place with highest symbolic significance when marketing Helsinki as one of the European Cities of Culture for the Year 2000. Helsinki City Tourist Office 1999.*

by the year 2000 when it was one of the European Cities of Culture. This new Helsinki is discussed primarily from a sociological perspective in a recently published book called *Urbs*. Here, some of the urban practices that have become significant for the young, trendy 1990's are described. The more liberal restaurant culture is emphasized and the new cafés are singled out as a newly emerging arena for self-representation and encounters (Ruoppila & Cantell 1999; Mäkelä & Rajanti 1999). In some cases, the new trends are described

39

enthusiastically and welcomed as a new kind of liberation (Mäenpää 1999). A corresponding ethnological view of the centre is, for its part, an analysis of the centre of Jyväskylä (Junkala & Sääskilahti 1999). This, too, accentuates the movements of the town dwellers, their consumption and the activity of strolling in the centre, but also processes of marginalisation are noted.

There is a feeling that Lefebvre's utopia has been realised. He advocated the meeting place and the priority of utility value, the city as a place for playfulness and festivity, rather than for culture as such (Lefebvre 1982, 152, 171). The main things for him were that the users, the city dwellers, were given preferential treatment. And it is expressly the users and their behaviour that have attracted the interest of researchers.

This interesting coincidence needs to be commented on. At the end of the 1960's, Lefebvre claimed that the then urban reality was characterised by features both from pure capitalism and "neo-capitalism". Within the latter, he argued, the centre of consumption is united with the centre of decision, that is, state power, and even if the consumption of goods is still important, information, nevertheless, is even more important. He further asserted that the use of the city, which I understand as the city dwellers' use of its places, cannot be totally reduced, and even if the convergence of the decisive power and the commercial power is strong, their power and its manifestations can also be evaded by the city dwellers (Lefebvre 1982, 170–171).

It was this irreducibility of the centre that also in the case of Helsinki allowed for resistance when the centre seemed to be stagnating. The fact that the merger between the decision-making power, the media world and the city's own bodies later made such clear marks in the urban landscape – and perhaps in future will do this even more strongly – and that the restructuring of the centre also took place through active planning, does not preclude the new spaces from also having benefited the city dwellers. But the process has had consequences that neither the utopian planner nor the bureaucratic planner have been able to imagine. The utopian Lefebvre would certainly think that it is, after all, the commercial powers that have the advantage and the planning, for its part, had hardly anticipated the resistance among active city dwellers against the further prioritising of state buildings in the absolute centre of the city (for example, offices for the secretaries of the members of parliament and a music house). This resistance had chosen as its weapon the old warehouses that still exist next to Kiasma and the *Helsingin Sanomat* building and which are planned to be demolished to give way to the new music house. Around the warehouses, a more lively urban culture with music, festivals, flea markets and art exhibitions has emerged which, rather than the projected music house, is reminiscent of Lefebvre's utopia.

The fact that the new trends toward urban living spaces – both public and subcultural ones – is to such a large extent aimed at youth and young adults, which is to say, primarily for one age category, is something that neither planning nor research has paid any great attention to. This means that it is not always taken into consideration that there are different kinds of city dwellers each of whom takes a different stance on its development (cf. Finnegan 1999, 58). Pensioners, the unemployed and children often lack both the resources

*The Helsinki City Tourist Office celebrated the new millennium with a brochure including two maps and three symbolically important buildings: the Parliament House, the Finlandia Hall and the tower of the National Museum. Helsinki City Tourist Office 1999.*

and the easy means of movement that are required for partaking of this new centre, where the supply is primarily aimed at the young or for those who are well off. The people belonging to the warehouse subculture have been accommodating when it comes to children, in providing circus events, a medieval market and snowboard competitions as main attractions. A detail suggestive of the emphasis of various central spaces and their shifting was

41

the snowboard event held in the winter of 2001: the event was not licensed to take place by the warehouses, but rather on the city's traditionally most venerable square, the Senaatintori. The roles had been switched; what is regarded as a youthful subculture was no longer allowed next to the area annexed by subcultural forces, but welcomed into the former centre of power.

## Which history and whose memories?

Urban trend theory makes the false basic assumption that "the city dweller" can be cultivated, that all city dwellers are included in the same generalisation. Particularly if the city dweller is regarded as a blank page that is only interested in getting experiences through consumption and entertainment, the complexity of urban life is obscured. In this context, the triad of memory, place and experience needs to be brought to the fore.

In the questionnaire material, there were certain reservations expressed about the present on the basis of what the writers had described. Here, the old city, as built in blocks with functioning networks of shops meeting daily needs as well as social focal points such as schools, sports grounds, skating rinks, parks and an attractive centre, functions as a nostalgic counterpoint to contemporary trendiness. It seems as if the narrators in their descriptions of the centre wish to emphasise that there has always been a city culture and a fashion consciousness even in earlier times. Most of the memories are expressly memories from their youth. In hindsight, the well-known culture of Helsinki gets a touch of the everyday and obvious, which the narrators want to deny today's urban reality. Specifically the lost spaces of the shops along Kaisaniemenkatu, are emphasised, as we saw above, and the memory of them also functions as a counterpoint to the new spaces.

And thus, we must also explore the other trend within the restructuring of the city centres, that is, that of polishing the historical surface. Ziehe points out that this ambition to preserve old environments does not aim at restoring abstractly declared values, but to enable the realisation of new modes of living, that is, lived and not only postulated modes of life (Ziehe 1993, 47).

In such a light, the memories of the centre of Helsinki of earlier decades as related above become interesting. In its unrestored form, the centre also made possible the existence of various life forms. Since memories are not fixed in the present, their aim is to convey something of the history of the city and not to look at the centre as only a surface for experiences of today. What information can they give us: what is the value of blurred memories of the centre? Which history do they convey?

Firstly, there are two different historical images of the centre of Helsinki. The everyday history that everybody can recount, can be seen in relation to the image of the historical Helsinki that the preservation processes within the restructuring of the centre produce. Each image refines something: the everyday image presents space as a backdrop for experiences, the historicising physical expression primarily underlines solidity, elegance and urbanity in combination with commercialism.

The sociologists Philo and Kearns have pointed out that there are at least three historical images of which one is the critically reflecting historical image, with a small h. This is supplemented by memory, with a small m, which lays claims to presenting its own truth. These two often stand together in conflict with the official, closed and legitimised History, which often occupies space at the expense of people's own memories and histories. These researchers also emphasize that the late modern trend to sell historical places tends to accentuate precisely such official History, which inevitably leads to conflicts with those who prefer memory. Ultimately, it is a question of whose city and whose history is spoken of or presented (Cantell 1999, 144).

I will in a few concluding paragraphs try to discuss the image of history as it is conveyed by these various media, "the stories of life in days of old" and the renovated buildings, and the nostalgia each of these possibly expresses. In this attempt, I myself aim at the critically reflecting view, which should be able to balance between memories and the official History.

## History and memories

Ethnological methodology should have something to contribute when it comes to the relation between recollection, narration and the history of places. The Jyväskylä study expressly emphasized movement in space. In my conclusion, I will therefore talk about movement in space, both in the present, but also in the past landscape. The excerpts above show a clear tendency in the narration: the narrators placed themselves in a position where they could move also in the Helsinki of yesterday. Not all of the responses are of this character, but several of them are. Through this movement, the writers were able to register in hindsight and convey what they had *seen* and observed. Thus they were able to paint the picture they had within themselves and so recreate something they had experienced. In this sense, the space does not exist without those who move in it and observe it, or historically seen, without those who have moved in it. The narrators remember themselves as a part of the life of the street rather than as observers of the façades of the buildings. Without this collective memory, a city or any other place loses the web of generations which constitutes the prerequisite for culture (cf. the memories of Viipuri before the war, which are only preserved with those evacuated to Finland). Benjamin says that this knowledge is usually presented orally from one to the other (Benjamin 1990, 345). The fact that the narratives used above are available to us must therefore be regarded as unusual.

Henri Lefebvre describes the space experienced as having a core, a self, or projection, a room, a house, a church, etc. In this material, there are clear projections partly onto the childhood home, and partly onto the house(s) where the narrator has lived. Other important places, too, become projections of the self. In the excerpts on the centre, there are also projections, often onto the most beautiful place of the city, the Senaatintori square, but usually the self moves and reflects the space along a walk, a route with streets as co-ordinates and certain buildings as landmarks, but, above all, with everyday, well known places to visit or stroll past. The dimension of architectural history is not very important, but through memories, the buildings are given the role of surrounding both urban life and the epochs this takes place in. This is what Benjamin refers to when he notes that to the flaneur, the city unfolds like a landscape and encloses him like a chamber (Benjamin 1990, 345; Åström 1999; 2000).

The new, trendy city centres are, for their part, *consciously* built and *improved* expressly in order to provide this backdrop: one should be able to stroll, drop into various places, sit down, observe. Both movement and gaze are as important also in the present for the flaneurship that is regarded as being one of the central dimensions of urban individuals (Benjamin 1990; Tester 1994). Certain extreme urban spaces, such as shopping centres, often in their interior world use the structure of the street and house-like façades for a cosy atmosphere. In addition, a historicizing surface is often created in order for the shopper and flaneur to feel at home, or, as Ziehe claims, to realise their own modes of living in the present (Ziehe 1993, 32).

In analogy with this, the historical façades in the centre, in their newly polished appearances, also get new meanings. They, too, become surfaces in which to reflect oneself in a new way. Helsinki has a relatively well-preserved exterior with blocks both from the early and the late 19th century, early 20th century and a functionalist era with some manifestations in the centre (Lasipalatsi, Tennispalatsi), but which left its thorough mark in the outskirts of the centre and the suburbs up to the end of the 1940's. The historical features of the centre stand out the more clearly as more new areas are built in the various peripheral parts of the city. The whole centre is elevated not only through the intensified supply of entertainment and consumption, but also through the opportunity to use the various style epochs in a new way. When the centre is remoulded into a relaxing living room for leisure, consumption and enjoyment of art, the historical environment plays an important part. It is in this light, that the new expertise in the area of city planning has been anxious to expose the historical layers.

From the ethnological material, for its part, the following emerges. A person who carries a memory of a landscape within himself or herself, can make continuous comparisons between the present and various past epochs. Thus diametrically different eras, such as the era of the city life lived in blocks, emerge clearly in relation to later decades closer in time. The one who remembers can actively take part in the new living space that the centre offers, while, at the same time, other images are there to be brought out. The centre's own appearance in the present is therefore always both a limited point in time (the present) *and* a choice between various eras. It is actually only the individual who is totally able to freely let different times pass by in relation to what he or she is observing. The historically critical view, for its part, is more systematisized and generalising – and of course longer than a life span.

Here, it is possible to refer both to Marcel Proust and to Walter Benjamin to further discuss the sensitive question as to whether reminiscences are always expressions of nostalgia. Marcel Proust claimed – specifically as interpreted by Georges Poulet – that a localisation always takes place in the memory process: a building, a city, a solid topographical unit emerges, often so that it feels neither blurred nor unclear (Poulet 1977, 16). However, Proust claimed that the worlds one remembers have, so to say, their own limits which cannot be bridged. In the informants' recollections of the cen- tre, this is manifested in that they often have chosen a certain epoch, which they remember clearly (often their youth in the case of the centre), while continuity and the gradual change seems indistinct. The "clear" images, on the other hand, can be compared to the present. The limits often also mean that the recollections are not only closed to gradual changes along the time axis, but also that space in reminiscence is not perceived as a continuum, but as a whole world, complete in itself (Poulet 1977, 33, 37–39). This, in fact, is true of the images both of the district where the informant grew up and of the centre (cf. Olsson, p. 84). In the reminiscences, these often constitute two separate worlds. And the way, the route, to the centre is included in the image of the centre and not in the image of the home district.

The idea of the whole and the feeling of completeness that such reminis- cences create, have been further developed by Walter Benjamin. He wants to see a connection between "superior" recollection and the possibility of ascribing something new to an object. This means that adults, when they become aware of having lost something, ascribe to the memory of this lost object a shimmer that it hardly had at the time when it was not yet lost. By this ascribed aura, their recollection becomes "superior". At the same time, they can see the irretrievably lost object and its relation to the approaching present and future. Ziehe claims that, in this, no return is simulated. Instead, a momentary object, here a place, is given a significance by its merging in the present with memories and something new, a third meaning arises (Ziehe 1993, 31). This new significance does not exist either in the place or the reminiscing individual, but in a constellation between them. The new glory appears as a shimmer or a veil.

When individuals write down their memories they lift the veil, but the glory can hardly be transformed, or actually conveyed. It exists only with the ascribing individual. It remains, according to Benjamin, a "secret", or, pertaining to places, a dimension in the position that de Certeau calls enig- matic (de Certeau 1988, 108). The shimmer or veil is possibly perceived by others as nostalgia, even if the aura that the one who remembers ascribes to the loss is a private emotion. The collective memory often remoulds and gives stability to the private. Something that is described – as in this article – also gets another character. Benjamin points out that if the object were ex- posed, it would actually appear as very insignificant (Ziehe 1993, 32). When reading the memories of Helsinki, fragments of which have been presented here, the recollections and the places described can also be thought of as "insignificant". However, in addition to being seemingly important for the writers, the attempt at conveying them is in itself significant.

It is memory with a small m that wants to get its voice heard in a situa- tion where so many other voices prevail. The fact that these voices originate in various selves, cores that have experienced the space, gives the image of the centre of Helsinki unique perspectives. Each narrative is an attempt at describing the comprehensive view of the writer, at, in hindsight, enticing the lost landscape. The quotations above do not do justice to this aspect, but it is in this that the fact is clear that the individual actually perceives of the city as a creative thing to participate in, as Lefebvre claims. This pertains to all city dwellers; the longer one lives in a city, the deeper is one's comprehensive image of it. The reminiscence is "superior" also in that only those who have memories can reflect and play with them. They can choose a certain perspective and eras, which is what these writers have done.[2]

Also when carrying out restoration work, one can choose to accentuate the historical dimension by *choosing* one epoch that the building or the buildings represent, and then consciously emphasizing this style. In the Esplanades as a whole this epoch is the turn of the 19th century and in the area around the Lasipalatsi, the 1930's. Modern architecture accentuates the present (Kiasma). According to this view, the architectural highlights and the periods of creation are emphasized, while the time during which the buildings have existed after this are often regarded as secondary. It is, however, often these periods that in the memories of the inhabitants form the backdrop for everyday life and the repeated appropriations of the centre that take place within the framework of them. Therefore the intervening periods are also interesting as such. Which is the history of these periods?

It is impossible to physically or socially recreate the Esplanades and the Mannerheiminkatu of the 1950's and 1960's – and probably not a desirable project. Their appearance can, however, be carefully revealed by historical studies that focus on the restructuring of, for example, the shops, the local fashion, the spirit of the times, etc. – and on the level of recollection within individuals. In their insignificance, the narratives provide information of certain features in the past street life. They are often factually descriptive and have, perhaps, a touch of tour guiding to them. There is something one wishes to "show". It has been pointed out that the motivation for autobiographical narrative can be that one, in a way, wants to present a story one is afraid will be lost. With one's own truth one wishes to rescue something. One is, on some level, aware that the lifestyles one describes are different from those of today. As the concept of youth can be used to represent the seeking for other lifestyles (Ziehe 1993, 51), the stories of one's own youth can, conversely, point to a historical diversity of lifestyles. The relation between "now" and "then" can even be taken to its extreme in that one, from today's horizon that can be regarded as full of simulations, by narrating that which is lost also wants to reach or convey something that feels more "real" (cf. Butler 1999, 153). As material, these different descriptions therefore also become parts of the image of the centre of Helsinki during past decades and, above all, of how the individual has perceived of the urban life.

To move in the new **living room** that post-modernism has resulted in, does not exclude the opportunity to move in and even find the **living space** that one has left behind:

I have thought whether there is anything in Helsinki that I would be particularly fond of, or whether everything drowns in the crowds of people and the traffic. Helsinki should be experienced early on a Sunday morning. Only then one is able to find behind everything else the true being of the city – or on a summer night. The parks and the shores! ... I look for typical streets and still find a few in Punavuori and Kallio, but they are far from the centre, where one usually moves. But perhaps it is good that they are far away. (Lecturer, b. 1945, IV:9, 3.)

## NOTES

1   Close to 500 long descriptions were submitted during three years, 1995-1997. The respondents were asked to describe in detail both their local environment and their activities in the centre during various decades: what they did, how they used the city's cultural and commercial supply, how they moved from place to place and how they perceived of the surrounding environment.
2   Rather than being nostalgic, reminiscences of places and shifts, for example, "in youthful situations", may be fetishist; this is the case if one denies the present and returns to the past in order to be "young again" (cf. Ziehe 1993, 31). Undeniably, there are such tendencies also in the present material. An appropriation of place in the memory might, if it is used and repeated, be an obstacle for perception in the present and the feeling for native place might be exaggerated.

## SOURCES AND BIBLIOGRPAHY

Questionnaires

I     Helsingfors som livsmiljö [Helsinki as living environment]. 1995. 182 answers.
II    Min generations Helsingfors [The Helsinki of my generation]. 1996. 90 answers.
III   Helsingfors, huvudstaden – min stad [Helsinki, the capital – my city]. 1997. 96 answers.
IV    Vad betyder Helsingfors för mig [What Helsinki means to me]. 1997. 128 answers.
      At the disposal of the author, to be transferred to the Helsinki City Archives.

## Literature

Åström, Anna-Maria 1993. Urban Culture – Consumer Culture – Cultural Criticism. On young people's interpretation of modern shopping centres in Helsinki. In Z. Sarvas (ed.): *Interacting Communities*. Budapest.

Åström, Anna-Maria 1995. Der Fishermarkt in Helsingfors (Helsinki) als Identitätsmerkmal der Schweden in Finnland. Ein Beitrag zur Diskussion über Symbolisches Kapital. *Schweizerisches Archiv für Volkskunde* 91(1995), H. 2, 129–142.

Åström, Anna-Maria, Olsson, Pia & Kivistö, Jorma 1998. *Elämää kaupungissa – Att bo i stan. Muistikuvia Helsingin keskustasta – Minnesbilder från centrum av Helsingfors.* [Living in the city. Memories from the centre of Helsinki]. Memoria 12. Helsinki: The City Museum of Helsinki.

Åström, Anna-Maria 1999. Ordinary People in Post-War Helsinki. Urban Popular Culture: Practices, Delimitations and Recent Elevations. In Kodolányi, János jr (ed.): *Ethnic Communities, Ethnic Studies, Ethnic Costumes Today*. Budapest: Hungarian Ethnographical Society, 101–115.

Åström, Anna-Maria 1999. Helsingfors anda – huvudstadens nationella och lokala betydelser. *Budkavlen* 1999, 26–55.

Åström, Anna-Maria 2000. The spirit of Helsinki. *Quarterly from the City of Helsinki Urban Facts. Kvartti. 2/2000, 33–39.*

Benjamin, Walter 1990. *Paris 1800-talets huvudstad. Passagearbetet* [Paris, the capital of the 19th century. The passage works]. Volume 1. Stockholm: Symposion.

Butler, Rex 1999. *Jean Baudrillard. The defence of the real.* London: Sage.

Cantell, Timo 1997. Konstens natt i Helsingfors på 1990-talet [The Night of the Arts in Helsinki in the 1990's]. *Laboratorium för folk och kultur* 1997/2, 19–20.

Cantell, Timo 1999. *Helsinki and a vision of place.* Helsinki: City of Helsinki Urban Facts.

Certeau, Michel de 1988. *The practice of everyday life.* Berkeley and Los Angeles: University of California Press.

Finnegan, Ruth 1999. *Tales of the city. A study of narrative and urban life.* Cambridge: Cambridge University Press.

Harvey, David 1989. *The condition of postmodernity. An Enquiry into the Origins of Cultural Change.* Cambridge, Mass: Blackwell.

Hewison, Robert 1987. *The heritage industry. Britain in a climate of decline.* London: Methuen.

Ilmonen, Mervi 1999. Helsingin Senaatintori muistiteatterina [The Senaatintori square in Helsinki as a theatre of memory]. In *Urbs – kirja Helsingin kaupunkikulttuurista* [Urbs – a book on the urban culture in Helsinki]. Helsinki: Helsingin kaupungin tietokeskus/Edita, 91–103.

Klein, Barbro (ed.) 1995. *Gatan är vår. Ritualer på offentliga platser* [The street is ours. Rituals in public places]. Stockholm: Carlssons.

Lefebvre, Henri 1982 [1968]. *Staden som rättighet* [The city as a Right]. Lund: Bokomotiv.

Lefebvre, Henri 1998 [1991]. *The Production of Space.* Oxford and Cambridge: Blackwell.

Linko, Maaria 1999. Taidetta(kin) olohuoneessa [Art (too) in the living room]. In *Urbs – kirja Helsingin kaupunkikulttuurista* [Urbs – a book on the urban culture in Helsinki]. Helsinki: Helsingin kaupungin tietokeskus/Edita, 73–87.

Mäenpää, Pasi 1993. *Niin moni tulee vastaan. Katutason tutkimus kaupunkijulkisuudesta* [One meets so many. A street level study of urban publicity]. Helsingin kaupunki-suunniteluviraston julkaisuja 1993:14. Helsinki.

Mäenpää, Pasi 1999. Viihtymisen kaupunki [A city of comfort]. In *Urbs – kirja Helsingin kaupunkikulttuurista* [Urbs – a book on the urban culture in Helsinki]. Helsinki: Helsingin kaupungin tietokeskus/Edita, 17–31.

Mäkelä, Johanna & Rajanti, Tiina 1999. Caféistuminen [Sitting in cafés]. In *Urbs – kirja Helsingin kaupunkikulttuurista* [Urbs – a book on the urban culture in Helsinki]. Helsinki: Helsingin kaupungin tietokeskus/Edita, 55–71.

Proust, Marcel 1982. *På spaning efter den tid som flytt I–V* [Orig. A la recherche du temps perdu]. Stockholm: Bonniers.

Ronneberger, Klaus 1990. Metropolitane Urbanität. Der "Plasterstrand" als Medium einer in die Städtische Elite aufsteigende Subkultur. In Heinz Schilling (ed.): *Urbane Zeiten. Lebensstilenwürfe und Kulturvandel in einer Stadtregion.* Notizen, Band 34. Frankfurt (Main): Universität Frankfurt am Main.

Ruoppila, Sampo & Cantell, Timo 1999. Ravintolat ja Helsingin elävöityminen [Restaurants and the livening of Helsinki]. In *Urbs – kirja Helsingin kaupunkikulttuurista* [Urbs – a book on the urban culture in Helsinki]. Helsinki: Helsingin kaupungin tietokeskus/Edita, 35–53.

Tester, Keith (ed.) 1994. *The Flaneur.* London and New York: Routledge.

Ziehe, Thomas 1993. *Kulturanalyser. Ungdom, utbildning, modernitet* [Cultural analyses. Youth, education, modernity]. Stockholm: Symposion.

Zukin, Sharon 1995. *The Cultures of Cities.* Cambridge, Mass: Blackwell Publications.

PIA OLSSON

# Constructing Local Identity

## The Folklorism of an Urban Workers Culture in Helsinki

*in the district (n'hood?) of Kallio.*

K allio is a fascinating district: distinctive, unknown and even scary. Kallio is the district of the poor, the arty people and the working class. Indeed, with its many faces, Kallio defies all generalisations. Even the newly elected president will continue to live in the neighbourhood, in Wallininkatu, for a few weeks. Kallio is Hakaniemi market square, Brahis and Kurvi. Kallio is the busy lottery cafés. Kallio is the small shops that offer individual service – familiar, personal and tiny. Aquarium fish, computer hardware, porn videos and children's clothes are sold cheerfully side by side. Just as in all big cities. (Helsingin Sanomat 21.2.2000.)

The "strange attraction" of Kallio was thus described in the city pages of Helsingin Sanomat (Finland's largest national newspaper) in February 2000. In the city-scape painted here, the life in the streets of a big city is identified with intimate social interaction, the traditional meeting-places of the district are situated alongside modern paraphernalia, and the area hitherto known as a working class district gains new esteem as the home of the president. "Kallio is a distinctive district of arty people and the working class" was the headline on the front page of the newspaper. This is also how an active member of the district association sees Kallio:

> - - I think Kallio has this wonderful feature, that everybody here accepts
> each other - - that we understand each other here and that is apparent in
> everyone – by contrast, for example with Töölö, where people don't speak
> that much to each other - - as one policeman said, there's a difference:
> when one goes to Kruununhaka, people there are so strict, in Töölö the
> ladies wear lace gloves even in summer, as well as a hat and a handbag,
> just so, but in Kallio people are open in a way, everybody feels at home - - I
> think this shows in the streets. When one compares it with other districts,
> Kallio is the most open and all in all one feels a kind of understanding and
> that's perhaps why all other activities are placed here, since we are relaxed,
> accepting and we respect each other - -. (Interview 12.10.1999.)

Should we draw the conclusion from these descriptions that Kallio is more pluralistic than other districts in Helsinki? And are the people in Kallio really exceptionally understanding and tolerant? It is probably impossible to answer such questions. The primary aim of descriptions such as those quoted

*The changed environment of Kallio described by many informants is visible in these two pictures taken from the same spot – the Kallio church tower. The low wooden houses from the beginning of the century are photographed in the 1920's. Fifty years later, the milieu is dominated by cars and blocks of flats. Photos: I. Timiriasev 1920, Kari Hakli 1972, Helsinki City Museum, Helsinki.*

above is to create an image of a unique district, distinct from its neighbours. The testimony of the "strange attraction" of Kallio and its atmosphere, which is described as tolerant, is part of a contemporary trend which aims at the mystification of places, and which manufactures images of the characteristic features of various districts. Facts are intertwined with images and the notions of the nature of the area may become blurred or simplified. Each one of us forms a conception of our surroundings on the basis of an area larger than our immediate, well-known environment. According to geographer Yi-Fu Tuan (1979, 88), the creation of such approximate notions of one's environment is necessary. Tuan claims that even these imprecise images help us form an understanding of the surrounding world and its structures.

"An area is not only a physical structure but also a symbolic construction", writes Mervi Ilmonen in her study of the differentiation of the housing areas in Helsinki. Theories of the segregation of housing districts have recently also taken into account cultural perspectives, according to which images and their accumulation, as well as ways of living, patterns of consumption and everyday practices influence the formation of the environment (Ilmonen 1997, 13, 15). The identity of an area is formed by its physical character, history, social structure, culture, language and dialects. The symbols, images and expectations connected to the area are, in turn, born on the basis of these (Riikonen 1997, 179). The images of the characters of different areas are shaped both by outsiders and by those living in the area. Pekka Kaunismaa has defined collective identity as being more of a cultural than a psychological phenomenon. As a cultural phenomenon, collective identity is intersubjective by nature and thus presupposes a shared understanding of the circumstances. According to Kaunismaa, collective identities consist of symbolic codes that, justifiably, can be called myths: stories, ways of expression and symbolic signs and habits. They are conceptions of groups, communities and social systems born out of the interaction between people. These myths signify the group or community to which people see themselves as belonging or would like to belong (Kaunismaa 1997, 41–43, 45, 49–50). Thus, there is reason to ask what concrete factors mould our perceptions of various districts, in this case Kallio in the inner city of Helsinki. What factors emerge when the aim is to make Kallio a distinctive district and what channels can be used for the creation of images?

## Kallio's identity as construction

Even if the differences between various districts in a city might seem small to the eyes of an outsider, the significance of these for the inhabitants of the areas should not be underestimated. On the contrary, according to Anthony P. Cohen, the borders surrounding a district or a community gain the more significance the closer they actually are to the group. Symbols perform a crucial role in this construction of borders. Their role is not to reveal final and real characteristics, but rather, they form an important resource for the creation of meaning. The members of the group all share the same symbols,

51

but their actual significance can vary greatly between the individual members of the community. In order for the symbols to function as a unifying resource despite the varying interpretation of them, they must actively be shaped in the desired direction (Cohen 1985, 13, 15).

One visible way of creating and strengthening local symbols is to erect memorials and statues. The statue entitled "A Working Class Mother", showing a mother wringing out washing together with her daughter was placed north of the Pitkäsilta bridge in Helsinki in the mid-90's. Ylermi Runko, director-general and member of the statue committee, expressed his own view of the meaning of the statue:

> Thanks to our mothers
>
> I have stopped to ponder what has driven us, men and women who have done our lives' work, to start this project for the Working Class Mother statue. We have left our old home environment. The world has taken us on to our own career paths. Few of us have kept in touch with the old neighbourhood and the boys and girls of our home blocks. Despite all this, we have felt a strange interest in our old quarters even if the wooden houses have disappeared and a stone village has grown in our old backyards. - -
>
> May this statue express our thanks to those mothers who with their extra work, washing and cleaning for wealthy families, opened the gates of education and the road to development for their offspring. We have not forgotten this, even if Finns so seldom say thank you. May this be the thanks of our generation to those who raised us. (Runko 1994.)

*One of the symbols of the history of the area north of the "Long Bridge" reflecting the values of constructed regional identity is the statue "A Working Class Mother" that was unveiled in the mid-1990's. Photo: Hely Rautiainen, Helsinki City Museum, Helsinki.*

The statue was realised as a joint project of the inhabitants of the Kallio and Vallila districts (Rautio 1998, 317), and thus for its own part it reflects the values and areas of the past that the former and present inhabitants of the districts wish to bring to the fore. Many of the other statues in the area seem also to have emerged as symbols expressly dedicated to the district's own past. There is a great contrast here in comparison with another inner city district, Töölö, where memorials are erected expressly to honour nationally prominent persons or state events. There is a long tradition of representing the working class and its ideology in the form of statues in Kallio. "The Boxers" was erected in the early 1930's and the models for this statue were boxers from the Jyry sports club for the districts north of the Pitkäsilta bridge. National politicians who are memorialised as statues in the district are the social democrat ministers Väinö Tanner and Miina Sillanpää. The Kallio Association has participated in the financing of memorials dedicated to the author and poet Arvo Turtianen, known for his descriptions of Kallio, and the actor Tauno Palo, who also grew up north of Pitkäsilta. The statue dedicated to war-time women was erected at a central location in front of the Kallio administration building in 1996. (Rautio 1998, 303–304, 307–308, 314.) These memorials emphasise, on the one hand, Kallio's past as working class district from the perspective of everyday life. On the other hand, the significance of ideological activity and political success are displayed through the statues of social democratic politicians from the district who have reached nationally influential positions. The past of Kallio is represented by the statues as characterised by sacrifice and work done in hope for a better life for future generations: as sacrifices, but also as achievements – as a form of heroic saga (see Snellman 1996, 236).

As can be concluded from the history of the statues, one of the creators of the image of Kallio is the Kallio Association. The predecessor of this association *Sörkän Gibat* (the Fellows of Sörkkä) was founded in the autumn 1940. Even if the association originally was open only to men, its aim was to function as a local district society. It was actually one of the first Finnish-speaking local societies on Helsinki (Koskinen 1990, 538–539). "Working for local ideology as a district association since 1940" is the motto quoted in the association's newsletter. In the emblem of the association, a relaxed fellow from Sörkkä walks towards Kallio church – one of the landmarks of the district. Using the terminology of Eric Hobsbawm and Terence Rangers, the Swedish historian of ideas, Bosse Sundin, has explored the construction, the conscious creation of local identity. He observes that, parallel to "the official writing of history", there is also a local identity which is formed spontaneously and is strongly tied to place. As an example of the shaping of such a spontaneous identity he describes the transfer of information in free conversation. Sundin believes that stories based on persons, family relations, past events and the local geography of an area create a sense of local identity in the listeners, often unconsciously, even in multicultural, large cities (Sundin 1997, 43–44). A district association can be seen as a kind of cross between the formation of spontaneous and of constructed identities. The founding of an association is a conscious decision for developing the local *[handwritten marginalia: — local identity forms from free-form interaction but also is constructed by institutional development (W provides for further free form interaction) + now even interactive web sites as constructed forms fo independent local identity formation]*

spirit. However, its various activities, such as the publishing of a district paper and the organising of various get-togethers, also offer opportunities for spontaneous identity development. The history of the place is no longer necessarily mediated through spontaneous discussions, but nevertheless in relatively free forms, and thus influences the feeling of local identity in the participants.

Carefully designed web pages based on research and fiction are a contemporary example of conscious constructions of a local identity. The local album "On the wrong side of Pitkäsilta bridge" on the Internet (www. pitkasilta.hai.fi/) repeats, but also enacts an ironic attitude to the features usually associated with Kallio. Presentations cover both the history of the district and its role as a working class area, "the romantic outskirts" as well as the poor and the bohemians. The voice of Kallio is supposed to stay alive on the "sounding-off" page where people can express their opinions about the happenings and conditions of the district or read what others think of the district. Again, the tool used is a *constructed* instrument for the spontaneous creation of local identity. The best "rants" preserved on the web page agree with the image of Kallio as a tolerant district, but, surprisingly, a majority of the comments dismiss the "atmosphere" and "elegance" of Kallio. The history of the district and its manifestations are well known. However, in the nostalgic remembrance the past problems of the district are not acknowledged and instead the negative conditions are associated exclusively with present day phenomena: *[handwritten: commonly knowledge]*

> I have lived in Kallio all my 43 years and now I am angry. I remember the men from who, in the 50's and 60's, used to hang around outside the Vaasa Hall with their mates from Kurvi who had a bit of a bad reputation. At 5 in the evening these men went home to their dinners of soup cooked by their wives, who had returned from washing the rugs. After that, the streets were quiet and empty until the buying of illegal booze started in Vaasa Park. So, what makes me angry now? The fact that all sorts of anti-social people who create disturbances wherever they go are systematically placed here. Within a few hundred metres there are places for former prisoners, the homeless, as well as a drugs clinic and a home for recovering drug addicts, etc. Do the authorities wish to turn this district into an area where normal, working people with families can no longer live? - -

> The elegant atmosphere of Kallio has disappeared because of the disgusting brawls of drunks and junkies that nowadays fill every bloody street. Parents do not want to let their children play in the parks amongst all the needles and bottles. - - The famous Kallio atmosphere is now only empty words. It doesn't exist anywhere but in people's imaginations. Good luck to those living there among that stupidity. Fortunately I got away and no longer have to pretend to be a tolerant citizen when a wino pisses through the fence of the children's park in the middle of the day.

> Kallio tolerant??? It is the only district where all sorts of abuse is shouted at anybody who dresses a bit differently from the basic boring style. - - The tolerance of Kallio is confined to drunks and other drop-outs puking/pissing/shaking/threatening all over the place. - - In reality, the

areas south of Pitkäsilta are considerably more tolerant. The people are friendlier and nicer.

Statistics show that in the 1990's Kallio, besides the city centre, was the area where most assaults happened (Tuominen 1999, 52). The comments on the home page characterise alcoholics and drug addicts as a threat to the atmosphere, but also to the safety of the area. The tolerance associated with the image of Kallio has in practice turned against itself. The tolerance is described as exaggerated when the inhabitants no longer feel safe in their own district.

Museums have traditionally held an important role in the official creation of local identity. Each place has a past of its own, which in one way or another is visible also in the present. Thus, not even an urban suburb is a truly rootless society. In addition, internationalisation and the modern perception of a world that feels boundless have created a new need to emphasise the characteristics of local environments. This is a kind of competitive profiling, where museums have an opportunity to take on a crucial role (Sundin 1997, 62). From this perspective, the Helsinki City Museum can be regarded as having also supported the profiling of the areas north of Pitkäsilta. An initiative to found a museum presenting working class housing was taken in the Helsinki City Council in 1980. The decision to open the museum in a wooden house in Alppiharju, which was built at the beginning of the 20th century, was taken in 1986. The last inhabitants of the building moved out a year later, when the renovation began. It is therefore appropriate that the museum comprises ten one-room flats which are furnished in styles ranging

*The coffee table for a christening party is laid in the home of a working family in 1948. The Working Class Housing Museum represents the ways of living profiling the special character of the area. Photo: Helsinki City Museum, Helsinki.*

55

from the 1920's to the 1980's. On show are, for example, the dwelling of an electrician of the 1930's, the home of a widow and her seven children of the 1920's and the room of a single man of the 1980's (Heino 1990a, 130; Heino 1990b, 174; Järvinen 1990, 168–169, 173). The museum thus represents the housing conditions of the working class not only in terms of a historical past, but also with a strong showing of recent developments in the area. The profiling of Kallio as a working class district does not only arise from historical conditions alone but is still an active feature of the present day, even in the museum.

In addition to the district association, the inhabitants of Kallio are able to mould their own local identity within the framework of another association. In 1995, the association Stadin Slangi (the Slang of the City) was founded in Helsinki. This association is intended for everybody who feels "the city to be their home". So, it is not an association for a certain district, but in spite of this, the majority of its members were born north of Pitkäsilta. This is natural to the extent that the slang is expressly the spoken language of the Helsinki working class and thus most likely to be found in that particular area (Paunonen 1995, 20). The nature of the activities of the association and its significance for its members is reflected in the fact that, in spite of repeated efforts, it is difficult to recruit young people as active members to the association, even if it already has a thousand members in all. Nostalgia is also a strong factor guiding the activities of this association. The relation between the Helsinki slang and the working class district is portrayed by the association's unofficial theme song "Niin gimis on Stadi" (The City is Really Great). The words of this popular song were written at the front-line of the war in the beginning of the 1940's and they expressly concentrate on describing Kallio and its surroundings: "Näkis Hagiksen platsit ja Brahiksen matsit ja Valgan – voi jebulis, se stemmaa" (To see the places in Hakaniemi and the matches in the Brahe park and Vallila – oh yeah, that would be great).

Anna-Maria Åström has suggested that the urban life-style north of Pitkäsilta was influenced by the simultaneous establishment of borders on two different levels. On one hand, a border was formed and consciously created within the city in relation to the wealthier districts, and on the other, in relation to the countryside and its rural dwellers. The urban slang, which explicitly was the language of young boys, was, according to Åström, a clear way of identifying with a certain district and its popular culture. The fact that a specific association has been founded for the slang, the members of which are no longer young boys, reflects the change in attitudes towards the phenomenon. The slang has nostalgically been elevated as a cultural phenomenon to the position of a kind of disappearing popular tradition. (Åström 2000, 161–162.) The margin has become a central part of the culture of the city. Popular urban culture is brought to the fore in social contexts. Its manifestations, such as its vernacular (slang) and local stories, achieve a cultural value, which can be manipulated according to various aims (Åström 1999b, 113).

The attainment of cultural esteem for the vernacular is partially influenced by the fact that researchers have directed their interest on phenomena within urban and working class culture. According to Timo J. Virtanen, it took a long time for urban culture to become the object of ethnological study since it was difficult to find a research object that forms a coherent whole among "cities and the city dwellers that have arisen at various times and taken on various roles". Urban traditions earned a part in the creation of a Finnish national identity only in the 1960's. (Virtanen 1997, 104–105.) Considering this background, the present symbolic use of urban tradition does not seem surprising. The rise of the phenomenon into becoming an object for research is one indication of its significance and has provided a means for increasing its perceived value.

## Constructed community and symbolic locality

According to Anthony P. Cohen (1982, 3–6), people become aware of their own culture at its border, at the point where they perceive another culture, with a set of behaviours that deviate from their own. These borders are always relative: they can be artificial and they might be created precisely in order to allow the group to stand out from their surroundings. However, this process not only results in an awareness of one's own culture; at the same time, it and the differing culture are evaluated either in positive or negative terms. Thus, the pragmatic function of tradition can be seen as more important than the significance of its contents: the past and its sectors might be safeguarded, not purely for their historical inherent value, but in order for us to be able to create an image of ourselves using these traditions. Cohen emphasises the importance of everyday life in the raising of the awareness of one's own culture. The feeling of belonging to a certain place can be awakened by the most various means: through spoken language, through the knowledge of genealogy or ecology, through jokes or a common religion. Cohen claims that these function as a counter-force against cultural imperialism and political and financial concentrations. Also peripherality and marginality can form a collective self-image. According to Robert Shields, the division of areas into centres and peripheries is not only based on geographical differences, but can be explained by their social value within a certain cultural system. The formation of cultural margins takes place through social and cultural activities. The dominant view of culture and its official discourses defines the area of social otherness, which is not only despised and abused, but also functions as the basis for the position of the governing culture. Our images of places are produced historically, but they also abide in contemporary history and are thus continuously questioned. (Shields 1991, 3–5, 18.)

In studying a district of the Maltese capital Valetta, which was regarded as a slum and was demolished and rebuilt in the 1970's, John P. Mitchell has noted that a communal solidarity and a feeling of safety associated with place are emphasised in the memories of the area. The former inhabitants of the district, who were placed in various sites around the city when their home area was demolished, had not only given up their primitive and cramped housing, but had, at the same time, lost the social structure that had formed itself in the district. The reforms, which were carried out with no regard

57

to the wishes of the inhabitants, meant that old neighbour relations were broken and that a new life had to be started in a new neighbourhood. In the reminiscence of the inhabitants, the lost district forms a whole, within which everything was shared and thus safe. Mitchell describes the feeling of the former inhabitants of an all-embracing solidarity using the image of family unity. He sees the phenomenon as belonging to the sphere of constructed nostalgia. (Mitchell 1998, 83, 85.) Constructed nostalgia refers to a way of thinking, where the past is seen as a paradise-like community consisting of pure social relations (Herzfeld 1997, 109). Mitchell claims that the memories of what is lost are connected to a larger Maltese social debate. The values associated with the demolished area are seen as the opposite of modernisation and party politics. By destroying through demolition a close community, the government also destroyed the opportunity of the community to defend itself against the features of modernisation that it experienced as dangerous. Thus, the inhabitants now have the possibility of using their loss as a political weapon: the measures that were intended as improvements have turned out to be a failure from the inhabitants' viewpoint. Mitchell emphasises that community and its symbolic or nostalgic construction are formed expressly in relation to general national and international processes.

So, we might ask, what national processes govern the formation of the local identity in the Kallio district in the centre of Helsinki? The Kallio Association, the Stadin Slangi association, the statues that reflect the district's past and even the museum founded on the initiative of the city council, can be seen as functioning as symbols for the local community and partly also as features of constructed nostalgia. At the same time, these are manifestations of a folklorism based on urban culture. By folklorism, I mean the re-use of phenomena of the past and the detachment of these from their historical context for aims corresponding to contemporary demands. Folklorism, which has largely drawn on peasant culture, has at times been seen explicitly as a tendentious romanticisation of rural culture and it has been felt to be a critical, negative feature of urbanisation (Korff 1980, 43). Furthermore, in Finland generally, phenomena from the rural folk tradition have usually been revived for cultural recycling. The revitalization of a peasant tradition became particularly common in the 1960's. In fact, Matti Räsänen asks whether this was a counter-reaction to the depopulation of the countryside and the perceived threat of a multinational culturalism. Räsänen notes that the ideas and elements of the folklorism of the 1960's resembled the forms of the rural folklore activities in the 19th century, but remarks that the actors had changed. While the activities in the 1800's were carried out by the intelligentsia, the actors in the latter half of the 20th century were "the people" themselves. (Räsänen 1989, 26.) Folklorism is an instrument which is often used expressly for the strengthening of local and national identities, the agents behind it being various local associations. In this form, folklorism has been seen as a protest against other general contemporary phenomena (Centergran 1992, 119, 121). Phenomena of popular culture, which have been detached from their original context and given folkloristic features, always have new meanings and functions (Bausinger 1969, 5).

Folklorism has been criticised, among other things, for almost exclusively focussing on phenomena that have been, or are being, experienced as positive in life. According to Ulla Centergran (Centergran 1992, 127), the basic significance of folklorism for modern people is to bring joy and festivity into life. In this respect, the urban working class culture as a form of folklorism forms an exception. Poverty, cramped housing and heavy work are a complete opposite to the usual folkloristic objects. The romanticised constructed nostalgia of the Kallio working class can be compared to other vocational groups, as Hanna Snellman has shown in the case of the rafters. The romanticisation of their profession improved the position of the rafters in society and at the same time it became an ingredient in the identity of Lapland as a whole: a threat turned into an opportunity. According to Snellman, the 20th century attitude to the rafter culture is a question of re-orientation: the heritage of the past is utilized as the stone base for belonging to a group. The utilisation can serve commercial, entertainment as well as ideological interests. (Snellman 1996, 245–246.)

What is the aim of the folklorism arising from the working class urban culture? What national or international processes at the turn of the millennium does it fulfil? The basics of the construction of identity can be sought in the individual's need to identify with a certain group but also in larger social processes. In the case of Kallio, what has to be observed is a strong identification with an urban working class tradition, where the past is revealed as being characterised by hard work, poverty and sacrifice. The financial boom during the 1980's elevated the status of Kallio; at least the image of the district became a middle-class one. During the last few years, a common trend in the change of urban space is its standardisation and the disappearance of local traditions. Culture has here been seen as holding an important role in the construction of positive urban images (Andersson 1997, 111, 117). Gentrification, that is, the social and physical change of the inner city areas surrounding the centre, is also connected to the creating of an image, where the history of the city is freely utilized. In Finland, the working class districts, which had become dilapidated in the 1960's and 1970's, were the objects of urban renovation in the 1980's and 1990's. One explanation given to the renewal of the inner city districts is the interest of the new middle class in individual living, which is assumed to increase one's symbolic capital (Jauhiainen 1997, 129–132, 134). The differences between the various areas of Helsinki were strongly evened out from 1960 to 1990. Working class districts with a very low status and districts of the upper classes and intelligentsia with a very high status are rare today (Lankinen 1997, 173–174).

Sociologist Pasi Mäenpää, who has studied the gentrification of Kallio, has suggested that the working class in the 1980's was no longer a characteristic feature of the district other than as "a diluted and romanticised fraction". In 1985, only 35 per cent of the inhabitants in the area were classified as working class. The level of education among the inhabitants of Kallio increased in the 1980's somewhat faster than in the rest of the inner city. The largest changes in the structure of the population in the 1980's were, on the one hand, the decreased number of children and young people, and on the other the increased numbers of young adults. Mäenpää assumes that migration has gentrified Kallio but with an inbuilt delay, since those moving into the area are themselves only in the process of becoming middle class. The district has attracted people because of its living environment and its atmosphere, as well as its location close to the city centre. Higher status professionals valued the liveliness and social diversity of the area. The working class found it important that Kallio was familiar and homely. The "age", "traditions", "beauty", "genuineness" and "atmosphere" of the district were quoted as reasons for choosing Kallio among all the groups studied by Mäenpää. The traffic and alcoholics were the environmental factors stated as decreasing the cosiness of the area also in this study. (Mäenpää 1991, 27, 31–32, 37, 46, 51.)

The emphasising of working class culture can thus be seen as part of the profiling of the district, which, in turn, is part of the gentrification of the area. However, Kallio has not definitely turned into a middle class district. The recession following the boom gave rise to a debate on the problems of the area: the unsafety of the streets, prostitution, drugs and drug addicts. At the same time, the strong wave of migration is reflected in the profile of the inhabitants of Kallio and the degree of their identification with the area. The financial boom and the "gentrification" of Kallio did not, after all, result in a permanent rise in the perceived value of the area. However, its status as a working class district has not lost its significance because of this development. On the contrary, the Kallio of the past and its values are seen as a solution to the district's new problems. The debate about ways of surviving the recession and on maintaining the support networks of society have brought to the fore the ideology of survival that was prevalent after the wars. The changes in working patterns and the ageing of the generation which still remembers the real working class Kallio are bound to support this development. The working class traditions from the times of the urban settlement of the area were seized upon as a natural means by which to develop the collective identity of Kallio.

"The working class community of Kallio has been destroyed, or rather, buried: but out of its ruins has risen a living urban city community", says Pasi Mäenpää of the Kallio of the 1980's. The working class community had only been buried in order to be recovered anew.

## BIBLIOGRAPHY

Andersson, Harri 1997. Kulttuuri ja paikan politiikka kaupunkiuudistuksessa [Culture and politics of place in city reforms]. In Tuukka Haarni, Marko Karvinen, Hille Koskela & Sirpa Tani (eds.): *Tila, paikka ja maisema. Tutkimusretkiä uuteen maantieteeseen* [Space, place and landscape. Explorations in the new geography]. Tampere: Vastapaino, 107–128.

Åström, Anna-Maria 1999a. Helsingfors anda – huvudstadens nationella och lokala betydelser [The spirit of Helsinki – the national and local meanings of the capital]. In *Budkavlen* 1999, 26–55.

Åström, Anna-Maria 1999b. Ordinary People in Post-War Helsinki. Urban Popular Culture: Practices, Delimitations, and Recent Elevation. In Kodolányi, János jr (ed.): *Ethnic Communities, Ethnic Studies, Ethnic Costumes Today*. Budapest: Hungarian

Ethnographical Society, 101–115.

Åström, Anna-Maria 2000. Finns det en folklig urban kategori? Stadskulturen norr om Långa bron i Helsingfors [Is there a popular urban category? City culture north of the Pitkäsilta bridge in Helsinki]. In *Det är det folk vi kallar vårt* [That is the people we call ours]. Helsingfors: Svenska litteratursällskapet i Finland, 151–166.

Bausinger, Hermann 1969. Folklorismus in Europa. Eine Umfrage. In *Zeitschrift für Volkskunde* 1969.

Centergran, Ulla 1992. Folklorism och revitalisering [Folkloristics and revitalisation]. In Birgitta Skarin Frykman & Helene Brembeck (eds.): *Brottningar med begrepp* [Wrestling with terminology]. Skrifter från Etnologiska föreningen i Västsverige 11. Göteborg: Etnologiska föreningen i Västsverige, 115–132.

Cohen, Anthony P. 1982. Belonging: the experience of culture. In *Belonging. Identity and social organisation in British rural cultures*. Manchester: Manchester University Press, 1–17.

Cohen, Anthony P. 1985. *The Symbolic Construction of Community*. Chichester: Ellis Horwood.

Heino, Tiina 1990a. Kunnalliset työväenasunnot [Council housing for the working class]. In *Narinkka* 1990. Helsinki: Helsingin kaupunginmuseo, 122–131.

Heino, Tiina 1990b. Museo Kirstinkujalla [The museum in Kirstinkuja]. In *Narinkka* 1990. Helsinki: Helsingin kaupunginmuseo, 174.

*Helsingin Sanomat* 2000.

Herzfeld, Michael 1997. *Cultural Intimacy. Social Poetics in the Nation-State*. New York: Routledge.

Ilmonen, Mervi 1997. *Mitä osoite osoittaa? Asuinalueiden erilaistuminen Helsingin seudulla* [What does an address tell? The differentiation of housing areas in the Helsinki region]. Pääkaupunkiseudun julkaisusarja B, 1997:2. Helsinki: Pääkaupunkiseudun yhteistyövaltuuskunta.

Jauhiainen, Jussi S. 1997. Kaupunkiuudistus ja gentrifikaatio [City reform and gentrification]. In Tuukka Haarni, Marko Karvinen, Hille Koskela & Sirpa Tani (eds.): *Tila, paikka ja maisema. Tutkimusretkiä uuteen maantieteeseen* [Space, place and landscape. Explorations in the new geography]. Tampere: Vastapaino, 129–142.

Järvinen, Jaana 1990. Rakennuksen korjaus ja entistys [The renovation and restoration of a building]. In *Narinkka* 1990. Helsinki: Helsingin kaupunginmuseo, 143–173.

Kaunismaa, Pekka 1997. Mitä on kollektiivinen identiteetti? [What is collective identity?]. In Kalle Virtapohja (ed.): *Puheenvuoroja identiteetistä. Johdatusta yhteisöllisyyden ymmärtämiseen* [Comments on identity. Introduction to understanding community]. Jyväskylä: Atena, 37–54.

Koskinen, Juha 1990. *Kallion historia. Kallio-Seura r.y. – Sörkän Gibat 50 v* [The history of Kallio. Kallio Association – Sörkän Gibat 50 years]. Helsinki: Kallio-Seura r.y. & Sörkan Gibat.

Korff, Gottfried 1980. Folklorismus und Regionalismus. Eine Skizze zum Problem der kulturellen Kompensation ökonomischer Rückständigkeit. In *Heimat und Idäntitet. Probleme regionaler Kultur.* 22. Deutscher Volkskunde-Kongress in Kiel vom 16. bis 21. Juni 1979. Herausgegeben im Auftrag der Deutschen Gesellschaft für Volkskunde von Konrad Köstlin und Hermann Bausinger. Studien zur Volkskunde und Kukturgeschichte Schleswig-Holsteins. Band 7. Neumünster: Wacholtz, 39–52.

Lankinen, Markku 1997. Asumisen segregaation tila ja kehityssuunnat [The situation and development of the segregation of housing]. In Kaarin Taipale & Harry Schulman (eds.): *Koti Helsingissä. Urbaanin asumisen tulevaisuus* [A home in Helsinki. The future of urban living]. Helsinki, 171–197.

Mitchell, John P. 1998. The Nostalgic Construction of Community: Memory and Social Identity in Urban Malta. In *Ethnos* 63 (1), 81–101.

Mäenpää, Pasi 1991. *Kallion keskiluokkaistuminen 1980-luvulla. Työläisyhteiskunnan tuho?* [The gentrification of Kallio in the 1980's. The destruction of a working class community?]. Helsinki: Helsingin kaupunkisuunnitteluviraston julkaisuja 1991:7.

Paunonen, Heikki 1995. *Suomen kieli Helsingissä. Huomioita Helsingin puhekielen historiallisesta taustasta ja nykyvariaatiosta* [The Finnish language in Helsinki. Observations on the historical background and contemporary variations of the spoken language in Helsinki]. Helsinki: Helsingin yliopiston suomen kielen laitos.

Riikonen, Heikki 1997. Aluetietoisuuden sisältö paikallisyhteisössä. Sukupolvet ja muistinvaraiset alueet [Contents of area consciousness in a local community. Generations and remembered areas]. In Tuukka Haarni, Marko Karvinen, Hille Koskela & Sirpa Tani (eds.): *Tila, paikka ja maisema. Tutkimusretkiä uuteen maantieteeseen* [Space, place and landscape. Explorations in the new geography]. Tampere: Vastapaino, 179–189.

Runko, Ylermi 1994. Kiitos äideillemme [Thanks to our mothers]. In *Patsas työläisäidille. Työläisäiti-patsastoimikunnan tiedote* [A statue to working class mothers. Newsletter from the statue committee] 3/94.

Räsänen, Matti 1989. Kansankulttuuri kansakunnan identiteetin rakennuspuuna [Folk culture as the building block of national identity]. In Teppo Korhonen & Matti Räsänen (eds.): *Kansa kuvastimessa. Etnisyys ja identiteetti* [People in the mirror. Ethnicity and identity]. Tietolipas 114. Helsinki: Suomalaisen Kirjallisuuden Seura, 10–28.

Shields, Rob. 1991. *Places on the Margin. Alternative geographies of modernity.* London: Routledge.

Snellman, Hanna 1996. *Tukkilaisen tulo ja lähtö. Kansatieteellinen tutkimus Kemijoen metsä- ja uittotyöstä* [The arrival and departure of the rafters. An ethnological study of the forestry and rafting work in Kemijoki]. Scripta Historica 25. Oulun Historiaseuran julkaisuja. Oulu: Pohjoinen.

Sundin, Bosse 1997. Hembygden som idé. Konstruktionen av lokal och regional identitet [Native place as idea. The construction of local and regional identity]. In Lennart Palmqvist & Stefan Bohman (eds.): *Museer och kulturarv. En museivetenskaplig antologi* [Museums and cultural heritage. A museological anthology]. Stockholm: Carlsson, 41–64.

Tuan, Yi-Fu 1979. *Space and Place. The Perspective of Experience.* London: Arnold.

Tuominen, Martti 1999. *Turvallinen Helsinki. Pahoinpitelyrikollisuus Helsingissä* [A safe Helsinki. Crimes of assault in Helsinki]. Tutkimuksia 1999:10. Helsinki: Helsingin kaupungin tietokeskus.

Virtanen, Timo J. 1997. Kirjoitetut kaupunkikuvat. Etnografiaa ja etnografiikkaa [Written urban images. Ethnography and ethnographics]. In Teppo Korhonen & Pekka Leimu (eds.): *Näkökulmia kulttuurin tutkimukseen* [Aspects on the study of culture]. Turku: Turun yliopiston täydennyskoulutuskeskus, 97–128.

Local Identity Practices in "Block Towns"

MONICA STÅHLS-HINDSBERG

# Vyborg – Town and Native Place

*based on recollections of Swedish former residents.*

In order to understand the relation of the inhabitants of Vyborg (Sw. Viborg) to their town, one has to know its history. It has in the past been a Swedish city and, during another period, a Russian border town; Vyborg has also been a city in the Grand Duchy of Finland as well as a city in the Republic of Finland. Vyborg was, and still is, a city built of stone, which today is regarded as lost to the people of Finland. In this article, I will use the voices of former inhabitants of Vyborg to describe how, by means of their memories, they symbolically appropriate their town. As material, I will use interviews with Swedish-speaking former Vyborgers.

The significance of the individual and his or her relation to the environment is the basis for ethnological research. The fundamental questions concern the ways in which the individual internalises his or her environment and creates an identity on the basis of this. Within urban research, interest is increasingly focused on the relation between town and individual. How do individuals create for themselves a place in the town and what practices do they use to turn the town into their home? The question gains interest when the native place is a city such as Vyborg during the first decades of the 20th century – which is also a city that is lost forever.

The aim of this article is not to write about Vyborg, but to present memories of the Swedish-speaking inhabitants of Vyborg about their native neighbourhoods and, in addition, to describe the symbolic meanings the individuals give the town.

Within German *Heimat* research native place is ascribed four functions. It can be associated with nostalgia; it can strengthen the identity of individuals; it can function as a compensation for something psycho-social which has been lost – for example as a result of modernisation or urbanisation – and it can also function as a focal point for activities. Native place provides territorial satisfaction (Bausinger 1985, 8–9).

In her research on the concept of native place, the German ethnologist Ina-Maria Greverus has described the ways in which individuals take possession of space (in this case the local environment), create an understanding of the space, and then place themselves in it, that is, make it their native place. In order to be able to root themselves in a place, human beings need spatial symbols that they can describe using language, that they can under-

65

stand, see as included in their everyday life, and to which they can conform (Greverus 1994, 28–33).

We continuously create places in our everyday lives. Places set the framework for what we can and cannot do in our everyday lives. There is an incessant interaction between what we produce and what we consume. The miniature model of Vyborg in the South Karelia Museum in Lappeenranta, which shows the central parts of the town before the Second World War, is an example of this. Following Bausinger, the model fulfils one of the criteria seen as typical for native place, that is, it has been the focus of specific interests and activities. At the same time, the model can also be said to form a place that has been re-produced. By visiting the museum and viewing the miniature model, the visitor is taken to the Vyborg of the mid-1930's. The miniature is constructed around the oldest parts of Vyborg, which also are the most interesting historically.

The experienced space, that is, the childhood memories of the inhabitants of Vyborg, have here been turned into a concrete memory, which can be constantly re-experienced through the miniature model. And it is the shaping of the model that decides what is worth remembering.

During the years 1996 and 1997 I interviewed "genuine" Swedish-speaking inhabitants of Vyborg. The interviews followed the life stories of the interviewees; we started in the informants' early childhood and ended at the time of the interview. The interview focused on three major themes: childhood, the evacuation from Vyborg and settling into a new place. 18 of the interviewees

*Miniature model of Vyborg in the 1930's. The miniature is kept in the Wyborg Collection in the South Karelia Museum in Lappeenranta. Photo: Vesa Mikkonen 2003, South Karelia Museum, Lappeenranta.*

were female and 16 were male. The average age of the informants was about 82 years and socially they could be categorised as middle class and upper middle class. The multicultural profile of the Swedish-speaking inhabitants of Vyborg has often been pointed out, and this was confirmed by the fact that the father or mother of 34 of the interviewees was of another nationality than Finnish, specifically either Russian, German, Norwegian, Swedish, Belgian or Baltic. Towards the end of the interview, many of the informants became very nostalgic and repeatedly described the Vyborg of their childhood and the carefree life there. The interviewees talked about their personal childhood memories and the significance of Vyborg as a border town, school town, garrison and finally as Finland's ultimate eastern outpost.[1]

## A brief history of the town of Vyborg

The history of Vyborg from the early Middle Ages up until 1944, when the city again became Russian territory, is well documented. Torkel Knutsson founded Vyborg Castle in 1293 as a base of the Swedish kingdom against the power of Novgorod. In 1403, Vyborg was granted its town charter and throughout the Middle Ages Vyborg and Karelia remained an area of dispute between east and west, but it also maintained its significance as an important port with contacts both to the east and the west.

In 1710, Peter I conquered Vyborg and the town became the Russian provincial capital of Vyborg County after the 1721 peace in Uusikaupunki. In 1812 the town was again incorporated in the new Grand Duchy of Finland and in 1839 the Vyborg Court of Appeal was founded, which meant that alongside German, Swedish gradually became the language of the governing classes. The Saimaa Canal was opened in 1856 and thus Vyborg became the centre for traffic and trade for all of eastern Finland. In 1860, the medieval town wall was demolished and the older ramparts were levelled. The railway between Helsinki and St Petersburg was opened in 1870, which increased Vyborg's importance as a trading town, and at the same time, it grew considerably, acquiring new suburbs, parks and squares. During the beginning of the 20th century no changes took place in the status of Vyborg. At the outbreak of the First World War, Vyborg functioned as a garrison for Russian military units. But the Russian revolution and Finland's independence in 1917 created an impenetrable boundary between Finland and Russia. During the Winter War in 1939–40 the acts of war resulted in a moving of the border, and Vyborg again became a Russian city. Although at the end of 1941, during the Continuation War, Vyborg was re-conquered by Finland, it was finally passed into Russian possession on 20 June 1944 (Ruuth 1906; WN 2000/1; Gardberg 1996, 11 ff).

Focusing on the 20th century, it can be noted that as Finland's new borders had been established after the First World War, the cosmopolitan character of Vyborg was, to begin with, strengthened because of the immigration from the east, but this faded away after a few decades. Vyborg maintained and strengthened its important position as a trading town and port, since the wood and other industries needed a port connected to the Saimaa Canal. At the end of the 1930's, the town prospered and capital moved; Vyborg was a typical Finnish industrial town, where the National Coalition Party and the Social Democrats fought for the seats in the town council. Thus, at the end of the 1930's, a quarter of all Finland's wood pulp was produced in Karelia, the company Enso-Gutzeit produced half of all the chlorine in the country, in Vyborg Havi Oy made 26 per cent of the country's soap, while the candle factory produced more than half of Finland's candles. In addition, there was a significant food industry. It is also worth mentioning that in 1939 there were, among others, 15 wholesale businesses, 161 shops for colonial products, 29 cafés, 18 restaurants, 14 motels and 5 hotels in Vyborg. (Knapas 1993, 10; Klinge 1993, 51; Karjala tutuksi 1997.)

Apart from trade and industry, Vyborg was also a city with a garrison and several schools. There were 8 upper secondary schools preparing for university studies, several comprehensive schools and 24 primary schools. Of these, one primary school and one secondary school were Swedish-speaking. Among the vocational schools in Vyborg was Finland's only maritime institute. The population of Vyborg and its surrounding areas amounted to 74 403 in 1939, which made it the second largest city in Finland. In the same year, the number of inhabitants in Helsinki was 219 842, in Tampere 69 500 and in Turku 61 000. As a result of the incorporation of surrounding areas, Finnish quickly became the dominant language in Vyborg and the large number of secondary schools created a strong Finnish-speaking middle class in the town. (Karjala tutuksi 1997.)

The Winter War and the Continuation War destroyed all previous traditions. The town was emptied of its Finnish population and obtained new Russian inhabitants. For a long time after the war, Vyborg's identity in the Soviet Union was that of a peripheral Russian industrial town. From 1958 and onwards, Finnish citizens have been able to visit Vyborg, but only in the 1990's did commercial tourism start on a larger scale (Knapas 1993, 10; Klinge 1993, 51).

## The Vyborgers: identity and native place

The images emerging from the interviews all show similar, recurring features. Most emphasis fell on the 1920's and 1930's, that is, the childhood, youth and early adulthood of the informants.

The intimate social relations between the families of the informants emerge clearly in all the interviews. The material shows that about two thirds of the interviewees lived in the old part of town and other districts adjacent to it. These facts might partly explain the nostalgic emotions that many of the informants associate with central Vyborg. They belonged to the same language group and the area where most of them lived was relatively small. When the informants were asked to characterise their childhood home, they often mentioned the old town, the school district and the ramparts; mentally, their Vyborg seemed to be limited to this area (SLS 1881).

Swedish middleclass
employed rural
Finnish women

There were servants in most of the informants' childhood homes and only in three families did both the mother and the father work outside the home. The servant girls usually came from the Finnish countryside and they were often recruited on the basis of verbal recommendations. When needed, temporary help was employed, for example the washer woman came regularly every fourth or sixth week, the seamstress a couple of times per year, party cooks and waiting staff at bigger celebrations. The groceries were bought in the market square and in the covered market, while the market Rödabrunnstorget was more of a narink (from Russian na.rinke = in the market). The informants said that until the 1930's it was possible to shop in Russian or German, instead of Finnish, if one knew where to go (SLS 1881).

The days of kindergarten and school are remembered in very happy terms. The circle of friends was usually exclusively Swedish-speaking, or mixed Finnish and Swedish. German was no longer used among the younger generation, but only when speaking to parents or an even older generation. The situation concerning the Russian language was similar. Contacts across the language groups were frequent among the generation of the informants' parents, but by the 1920's and 1930's the contacts had decreased considerably. There was an invisible wall between them and the Russian speakers and the Jews. Particularly the older informants expressed a clear suspicion of anything Russian. Many found it difficult to talk about the evacuation and all its hardships. They had not only lost their material belongings, but also the social and cultural identity that gives individuals their place in society (SLS 1881).

*The relation between the servants and the family was generally very good and many stayed with the family until old age. The servant girls often came from the countryside surrounding Vyborg. This picture is taken at the Pulkkinen family in Torkelsgatan 7 in the mid-1920's. Photo: South Karelia Museum, Lappeenranta.*

Normal everyday life usually followed a clear pattern: school in the morning, then home for lunch and back to school for the afternoon, and when the day was finished perhaps a coffee in a café and then home again. In the evenings, homework, dinner, skating in the winter, possibly a stroll down the Torkelsgatan street and then everybody went home. In the summer, practically all families moved out to their summerhouses as soon as school was over and stayed in the countryside until school started again in the autumn (SLS 1881).

It is striking how much the interviews resemble each other in the details of the description of everyday life. Even if each interview is unique and forms a single entity, certain common cultural patterns emerge clearly. These are based on the social class and the bourgeois background that the families represent. As mentioned above, both the physical and mental space for social relations, for children as well as adults, was small and intimate. In actual fact, the multilingual background had, by the 1930's, largely lost its significance, even if some of the oldest informants referred to it a few times. The Swedish-speaking minority diminished quickly in size, as did the German-speaking one. The community strove to maintain its cultural tradition by organising an annual celebration on the 7th of January, which was intended for Swedish and German speakers. The 7th of January Festival, as it has always been called, is still organised every year at the beginning of January in Helsinki. Today, the common denominator is Vyborg (SLS 1881).

The sociologist Maurice Halbwachs (Halbwachs 1992 [1952], 50 ff) has emphasised the significance of collective memory in various groups. By collective remembrance, affinities within the group are strengthened and the unique position of the group in relation to others is emphasised. According to Halbwachs, individual members do the work of remembering, but it is the group that decides what is worth retaining of those memories. Recollections also function the other way around. By focusing on a single event that was important for the group, the collective memory becomes private and the individuals feel as if they had participated in the event.

In her article "Identity, local community and local identity" (1988), the Swedish ethnologist Ulla Bruck discusses the need that human beings have to be confirmed and affirmed by their neighbours in order to be able to experience local community and feel that they have a local identity. It is important for local identity that there is a feeling of continuity in everyday life and that one feels a similarity to those that oneself or one's family has social relations with. Similarity also presupposes that there are those who are dissimilar, that is, such groups are based on perceptions of 'us and them'. Bruck confirms what Herman Bausinger has noted on native place: native places and identities represent intact social relations. Bruck also thinks that local identity can be understood as continuity and similarity, while Bausinger talks about trust, security and confidence in life. The self-image that the individual creates thus stands in direct relation to the local environment, where the factors mentioned above form the basis for the ability to feel affinity with the place and the people. Local identity also means that in discussions with others people can refer to the same things and events, which furthers the concentration of memories and makes them the individual's own. Discussions about the past where all parties can participate on an equal level strengthen their self-image. It is also possible to define oneself in relation to "the others", according to characteristics one does not possess. In the case of the interviewed former inhabitants of Vyborg, we must take into account that the continuity is broken forever and that their local identity is totally based on memories of their native place. But even in this case, Bruck's argument is of certain relevance. (Bruck 1988, 78; Åström 2001, 104–105.)

The everyday life of the Vyborgers was characterised by continuity and similarity. Recurring events such as the 7th of January Festival, the districts they moved in, the stable social relations and the feeling of belonging to a certain group, are all factors that invoke a strong local identity. The self-image stands in relation to and is based on the nearest local environment, the neighbourhood. The relations between the language groups are seldom seen as a problem, but rather as a natural part of the childhood environment, even if a certain awareness of "Us and the Others" can be discerned. Since self-image is in direct relation to the local environment, the self-image of the interviewees has a strong historical connection. Signs of small town mentality, strong local identity and feelings for their native place emerge in the self-image of the interviewed inhabitants of Vyborg, precisely through the experiences they share of continuity, similarity, trust and confidence.

In the next section, I will analyse the interviews in relation to Ina-Maria Greverus' typology of urban places and thus explore the ways in which the group of former inhabitants of Vyborg that I have interviewed moved within the town; which places were important for them and what their attitudes towards their environment was.

## The Vyborgers' appropriation of place: the neighbourhood of the Fortress district

Ina-Maria Greverus' characterisation of urban places is based on, or rather, seeks support from, Helge Gerndt's theory of fields of communication and action. Greverus has focused on four types of urban place in which the inhabitants of a city create their everyday life: for example, where they move, which places are most important and where they think it is possible to experience something out of the ordinary (Greverus 1994, 25–33).

Greverus also thinks that the structure of everyday life reveals the ways in which boundaries are drawn and how these boundaries can be circumvented and changed. If the borders give the individuals the framework for their everyday actions, by, for example, defining where and when it is acceptable to be in a certain place, with whom they spend time and how they move around, these elements also constitutes the framework of their identity. Further, such frames are surpassed every time the individuals do not conform to the boundaries set up by their group. (Greverus 1994, 25–33.) What characterised the territory of the interviewed inhabitants of Vyborg and how did they move within the town?

According to Greverus, there are so called *actual places*, that is, meeting places and points that attract various groups and various sorts of people. She is referring to a socio-cultural pattern of dominating a certain place. People can also create their identity on the basis of these places, which in large cities can be, for example, the local shop or the local pub. These places give both the individual and the place an identity. (Greverus 1994, 25–33.)

As mentioned above, most of the former inhabitants of Vyborg interviewed for this article, lived in and mainly moved around in the most central area of the town, a district called the Fortress. In the interviews, they often refer to the long history of the Fortress, to the Swedish-speaking group that first settled there and the significance to them of the fact that this was truly their area.

> It is interesting that when we, most of my mates from Vyborg, or relatives from Vyborg, when we talk about Vyborg we think in terms of a very small area, and also afterwards one realises that one has forgotten the names of the more peripheral… [districts] Batteribacken and all those. But when we talk about Vyborg it is between Neitsytniemi and the fire station, within this area and everything we did, such as scouting, skating, school… the schools and so on, the tennis hall, everything was within this area […] so we must remember that we idealise Vyborg in that we only talk about these neighbourhoods which also happen to be the most valuable neighbourhoods from a historical perspective. But we mustn't forget that the majority of the population of Vyborg lived outside this area and that was the so-called humble folk. (SLS 1881, 1996:99, male, b. 1920.)

The home neighbourhood can also be an actual place. Depending on which district it is situated in, it reflects the social status of the individual. In the Vyborg of the 1930's, every block usually had its own dairy shop, bakery, butcher, etc., which is to say, a group of small local shops that were seen as belonging to their own sphere. Every house also had its own caretaker, who acted as part of a network of many inhabitants. Usually, neighbours knew each other and in general belonged to the same social group.

> For example, in Vakttornsgatan street where we lived in that house, there were only Swedish families… And like, yes, there were also German-speaking. (SLS 1881, 1996:51, female, b. 1915.)

Judging from the interviews, people moved in small circles, usually within their own neighbourhood, which is totally natural, since that was the safest place to be.

The long history of Vyborg is often reflected in the informants' answers.

> If I talk about the old town, there is nothing like that here, no, so there were stone buildings and originally it had been there that Gustav Vasa had built, that ring-wall like that (SLS 1881, 1996:54, female, b. 1915).

> Yes almost all were buildings of stone and a few houses were from the Middle Ages […] (SLS 1881, 1996:133, male, b. 1919.)

*The north shore of the Salakkalahti bay in the early 1930's. In the background, the Vyborg Castle that dominated the skyline of the town in all directions. Photo: OY Helios, South Karelia Museum, Lappeenranta.*

A child could go to another part of town because of a hobby.

> No, no I only passed the market Rödabrunnstorget when I walked to the music institute. I have not experienced it and I didn't go there either. (SLS 1881, 1996:58, female, b. 1912.)

The informants who lived in the "new town" usually stayed there.

> But I lived on the other side in a way, so I didn't really very often go to those [old neighbourhoods]… (SLS 1881, 1996:86, female, b. 1920.)

If actual places are understood as places that attract various groups, the school dances that the informants frequented fall into this category. The schools in Vyborg usually organised dances every Saturday, each school in turn following a set schedule. According to the informants, these dances were often the highlight of the week, and the dances at certain schools were more popular than others.

> And then it was very important in Vyborg, that since there were so many schools, there was always a school dance on Saturday and one went to these parties at the various schools. One could only go to those real schools, for example those kinds of commercial colleges and the like, those one didn't go to … but to the ordinary school dances on Saturday and we thought they were great fun. (SLS 1881, 1996:102, female, b. 1921.)

The informants only visited the school dances of the Finnish and Swedish speaking secondary schools.

The patterns of moving about in the town were also reflected in the ways children took to school in Vyborg. Since most of them lived within a relatively small area, and Vyborg as a whole was not very widespread, the way to school was not very long either. Most of the children walked through the Esplanade and the Torkelsparken park, perhaps crossed the Rödabrunnstorget or the Paradplan square.

> Yes, the normal thing was school and the way to work. And that meant, the school was in the centre in Karjalagatan. I walked past the cathedral and that … the County Governor's residence and the post office on my way to school. Oh yes, at one time we lived in the house next to the school. That was when one arrived late since it was a bit too close, slid in through the door and the porter stood there and held it open and grrr… (SLS 1881, 1997:4, female, b. 1907.)

 A second category of places, according to Greverus, are the opposite of actual place, that is, places which lack an identity, so called *non-places*. These *non-places* non-places are not social meeting points but exist for some other purpose; for example, railway stations and ports can belong to this category. Non-places can be planned and placed within actual places and thus weaken or erase the identity of the actual places. Non-places are also formed when different places start resembling each other to an extent that they can no longer be told apart. Even if a certain amount of communication takes place in these places, the place itself does not offer people any opportunity to ground themselves here, on the contrary, they strengthen the feeling of rootlessness. However, on the mental map drawn by Marc Augé, these non-places represent "the world". His point is that it is, after all, possible to experience something in these meaningless spaces, but on an internal level. It is possible to undertake

*The Railway Station designed by Eliel Saarinen and Herman Gesellius. The beautiful station building was blown up during the retreat of the Russians in 1941. Photo: South Karelia Museum, Lappeenranta.*

an inner journey to wherever one wishes. Spaces that exist only in order to transport people to another place are often so insignificant that individuals flee the place mentally by going on an inner journey.

The railway station in Vyborg might also belong to this category. People only visited the railway station temporarily; it was not a place for social meetings and existed only for getting on and off trains. Parallels can be drawn to non-places since the station was a place for passing through only and did thus not have an identity of its own. However, this theory is challenged by the fact that the building itself was not an anonymous place lacking an identity; on the contrary, several of the informants refer to the railway station as a beautiful building worth showing to visitors: "Yes, it was a fine building. It was by Eliel Saarinen". (SLS 1882, 1996:57, female, b. 1912.)

In my opinion, there were no non-places in Vyborg in the sense defined by Greverus; in fact, her examples refer to later urban variations. For the Swedish-speaking inhabitants of Vyborg, the town was not a place for only passing through. However, if the aspect of ethnicity is added to non-places, the mental maps of the Swedish-speaking inhabitants of Vyborg reveal places that they did not visit. Thus, I define places and non-places on the basis of how the various language groups moved around within the town. One such non-place for the Swedish-speakers was the market Rödabrunnstorget, which they usually only passed through or would visit in order to buy their Christmas tree.

## Change and transition in the centre

There are also places that are constantly forming and being recreated, which are short-lived, and which may be termed *transitory places*. City centres as a whole can, in a certain respect, be regarded as transitory places. These parts of a city can very quickly change their appearance and image. Conversions into offices and constantly changing patterns of consumption can change the various neighbourhoods of a city very quickly. It is a process which also involves displacement. The core of actual places is the everyday local shops of the city. But in the centre fashion dictates which shop should be favoured. The people that appear in such places come and go, people meet and separate. The urban inhabitants choose which shops they go to and which they do not go to. There can be a repair shop next to a fashionable jewellery shop and even if the clients of the two shops belong to, for example, different age categories, they can meet and part without any problems. Greverus (1994, 25–33) wants to emphasise that this is not a question of indifference towards each other but of the fact that different places have the same right to exist. They just exist in different ways. Thus, high and low features of culture can exist side-by-side in big cities. Various ethnic groups and artistic circles each find their transitory slots or places.

Vyborg, as was the rest of Finland, was characterised by a quick *Fortschritt*, as they called it: a rapid social development during the latter half of the 1930's. The town expanded and, for example, new office buildings were continually being built. However, the neighbourhoods where my informants moved were not subject to the same change as the newer parts of Vyborg. On the contrary, very few changes took place in the oldest parts of Vyborg throughout the 1930's.

> And then one noticed on the whole that the standard of living began to rise slowly but steadily. One noticed this from the way people dressed and from the selection of products and shops and the whole atmosphere that things were finally moving upwards in a way. So I would say that in '36, '37, '38, '39 it was when the town experienced a short but intensive period of prosperity in all areas, also within culture and so on, and this was perhaps the last, one more last time. One noticed that there was an enormous hustle and bustle everywhere and a lot happened and people were happy. And then one must remember that this was not an industrial town, but a trading and shipping town. (SLS 1881, 1996:81, male, b. 1920.)

Many point out that a typical feature of Vyborg was its great number of shops with owners of various nationalities. For example, some informants refer to the fact that the clothing shops were owned by Jews.

> And then of course there were the Jewish shops. There was a shop with the absolutely best, the best clothing; that was a Jewish shop. (SLS 1771, 1993:26, female, b. 1916.)

On the other hand, some of the informants are irritated by the emphasis on the international character of the shops, which is typical of a stereotype image of Vyborg. They do remember the commerce, but underline that it was modest.

> It has irritated my generation that the Vyborg News is full of that kind of thing: what it was like in good old Vyborg, you know, that one went in … *hinten Zimmer offen* … that one went in and bought all sorts of delicacies. And that there were crab and lobster and wines and whatever was available in those shops. That was no longer the case in my time: no, the shops had completely normal opening hours and they were perfectly ordinary… (SLS 1771, 1993:26, female, b. 1916.)

Some remember the names of certain shops and refer to the fact that there was or had been tradesmen of several nationalities in Vyborg.

> Yes and then in the same yard Elfström's ancient watchmaker's shop had their – what should one call it – where they pottered with their clocks and watches and there was a window and from the yard one could always study the guys when they were working [...] And then there was, on street level, there were shops. There was Singer and then there was Fazer's music and then there was, I think, Domadetsky's shoe shop and then Arne's jewellers and then Paul Stude's tobacconist and then came Strandell's men's outfitters. And then after that came some sort of Pimenoff's hat shop. (SLS 1881, 1996:81, male, b. 1920.)

Families usually had regular stalls to which they frequently went at the market square and in the covered market. Many informants describe how their mother went out daily on her usual shopping round. Often language was the crucial factor in the decision as to who to shop at:

> Yes and then for example in the shops everybody had their own salesperson. I often went with mummy to the market and she always went to certain stalls. (SLS 1881, 1996:89, female, b. 1920.)

> I always spoke Finnish in the shops in Vyborg. In my time one spoke Finnish. But earlier it was German or perhaps even some sort of Russian, I don't know. (SLS 1881, 1993:25, female, b. 1916.)

The shops gradually were taken over by Finnish owners until the whole market trade had practically been taken over by Karelian sellers. There were no longer any Russian ice cream vendors. Transitory places were created and disappeared. Shops changed owners, the trade in the market square and the covered market was dominated by temporary vendors from the countryside who came to Vyborg with their produce.

The inhabitants of Vyborg constantly looked for their roots, strived to create places that would give them as strong a feeling of native place as possible. When this did not succeed, people moved to other places. The wave of fennicisation that swept over Vyborg in the 1930's resulted in many older Swedish-speakers moving to Helsinki. The fennicisation was hardly the only reason for this, but it was certainly one of the contributing factors.

> Yes, so there was a wave of fennicisation, the competition hardened in certain cases. […] Friends and acquaintances still lived there, but many had moved to Helsinki. The Swedish-speaking population, especially, diminished. The school suffered from a lack of pupils already in my time. (SLS 1881, 1996:114, male, b. 1919.)

> They had a rather small circle and over the years this shrank considerably since many had the bad habit of moving to Helsinki when they retired. So my parents had a very small circle of friends. (SLS 1881, 1996:59, female, b. 1923.)

### The skating-rink, the Esplanade and the cafés

Finally, Ina-Maria Greverus includes in her typology *the places of possibility*. These pertain to various groups trying to find or create *various important places* for themselves, where the groups can open up their senses and experience new things. According to Greverus, an alternative group can create a place of possibility out of a non-place by occupying it and providing various groups with the possibility of practicing some form of artistic activity there. However, conflicts often arise between these new actors and the urban inhabitants who already have their set places in the city. A place of possibility can also be an old established space such as churches, art galleries, swimming pools, parks and other places for renewal and recreation. Places of possibility provide people with an experience out of their ordinary everyday lives. (Greverus 1994, 25–33, Augé 1995, 93.)

There are a few places that the old Vyborgers mention time and time again: the Torkelsgatan, the skating-rink and the Esplanade park. According to their stories, these places were visited in order to meet new people and for recreation; not necessarily always for new and unusual experiences, but in order to be in a place where one could experience a new, even if temporary, feeling of affinity or of excitement. For example, the empty skating-rink could be filled in a moment by young people who amongst themselves created relations that gave opportunities for new experiences.

The places that young people went to and the way they moved around in their leisure time reflects the way in which middle class, secondary school children moved around in other towns in the 1950's. Most of the informants describe a similar pattern in their everyday lives: school, lunch at home, school, home, homework, dinner, skating and finally home.

> In winter, as soon as school was finished, home and then quickly to Salakkalahti Bay to skate and play bandy. Every single day – home, eat, homework and then to the skating-rink with chums, with or without girls, round, round, round. And then Torkeln and then home. (SLS 1881, 1996:99, male, b. 1920.)

The Esplanade was a popular place. The way to school or the way to the skating-rink often passed through the park. Most friends lived on the other side of the Esplanade or close to it. Everybody describes it as long and beautiful and notes that, for example, the Esplanade in Helsinki does not compare to it at all. Here, friends and acquaintances met and "everybody" who was at school was there. A stroll down the Torkelsgatan was a part of every evening. The oldest informants said that the Esplanade "was invaded" every evening by young people who walked up and down the streets lining the park. The tradition was to walk on one side of the Esplanade in the winter and on the other in autumn and spring. Nobody could say exactly when and why the change happened. It was just done.

> Yes, it was absolutely customary […] one must have been around 10–12 years when one started walking, strolling there, up and down. But first one always went to the skating-rink in winter and then after the skating, back for a stroll. (SLS 1881, 1996:91, female, b. 1915.)

People went to the Esplanade for other purposes too. During the summer months there were often musical performances close to the restaurant Espilä. Usually a brass band played at certain times during the evening.

> Yes, yes and large and long besides and it was wide. And then there was this … restaurant Espilä. And then there was that music that was always played there and then we often went there, when it was the summer, and when it came to 6 December, then we stood there and listened to the music play and it was so nice and I would so wish that people could experience

a life that is totally different. Also the small things that are nice. (SLS 1881, 1996:54, female, b. 1905.)

The Esplanade offered many dimensions to the inhabitants of Vyborg. There was music, nature, people, a restaurant and new, exciting experiences in the form of new acquaintances. The cafés, for example, offered the inhabitants of Vyborg new dimensions of taste and experience. Only in the 1930's did visiting cafés become an everyday event, according to the informants. Until then, going to a café was unusual and the visit was always associated with excitement and something new. Many talked nostalgically about various cakes.

> Yes, Pursiainen's café in the Torkelsgatan was definitely number one. And it was also a good bakery and … It was where one went if one went to a café, which didn't happen very often. (SLS 1881, 1997:4, female, b. 1907.)

> Yes one went to cafés, but it was a bit later in a way, I would say, there was still that Aula café and the Colombia café, but I would say that one was, one wasn't so, yes it was that kind of old […] that one went to in the afternoons, very seldom in the evenings actually. One went there in the afternoon, after school one could go, if one had a little money one went there to have a cake. (SLS 1881, 1996:91, female, b. 1915.)

As I have pointed out above, the everyday life of the Swedish-speaking inhabitants of Vyborg was characterised by middle class cultural patterns. This emerges again when studying the café culture of Vyborg. Everybody had their regular cafés that they visited. Usually people frequented Pursiainen's in the Torkelsgatan, but Colombia was also popular. These cafés which people visited practically every day were situated in the centre of town and close to their homes. The fact that the informants clearly favoured certain cafés also shows that they thought of these cafés as their territory and by thus appropriating them, the memory is further concentrated and these cafés are experienced as their own.

Café visits can be said to represent a cultural pattern that is based on the informants' social class; in this case middle class and upper middle class. In order to be able to visit cafés every day to sit and chat and perhaps have a cup of coffee or an ice cream one had to have money, which not everybody had.

The short distance to school enabled the pupils to go home for lunch, which often was quite a simple meal, but still prepared by somebody employed in the household. The mother was usually at home, the father worked. Life went on every day in the same streets, in the same blocks that looked the same day after day. The recurrent, regular events must have created a strong sense of security in everyday life. To recreate such a safe and static childhood in one's memories must most probably result in a powerful yearning for that period.

The old town of Vyborg became a symbol for Vyborg as a whole for the Swedish-speaking informants. The music in the park, the social networks

79

*The Salakkalahti bay was an important place for young people. In winter, for example, there was a chance to make new acquaintances while skating. Photo: South Karelia Museum, Lappeenranta.*

and the short distances, the stereotypically middle class everyday life, the strolls in Torkelsgatan, the school dances, the skating, all this that was experienced time and time again in a historical environment is manifested in the stories of the happy and carefree Vyborg, which in this way is recreated again and again. The oldest parts of Vyborg belonged to those who were multicultural, tolerant and spoke many languages. The oldest informants hardly ever moved outside this area, while the younger ones looked with confidence and interest to the financial development that boomed in the 1930's. The younger informants also realised that Vyborg was no longer the historical and multicultural town it had once been, but that what remained of it were in the memory alone.

## Memories and symbols

How do individuals create a place for themselves in the city and what symbolic significance do they give the concept of native place, when the native place is a city, in this case Vyborg during the first decades of the 20th century? This was one of the questions that I posed in the introduction to this article. In the German research on native place, these places are ascribed four functions: nostalgia, strengthening of one's own identity, compensation for something lost and, in addition, they can function as objects for activities around something that has been lost. According to Herman Bausinger (1985, 89–98), native place is understood as the place that one feels a deep trust in and it forms the basis for one's whole identity. Native place refers to a spatial relation, which cannot be limited, but it can be localised, while identity refers to the internal structure. Identity means, among other things, that the individuals are sure of themselves, are able to connect their past with their future and are fully accepted by others, which in a metaphorical sense means that they have a native place. Identity and native place mean, following Bausinger's definition, that the social relations of individuals are intact. Ulla Bruck (1988, 78) also mentions continuity and similarity between people as a breeding ground for a local identity.

The Swedish-speaking former inhabitants of Vyborg have a strong local identity, which is based on comparatively very similar childhood experiences. The similar middle class background, the mental and physical social relations that to a large extent were limited to the oldest parts of Vyborg, the intimate contacts and the feeling that "everybody knew each other" are factors ascribed to Vyborg. These factors also coincide with the criteria for nostalgia and identity defined by research on native place. The miniature model of Vyborg in the South Karelia Museum can stand as an example of an object for activities, it functions as a connecting factor and it compensates something that has been lost. The 7th of January Festival, which is still celebrated every year in Helsinki, is another good example of a cohering social activity.

There was a shared experience of space that was formed by the oldest parts of Vyborg, where most of my informants lived and moved around. By moving every day more or less according to the same pattern and by repeating their actions, the town dwellers gradually appropriated their town and regarded it as "their own". They possessed the space, then later concretised it in their memories and carry the memory with them throughout their lives. Each time the inhabitants of Vyborg describe their town, they recreate in their minds an image of what it was like.

In analogy with Halbwachs' assumption that individuals have a tendency, or an ability, to generalise their memories, I would say that the inhabitants of Vyborg whom I interviewed described many coincidental features in their childhood environment and thus revealed very similar childhood experiences and memories. It is difficult to define where the border between individual memories and collective memory lies, as it is to tell what the individuals themselves find it important to remember. Collective memories can be similar out of necessity. It is clear that memories of a so-called flashbulb character – of sudden, strong and vivid events – often hold an essential place in reminiscence. Everyday events can also be of a flashbulb character, if the person in question experiences them very strongly. This was confirmed in the interviews, where descriptions of the evacuation held a very central position. Likewise, memories of a strong emotional nature claim more space in a person's life story than everyday and recurrent happenings (Conway 1995).

According to Anthony P. Cohen (1982, 3–6), one becomes aware of one's own culture at the border zones with other cultures. At the same time, one's sense of one's own culture is strengthened. These borders are often relative and frequently created in order to indicate one's own culture. The former inhabitants of Vyborg often mentioned at the end of the interview that they were still Vyborgers and would always remain Vyborgers. Very few said that the town would be a closed chapter for them.

For the Vyborgers, the town represents continuity, intimacy, security and intact social relations, but also a strong historical connection. They affirm each other in their memories since they used to belong to the same group. In Vyborg they had a place, both historically and socially, contrary to the world they were forced to confront after the evacuation. In contrast to the experiences of continuity, similarity, trust and confidence, the informants say that the sudden, often traumatic departure made it difficult to adjust to the new place. Even if the practical settling in was relatively effortless, the world felt chaotic and alien. Still, they carried with them an image of how one should live and move in a town. However, many mentioned that they longed for a continental element in their everyday life in the new town and that they missed their given places in society. Thus, the Vyborg identity and feeling of native place was accentuated in relation to everything new that they were confronted with. It can therefore be claimed that the Vyborgers walk in the landscape of their memories and through these memories of their town they maintain their Vyborg identity.

An abundance of social clubs and associations for Karelians and Vyborgers sprang up after the war. Many former inhabitants of Vyborg participate actively in those of the associations which still exist. Here, they can talk about their lost native place, they can reminisce and laugh together. The associations fulfil an important function since the members can revitalise their memories at the get-togethers, a social activity which also strengthens their Vyborg identity.

## NOTES

[1]    The original Swedish interviews have been transcribed word by word without any editing or revision. They are archived at the folk culture archives of the Swedish Literature Association (Svenska litteratursällskapet) in collections number SLS 1771 and 1881. Any omissions in the quotes from the interviews are marked […], and my comments are also inserted in quotes within square brackets. The references of the quotes give the collection number, tape number, and the gender and year of birth of the informant. The total length of the transcribed material is about 1 200 pages.

## SOURCES AND BIBLIOGRAPHY

### Interviews

Svenska litteratursällskapets i Finland folkkultursarkiv (SLS):
SLS 1771 "Språken i Wiborg och wiborgssvenskan" [The languages in Vyborg and the Vyborg Swedish] (band 1993: 24–32)
SLS 1881 "Wiborgsliv och wiborgaröden" [Lives and fates in Vyborg] (band 1996:50–60, 81–115, 127–134; 1997:1–11, 69–70).

### Literature

Åström, Anna-Maria 2001. Språk, klass och kultur i småstaden [Language, class and culture in small towns]. In Anna-Maria Åström, Bo Lönnqvist & Yrsa Lindqvist (eds.):

*Gränsfolkets barn – Finlandssvensk marginalitet och självhävdelse i kulturanalytiskt perspektiv.* [The children of the border people. Finland-Swedish marginality and self-assertion in a cultural analytical perspective]. Folklivsstudier 21. Helsingfors: Svenska litteratursällskapet i Finland, 100–141.

Augé, Marc 1995. *Non-places. Introduction to an anthropology of supermodernity.* London: Verso.

Bausinger, Herman 1985. Hembygd och identitet. Kulturmöten och kulturell förändring [Native place and identity. Cultural encounters and cultural change]. In A. Gustavsson (ed.): *Nutida tysk etnologi i urval av A. Gustavsson* [A selection of contemporary German ethnology]. Malmö: Liber förlag.

Bruck, Ulla 1988. Identity, local community and local identity. In Lauri Honko (ed.): *Tradition and cultural identity.* NIF publ. 20. Turku: Nordic Institute of Folklore, 77–92.

Cohen, Anthony P. 1982. *Belonging: the experience of culture. Belonging, identity and social organisation in British rural society.* Manchester: Manchester University Press.

Conway, Martin 1995. *Flashbulb memories.* Howe: Laurence Erlbaum Associates.

Ehn, Billy 1992. Livet som intervjukonstruktion [Life as a construction in interviews]. In Ch.Tigerstedt, J. P. Roos & Anni Vilkko (eds.): *Självbiografi, kultur, liv. Levnadshistoriska studier inom human- och samhällsvetenskap* [Autobiography, culture, life. Studies of life stories within human and social sciences]. Stockholm: Symposion.

Gardberg, Carl-Jakob 1996. *Vyborg. En stad i sten* [Vyborg. A city of stone]. Helsingfors: Schildts Förlags Ab.

Greverus, Ina-Maria 1994. Was sucht der Anthropologe in der Stadt? Eine Collage. In Ina-Maria Greverus, Johannes Moser & Kirstein Salein (eds.): *Stadtgedanken, aus und über Frankfurt am Main.* Frankfurt am Main: Institut für Kulturanthropologie und Europäische Ethnologie der Johann Wolfgang Goethe-Universität Frankfurt am Main, 11–74.

Halbwachs, Maurice 1992 [1941/1952]. *On collective memory.* Chicago: The University of Chicago Press.

Karjala 1997. *Karjala tutuksi.* [Presenting Karelia] Helsinki: Karjalan liitto ry.

Klinge, Matti 1993. Viipurin kulttuuritraditiosta [On the cultural traditions in Vyborg]. In Tuomas Forsberg et al. (eds.): *Ikuinen Viipuri* [Eternal Vyborg]. Helsinki: Otava.

Knapas, Rainer 1993. Viipuri – vanha ruotsalainen, venäläinen ja suomalainen kaupunki [Vyborg – an old Swedish, Russian and Finnish city]. In Tuomas Forsblom et al. (eds.): *Ikuinen Viipuri* [Eternal Vyborg]. Helsinki: Otava.

Ruuth 1906. *Wiborgs stads historia* [History of the city of Vyborg]. Helsingfors.

PIA OLSSON

# Modes of Living and Local Identity

## Formations in Two Districts in Helsinki

Then in Helsinki I was alone. I started to get to know the new district, Etu-Töölö. In the evenings I would walk through the maze of streets in the neighbourhood further and further from Arkadiankatu all the way to Hesperiankatu, where I later also learned to walk through the backyards. I often sat and read on a bench in the Väinämöinen Park, to the south, I went all the way to Bulevardi. Once I even ended up in Mustasaari, but the church youth were a cliquish bunch. Then when I brought my bike to town, I used to go to the ladies' beach on Seurasaari. Over the years my area expanded as I got friends to visit from Tapanila to Tapiola and from Meilahti to Kaivopuisto. People always remembered to warn me against going to the other side of the Pitkäsilta bridge, and especially against moving there! (Response I:97. Töölö, female, b. 1926.)

In the summer of 1946, a young woman who had just finished her matriculation examination moved to the Töölö district in Helsinki. Helsinki became her home city for the next 18 years. She explored and got to know her new environment step by step, by exploring and gradually expanding her territory. This reminiscence documents an unusual occurrence amongst those recorded in the research material used in this article, in that it describes the discovery of Helsinki from the viewpoint of a young adult. Most of the memories focus on a childhood spent in the city. However, in both cases, the personal discovery of an environment which is described has taken place according to the same principle – albeit less consciously among the children – by gradually mapping their surroundings and appropriating them.

In her study of the mindscapes described in films set in Helsinki, the geographer Sirpa Tani (1995, 66–67) has explored meanings associated with the city and its inhabitants in post-war Finnish cinema. She notes that in many films the city only functions as a backdrop for the story of the film, without any role or character of its own. Helsinki lacks an identity in the world of film. In their reminiscences of their childhood localities, the inhabitants of Helsinki create a completely different image of the urban framework of their lives. In these memories, there is hardly any sign of the environment as a mere static setting. On the contrary, the childhood landscape is closely connected with action that was once experienced as interesting and important. The place where these actions took place is not irrelevant. How is the role of an urban environment formed in real life and what is the nature of this role? What factors influence the birth of a personal relation to a certain place, in this case, a certain place in the city?

"Native place provides the models for language, ways of thinking, values. Native place and its landscape are a way of life," notes Yrjö Sepänmaa as he considers the meaning of native place. According to him, native place has a personality which is reflected onto human beings, and thus every change happening in its built environment is also transmitted to this relation (Sepänmaa 1986, 7–8). So, our native place is seen as reflected in our mode of living, but what does the relationship look like the other way around: how does our way of life influence the formation of a feeling for native place? To what extent is our image of our native place formed through our mode of living?

The Swedish ethnologist Magnus Mörck has used material from Gothenburg to study the way mode of living is reflected in the way various groups utilise, among other things, their environment. According to him, the mode of utilisation represents the person's way of life in terms of social relations, clothing or the objects he or she has chosen. In the urban environments of the city, places also become important for people through the significances attributed to them, even if the mobility of the urban lifestyle, on the other hand, creates less significant spaces of transition as well. Mörck claims that lifestyle is always rooted in space; it is constructed from daily routines, circles of friends and acquaintances, objects and time usage (Mörck 1998, 153, 155, 255). Factors that essentially influence the mode of living of a person are his or her profession and stage of life, but the native places and status of his or her parents are also of central importance. Housing is ascribed a conscious significance for lifestyle only when life has stabilised, when one wants to interpret and reflect lifestyle through one's dwelling (Roos 1985a, 28).

In this article, I will explore the meaning of modes of living for the creation of a feeling for native place in an urban environment. Two districts in central Helsinki, Kallio and Töölö, are the objects of research. Timewise, I will focus on the period after the Second World War, particularly the 1940's and the 1950's. The main material for the article consists in the responses concerning Töölö and Kallio to the questionnaire "Helsinki as living environment", compiled by Anna-Maria Åström.[1]

The same housing area, the same age group and a shared socio-economic background are factors that facilitate a collective identity connected with a certain location and group of people (Riikonen 1997, 182). The informants born in the 1920's and 1930's (24 responses) are, according to J. P. Roos's generation categories, part of the so-called post-war generation of regeneration and growth, in whom memories of the war are still strongly present. The childhood experiences of this generation include many of the same factors as those of the generation before them: poverty, illness and insecurity. However, change is brought about by the economic development, which has given this generation a financially secure life (Roos, 1985a, 24–25; Roos 1987, 54–55). In Roos's categorisation, the respondents born in the 1940's (13 responses) belong to "the generation of the great change". According to Roos, the childhood experiences of those born during or after the war differ

85

significantly from the experiences of earlier generations. Illness and insecurity no longer characterised the years of childhood: rather they were lived in a spirit of optimism and with the benefit of the beginnings of welfare (Roos 1985a, 25; Roos 1987, 55–56). These factors, which influenced the lives of both generations, are also reflected in the informants' descriptions of their relation to their childhood environment. However, a comparison of the two districts studied also reveals the differences between the opportunities provided by differing childhood circumstances to meet the challenges posed by society, and how these different circumstances have influenced experiences of the same events (see Snellman 1996, 215).

The questionnaire responses are supplemented by interviews that were conducted in the spring of 1999.[2] Both the questionnaire and interview material also demonstrate the "basic dilemma of everyday life": it is familiar to us all, but still very difficult to analyse (Roos 1985b, 63). It is clearly easier for the informants to describe the everyday life of the past in their memories than to survey the corresponding phenomena and changes of the last few years or even recent decades. These reminiscences are also characterised by a nostalgic attitude to the past. Earlier times are remembered with pleasure and even any troubles that might have occurred during those times are given a positive tone. Childhood is a typical object for nostalgia: a sense of loss and longing for a time past is associated with it in the reminiscences (Korkiakangas 1999, 171–172).

## The Helsinki of Töölö and Kallio

The districts studied here, Kallio and Töölö, both achieved their urban character during a period of expansion for Helsinki at the turn of the previous century. Over time, they have developed their present character alongside each other. Both districts have a reputation for being distinctive areas – sometimes even in opposition to each other. Therefore they form an interesting pair when comparing the significance of the environment of central Helsinki for the lives of its inhabitants.

When the building of the old centre of Helsinki had been almost completed at the beginning of the 20th century, construction activities were moved to Töölö and the areas north of the Pitkäsilta bridge in the 1920's. In 1913, for example, the city had about 250 sites for sale or rent; of these, 94 were situated in Töölö and 97 in Kallio and its surroundings (af Schultén 1955, 95). The shaping of the various districts of Helsinki as housing areas for certain population groups had started in the 1880's, when it was a natural attitude within town planning that different social classes should live in their own areas. According to the population register of 1922, under 2/5 of the inhabitants of Etu-Töölö belonged to the working class. However, the northernmost parts of Töölö, which were situated outside the actual urban district, belonged to an area where about half of the population was working class. Kallio, for its part, was situated in a sector where more than 70 per cent of the inhabitants were working class. Thirty years later, the situation

*The two areas in focus – Kallio and Töölö – are separated only by a bay and by the railway. Despite their geographical nearness, both districts have distinctive characteristics. Photo: A. Pietinen 1930's, Helsinki City Museum, Helsinki.*

had changed, particularly in Kallio, where the proportion of working class inhabitants had clearly diminished. The probable reason for this development, apart from the emergence of a new generation of inhabitants with better education than their parents, is Kallio's location, which is close to the very centre of Helsinki. In general, by the 1950's there was a more even distribution than before of working class inhabitants among the various districts, so that at least one fourth of the population in all districts was working class. At the same time, however, the amount of wealthy inhabitants increased in Töölö. The old buildings in the northern parts of Töölö had disappeared and the whole area was now mostly inhabited by non-working class populations. During the first half of the 20th century, the areas north of Pitkäsilta developed politically into an area which supported left-wing parties, while Töölö became an area of support for right-wing politics. (Lankinen s.a., 76; Siipi 1962, 276–277, 279, 288.)

The strongly marked social segregation of the districts is, above all, visible in the development of the population density in various areas. The new housing developments of the district lifted the living conditions in Töölö to a level above the average for the city as a whole. The population density in Kallio also decreased throughout the 20th century, but a more rapid improvement in the living conditions of the district began only in the 1960's (Koskinen 1990, 38; Lankinen s.a., 70). At the beginning of the 1930's, half the population of Kallio still lived in overcrowded housing (Siipi 1962, 266–267). In 1955, it was estimated that there were 1,8 inhabitants per room in Kallio and Sörnäinen. 30 per cent of the population in these districts still lived in cramped

Pia Olsson

quarters. The population in Kallio remained relatively stable – about 40 000 inhabitants – from the 1930's to the mid-1960's. Because of more people moving out than in to the district, as well as the increased spaciousness of apartments, the population of the district began to decrease sharply during the latter half of the 1960's. Although Kallio in the 1970's still had the largest population of all the districts in Helsinki, it formed only seven per cent of the city's whole population. By the end of the 1980's the population of Kallio and Sörnäinen had diminished to about 25 000 inhabitants (Koskinen 1990, 34). The size of the population in Töölö also varied greatly during the last century. In 1930, the district had approximately 13 500 inhabitants. The building of Etu-Töölö had resulted in a rapid increase of the population. The population of Töölö reached its peak at the end of the 1940's, partly because of the housing regulations. Since then, the population has gradually diminished (Lankinen s.a., 72). Jouko Siipi has noted as a special feature of Etu-Töölö that it joined the group of districts with a majority of female inhabitants in the 1920's. Etu-Töölö became the home district especially of independent women with their own income. The female inhabitants still dominated the district in the 1950's. (Siipi 1962, 154.)

During a relatively short period of time, the physical environment of Kallio has undergone several changes that have influenced the general landscape of the district. The extensive building that took place at the beginning of the century is well illustrated by the figures from the census years: during 1926–1930 more than 4 000 flats were built in Kallio and Sörnäinen. Almost the same production was achieved again ten years later. Already at this stage all the housing areas in Kallio were in use, so the construction of new buildings meant utilising single empty sites and tearing down old wooden houses. After this, Kallio has experienced another two changes brought about by new building projects: the first happened after the Second World War, when the wooden houses from the beginning of the century finally had to give way to modern blocks of flats. In 1961, a building ban was placed on Kallio. In the 1980's Kallio underwent yet another renewal as some of the blocks were rebuilt. Kallio's popularity as a residential area increased significantly in the 80's, and the price of flats rose almost to the level of the prices in the western districts of Helsinki, which are traditionally the most expensive in the inner city (Koskinen 1990, 32, 34–37, 40). Despite the elevated status of Kallio, it is still expressly the district for people with a low income. The proportion of different social groups within the population of the area was further balanced by the 1980's, but the majority of the district's inhabitants worked within production or mid-management. Trade and industry were the largest employers, even if service occupations have increased among the inhabitants of Kallio. (Koskinen 1990, 201, 204–205.)

Together with Vallila, Töölö is considered the greatest achievement of the housing production in the 1920's. The architecture of the period with its classic apartment buildings of red brick is represented by Etu-Töölö, where six- or seven-story houses were built along all sides of the blocks. The size of the apartments varied from one to several rooms (Nikula 1990, 151). However, the densely built area has also been criticised for unsuccessful architecture

88

(Ekelund 1962, 103; af Schultén 1955, 90). Taka-Töölö only received town planning under the supervision of Birger Brunila during 1937, and its low-rise lamellar houses formed the first open-plan housing district in Helsinki. The town plan was based on the new international ideals of the time, according to which a city should be spacious, green, light and hygienic (Nikula 1990, 105–106). The physical environment of Töölö has, in fact, not experienced changes comparable to those in Kallio since the 1920's and 1930's, so its general landscape still consists of the same architectural scheme as in the childhood of the informants.

## Jaakko and Anna

Jaakko Lahtinen and Anna Mäntylä were born in the 1920's and thus belong to the post-war period of regeneration and growth.[3] Alongside their shared experiences, their life cycles reflect ways of life that have followed from their private choices and social backgrounds. They represent not only their own generation, but also, and above all, two different lifestyles and thus two different ways of encountering one's local environment.

Jaakko Lahtinen was born in 1928 in a working class family in Pasila. His older brother had been born six years earlier and the family's third son was born in 1930. The father of the family was a carpenter and did temporary work until he fell seriously ill at the end of the 1930's. Before the sons were born, the mother had worked as a cook, and later, as the children grew older, she did various cleaning jobs. The family had to move several times, particularly during the years of the depression at the beginning of the 1930's, when they found it difficult to scrape together the money for rent. From Pasila they moved to Alppila and then on to the Kolmas linja street in Kallio when Jaakko was six years old. After a short time in Vilhovuorenkatu the family finally settled in Alppikatu at the end of the Winter War:

> We stayed there for a long time: we lived in that house until the 1950's. There I got married and from there my brother left to fight in the Continuation War. I became a sportsman and started working. I got my first job when I was around 12, as a shoe-cleaner – one started young in those days – times were hard, the money was needed. So, I started as a shoe-cleaner when I was 12 and did that for two summers and then went to vocational school and was there for two years and then got a job - -.

The boy learnt to know his environment through his sports hobby and relatively uncontrolled free time. Life was presented to him exactly as it was. Children were not especially protected from seeing its different sides. The boys used their environment creatively and also played in areas which were primarily intended for other uses, for example harbours and their timber yards. Jaakko got to know his local environment through the free adventures, and the sports, for their part, widened his knowledge of the city as whole – and his territory – when going to sports grounds situated in various areas.

*The use of the environment is described as uncontrolled and free in many of the reminiscences from Kallio. A playground could be found, for example, on a street corner. Photo: Eino Heinonen 1950's, Helsinki City Museum, Helsinki.*

Well, you know how the working class lived in those days. One saw many dark sides, but I think it seemed nice through the eyes of a child: there was such a variety of things. I couldn't think badly of it and I have never been ashamed of being born in a working class family which lived in Sörkka and I have friends from many circles – I have been able to get along with everybody. - - I remember how nice it was in those days: when we played hide-and-seek, there were girls and guys. - - There were nice places, when the houses were so close together, there were alleys. And then when one was older, one was with girls a bit, as young people usually are. Everybody has had these games of their own. - - I had in the sense that I had very liberal parents. I have never had an upbringing. - - With dad I wasn't like that, but my mum knew all I did, dad didn't know a thing.

Yes my playgrounds were those, they were those sports grounds, the Eläintarha sports grounds, the Kallio skating-rink, the Töölö sports grounds and all fields nearby. We went to Vilhovuorenkatu, to the Sörkka harbours. It was fun there, there were timber yards and other things... and sailors.

Areas which to an outsider felt frightening do not seem to have limited Jaakko Lahtinen's life. The familiar environment and its familiar inhabitants created a feeling of security that could not be disturbed even by the negative reputation of the area.

When we lived in Sörnäinen there were all sorts of people, all sorts of wasters. It never crossed my mind to go there. - - I've got a great deal from the example of my mum, that's how I've become what I am. And I appreciate it. - - Well, that Vaasankatu is also - - that was the dodgiest place of them all. But in those days I knew many people who lived there too. And I never, as others did, wondered whether one could go there without immediately getting beaten up. But I said that yes, one can go there – I know everybody there, nobody has ever got beaten up there...

After his childhood job as shoe cleaner, Jaakko Lahtinen went to vocational school at the beginning of the 1940's and trained as a metalworker. Sports held an important position in his life from when he was a young boy – and still does, the Kullervo sports club has "maintained its grip". He also met his future wife – "a really nice woman" – through the activities of the club. They were married in early spring 1951 and have two sons. The family found their first home in Fleminginkatu: two rooms and a kitchenette. "My wife was a book-keeper and I was a sheet-metal worker. Both of us hard-working, neither one smoked or was keen on the drink. I did sports and my wife went to meetings, she was active in many associations." Over time, the savings of the family grew and in 1961 they moved to their own flat in Vaasankatu. Six years later, they left the childhood environment as the family decided to move to Roihuvuori "to better circumstances". At that point, Jaakko Lahtinen had lived for more than 30 years in the area north of Pitkäsilta.

91

*The inner courtyard of a block in Töölö is spacious, which was not often the case in the inner city. Parking cars, drying the laundry and emptying the garbage bags were some of the many functions concentrated in the yard. Photo: Kari Hakli 1969, Helsinki City Museum, Helsinki.*

The parents of Anna Mäntylä from Töölö had met while they both worked for the railways; her mother had, among other things, been only the second female train-dispatcher in Finland. Her father studied alongside his job; first he finished his matriculation examination and then studied law at the University of Helsinki. After graduation, he worked in banking for the rest of his life. The family's first child, Anna, was born in 1926 and at that point the mother left her job. The family had a second daughter in 1928 and a third in 1939. A housemaid also lived with the family. They moved to the apartment in Töölö, where Anna Mäntylä still lives, in 1927. In this home, she first lived until she got married in 1950 and moved back there in 1970. Throughout her life, Anna Mäntylä has lived away from Töölö for about ten years and from her present apartment for about 20 years.

Her childhood environment felt safe as long as it was familiar and she was allowed to use it. The backyard and block and the change of seasons were important in Töölö, too: the children channelled their energy by running around the block and digging tunnels and caves in the heaps of snow gathered along the streets. However, a girl in Töölö was not totally free to use her environment as she wished, and there was nothing like the free adventures of the children in Kallio. Outings to the Hesperia Park were made together with her younger sister and mother, and even as a schoolchild, Anna was forbidden to make any detours on her way to or from school, even if the temptations of vacant sites sometimes were stronger than her parents' orders.

> And then of course our yard was safe and when I was very small I wasn't really allowed to leave the yard. - - Then when I was in primary school I wasn't allowed to go anywhere further, but with this Anja, who was my classmate - - with her we once went to the Hiekkaranta beach, it was somehow exciting, since it was forbidden.

But this adventure ended unhappily in a fall, which made the girls feel that "this was their punishment for going there". The restricted movement in the environment was compensated for by visits to the homes of friends, which seemed to have been an unknown pastime for the child growing up in Kallio. In the responses describing the areas north of Pitkäsilta, home is more of a springboard to external activities than a place for cosy family life. The eventful life in the block and use of the local environment compensated for the inner life of the home in Kallio (Åström 1997, 27). Films were Anna Mäntylä's hobby in her teens and now adventures in the city enter her life: "We had adventures, walked in the city, and when the streets were blacked out it was awfully exciting - - In the Esplanade we strolled up and down - - we walked and looked at boys."

Changes in the environment have not disturbed the long-term inhabitant of Töölö, since the outer appearance of her childhood environment has largely remained the same, even if some of the buildings are now used for other purposes.

## Urban childhood environments

Jaakko's and Anna's experiences of their own childhood native place reveal how a mode of living adopted already as a child influence the experience of one's environment. In both cases described above, the immediate local environment is very important for the child's creation of a relationship to his or her environment. The backyard and the block emerge strongly also in other reminiscences of the study. The informants remember exactly what that local environment looked like. It is not, however, valued for its aesthetic aspects, but its important feature is the framework it provided for various activities. When building up their relationship to their environment, children do not, according to the cultural geographer Yi-Fu Tuan, pay attention to its aesthetic qualities as adults do. The fact that children are open-minded, carefree and indifferent to common notions of beauty, enable them to experience positive sensations of their environment, even if this does not correspond to standard expectations of a positive environment (Tuan 1990, 96). "Childhood native place is accepted unconditionally", observes Yrjö Sepänmaa for his part (Sepänmaa 1986, 6).

In the city, the most immediate – even if forbidden – local environments were the stairways, lifts and dark attics and basements of the blocks of flats.[4] The backyard of the house was a natural continuation to these. Even if the backyard is often described in reminiscences as outwardly humble, even repellent to outsiders, its greatest significance was as home base for various activities. The function of the yard was defined and sometimes limited by its physical environment – not always in a negative sense, though, for it also provided inspiration and opportunities (see Knuuttila 1981, 232). The yard connected the activities of the inhabitants of the house with the children's meeting place, as in the following examples from Töölö:

> The asphalted yard was where the children mostly played. The large wooden waste bin was alive with rats. In the yard rugs were aired and somebody even varnished their boat there. (Response I:86. Töölö, female, b. 1946.)

> By the other fence there was a shrubbery or a kind of flowerbed, which we kids trampled quite efficiently, despite the caretaker's warnings. There, for example, we put on a play, where I sometimes was director as well as actor. We improvised the lines as the play went on. In the yard we also played "church rat" or some other ball game, where the ball was thrown against the wall and then "stoi" was shouted. The war had thus also widened the children's vocabulary. In the street, particularly the girls played hopscotch. With a chalk or a barbiturate stone from the gravestone shop in Mechelininkatu a grid was drawn on the asphalt of the street, and there we boys also played a little. (Response I:88. Töölö, male, b. 1939.)

Even if the backyards in Töölö are often also described as sunless asphalted yards, the unattractiveness of the yards is particularly emphasised in the reminiscences of those who spent their childhood in Kallio. Therefore the children made use of the wider local environment as their playground. Tiina-Riitta Lappi has noted that individual elements characterising the landscape often emerge as more important than the environment as a whole when interviewees talk about their relationship to the environment: the landscape is constructed through details. The same phenomenon appears in the memories of the informants from Helsinki. However, the stage of life these describe differs from that in Lappi's material. In her study, adult interviewees describe the present and talk about landscape from the perspective of external onlookers, while a strong functional connection between the informant and the landscape is emphasised in childhood memories (Lappi 1999, 62).

> There were no shared hobby rooms, the yard was only the bottom of a shaft surrounded by waste bins and racks for airing rugs, where one couldn't and wasn't even allowed to play. Strict order was kept by the caretaker, Mr Kuusinen, who chased away both girls and boys from the yard. No bouncing balls against the walls, no drawing hopscotch grids on the asphalt. One wasn't even allowed to lean against the walls. - - But we had something that the children in Kallio today lack. There were the wonderful and oh so steep cliffs of Vesilinna, where we used to climb. In the area where the Linnanmäki amusement park is today, there was even a small pond, where we tried to catch small "shittyfish" the size of matches by hand. We had the Linja cliffs, which is where the City Theatre is today and the "ruins", the wild areas nearby, where the houses had been bombed and burned into strange hills of rubbish and tumbled down chimneys. We climbed, played hide-and-seek and "spying" and above all we could be as rowdy and noisy as we wanted. On the cliffs, particularly those of Vesilinna, one saw trees and bushes and noticed the change of the seasons, while from the window at home one saw only the wall of the opposite house and the black shaft of the yard. (Response I:70. Kallio, female, b. 1933.)

*The milieu in Töölö in the 1970's (as well as in the 2000's) retains many of the same features as in the years often remembered in the reminiscences: e.g. the 1920's architecture and the many corner shops. Photo: Kari Hakli 1970, Helsinki City Museum, Helsinki.*

The way the environment is used both in Töölö and Kallio is influenced by a mode of living connected to a city consisting of neighbourhoods, which was prevalent in Helsinki until the 1960's (Åström 1997, 23). Businesses that changed several times and many of which have disappeared by now – restaurants, shops for colonial products, public saunas – formed a part of everyday life. Apart from the shops in their own house, the other shops of the neighbourhood were also part of the everyday life of the children and were often visited daily. The concentration of activities is typical for a city built around densely populated neighbourhoods. It is almost impossible to find a space were no human activity takes place in this kind of environment. This is, naturally, reflected on the way the city space is utilised, experienced and valued (Franzén 1992, 48). Shopping rounds, and the choice of route are one way of creating a perception of the city. The opportunities for leisure activities, for their part, reveal choices governed by earlier decisions on which of the possibilities offered by the environment one wants to utilise (Mörck 1998, 187, 201). In the eyes of children, everyday actions were not only practical chores to be carried out: they had their own significance and a hint of adventure:

> The yard was the centre for events and activities. Its busyness was increased by the restaurant Canjon, the kitchen of which faced the yard, and the public sauna. There was all sorts of service traffic: a speciality was the ice van that came in the summer and from which men wearing leather capes carried big blocks of ice by means of their ice tongs. - - The butcher's

95

van, the dairy van, the coal van, the drinks van, all these providing for the needs of the restaurant. As an aural memory, the everyday beating of steaks echoes in our ears. Firewood and bunches of birch twigs were delivered to the public sauna. The children of the house were allowed to help in unloading and were given a bit of money for sweets. With our earnings we bought pineapple sweets in Ronkainen's colonial goods shop across the street. Most of the children bartered rather than shared their sweets. (Response I:74. Kallio, male, b. 1950. See also e.g. response I:70. Kallio, female, b. 1933.)

Whereas simply to find a place to play required that the children in Kallio independently explored their local environment, reminiscences from Töölö emphasise family walks as a way of getting to know the district and the city beyond it. The choices of route were more official during these walks than was the case with the children's independent mapping of their surroundings:

> The family went for a walk on Sunday mornings. Since we had family graves in the Old Cemetery, we often headed there. I also often went with my dad to his office in Fabianinkatu on Sundays. The post-war period was very violent. Disbandment allowances were spent on drink. The streets and yards were still blacked-out. Between woodpiles and in street corners these men who had been treated badly by the war held their drinking bouts. To feel safe, old women carried a frying pan in their bag when moving in the streets. - - Sometimes I went out for Sunday lunch with mother and father: there were the Co-op restaurants in the Lasipalatsi, in Arkadiankatu and next to the Exhibition Hall. Espilä (now KY) and Lehtovaara were slightly better places. And of course the brothers-in-arms restaurant Motti. (Response I:87. Töölö, female, b.1933.)

> On Sunday mornings, mother did the housework and cooked the meal of the week, which is to say, a roast  - -. Meanwhile, father took me for the Astra walk, which means that we went to Tunturikatu to look at the posters outside the Astra cinema. In summer, we walked to the eastern shore of the Töölö Bay to feed the swans and the ducks, sometimes we went to the City Gardens. There was a ski-track in the Hesperia Park, leading to the Laakso sports grounds, where sausages were grilled and they sold juice and national skiing campaign cloth badges for sewing onto one's anorak sleeve. When the snow was good for skiing we went all the way to Ilmala. - - Later in the evening (on Sundays) the whole family went for a Sunday walk to look at the shop windows of Forum, Stockmann and Sokos. (Response I:90. Töölö, female, b. 1947.)

The territory expanded and the independent use of the city increased when children started school, as well as through their hobbies, especially films and sports[5] (Åström 1999b, 106). The city itself is seldom described as threatening: the familiar is safe while the unknown is frightening. A relaxed attitude towards the traffic of the city is emphasised in the reminiscences, whereas the children were warned against the seashore, drunks and dirty old men as well as the dangerous but tempting stacks of wood: "In the 40's I was never warned against cars, and neither were the other children in the neighbourhood. The greatest fun in winter was to ride a sledge down the Vänrikki

*One of the objects the inhabitants became acquainted with in their environment were the places for outings and sports. The skating rink in Töölö has gathered both youngster and families on a bright winter day. Photo: Novofoto 1930's, Helsinki City Museum, Helsinki.*

Stool slope onto Hesperiankatu, and that was totally allowed" (Response I:100. Töölö, female, b. 1941). The area that felt familiar expanded yard by yard and block by block:

> In the beginning the area where I moved comprised our own yard. There was a sandpit, a rack for washing, a big birch tree and a small slope. There is still a vacant site between Mannerheimintie 49 and 47, which created plenty of space. - - As I grew older, my territory expanded to the neighbouring yards. We easily climbed the fence to the yards opposite, in Urheilukatu. - - It was not allowed to cross Mannerheimintie on one's own. (Response I:105. Töölö, female, b. 1954.)

> Then, when we were allowed to leave our own home yard, we got to play in the "field". - - There we rode the sledge run and there we learned to ski. - - The following step in life was to be allowed to play on the cliffs where there were pine trees, "the forest", where the Social Insurance Office is now. - - When I had learnt to ride a bike, my sister's BIG black one, the world grew larger. I was over ten before I was allowed to go for a ride - -. (Response I:109. Töölö, female, b. 1937.)

## Environment as a place of security

There are several differences to be found between Jaakko's and Anna's, the two sample interviewees', experiences. Even if children strive for independ-

97

ence, their behaviour at various stages of development is governed by the demands and expectations of adults. These, in turn, are based on characteristics valued by the broader community. Thus, according to Seppo Knuuttila, the upbringing of children stands in direct relation to the socio-economic structure and cultural heritage of the community (Knuuttila 1981, 198). Gender alone sometimes seems to have largely defined the child's freedom of movement. It has been more appropriate for boys than for girls to freely explore their environment. Typical boys' games, with their emphasis on physical activity take a form that requires extensive space. Knuuttila's material from the 1970's shows that boys clearly combined various games and environments in more ways than the girls did. In addition, the liberation of small groups and their conscious attempts to revolt against the norms of the adult world is regarded as particularly typical for groups of boys (Knuuttila 1981, 198, 203, 232). This difference is further strengthened by the financial and social backgrounds of the families. Just as clearly as the ideal of a family-centred home, created in the 19th century, shows in the reminiscences of the children in Töölö, the consequences of the physical environment of the home on the use of the environment are evident in the memories from Kallio. In working class families, the small flats alone limited the opportunity for socialising with friends – and even members of one's own family – at home; meeting places had to be found somewhere else. It is also obvious that the families' individual choices concerning their lifestyle and influencing their relation to the environment have varied within the districts; therefore, there is no reason to try to define a homogenous attitude to the environment prevalent either in Kallio or in Töölö. The reflection of their way of life on the way people relate to their surroundings is, in any case, apparent in the material. The way in which the environment is used, in turn, influences what the native place is experienced as: which places become personally significant, how the area experienced as one's own is expanded and which areas are experienced as safe, which as threatening.

Michel de Certeau (de Certeau 1988, 117) has divided the environment into place and space. Place represents continuity, stability. It forms a kind of outline or set of outlines around space. Space, for its part, is created when different variable aspects of place are considered. Place becomes space through its usage. de Certeau exemplifies this with a street formed by town planning, which gains a spatial significance only when its users, the pedestrians, have found it. Human geography, among other things, has also separated the concepts of place and space, using the difference created by action as the basis for the definitions. However, the use of the terms within this discipline differs from de Certeau's definition. For Tuan, for example, place means security while space represents freedom. We are attached to place and long for space, for freedom (Tuan 1979, 3). According to human geography, place becomes meaningful only through the experiences and interpretations of human beings. Thus, space represents a neutral environment, which is formed into a subjective place by the personal experiences connected to it (Karjalainen 1986, 113–114; Tani 1995, 19). However, in order to understand how an emotional attachment to the environment is formed, it is of secondary importance which way around we want to define space and place. The essential point to understand is that the creation of an attachment requires experiences or a lived world connected to the place.[6] According to de Certeau, the attitude of people to their environment can be either tactical or strategic. A strategic approach is adopted to an environment that can be limited to form a personal area and that offers a home base from which external areas – which can be experienced either as opportunities or as threats – can be manipulated. Following strategic rationality, people separate a certain area in their environment as their personal territory. The aim is to be able to control the area that is experienced as personal, and which is surrounded by an alien world with unknown forces. The opposite of strategic action, following de Certeau, is tactical. Tactics are calculated actions, defined by their independence from any given place. Thus, the space of tactics is found outside the strategic sphere of action. (de Certeau 1988, xix, 36–37.)

In landscape semiotics, the interaction between the environment and its observer is interpreted as a communicative relation. Here, the environment is the sender of the message, the landscape, the environment, is the message itself and the observer, the user of the environment, is the receiver of the message (Tarasti 1992, 164–155). The reminiscences utilized here show that the environment communicates not only through the present, but also through the past. de Certeau has observed that housing areas often become presences of diverse absences for their inhabitants. The environment we see today also communicates a vanished landscape. Everything has not always been what its looks like at the present moment. Places are associated with fragmentary and introvert histories, which unfold in different ways to observers with different experiences (de Certeau 1988, 108). According to Tuan, familiarity creates attachment, given that it does not give rise to disdain or contempt, and the awareness of the past of the place is an important factor for the creation of an emotional bond. People invest their own emotional life in their homes and in the surrounding local environment, and thus these become a kind of protection against the outside world – in de Certeau's terms a strategic space. (Tuan 1990, 99.)

The differences in lifestyles between Töölö and Kallio, and the influence of these on the inhabitants' relation to their local environment can be seen expressly as differences in the experience of place and space. Free exploration of the environment has, already at an early stage, made the district a safe, strategic area. On the other hand, when the appropriation of place has been limited, the strategic space has been smaller and tactical space has approached the immediate local environment. At the same time, the significance of home as one strategic area has been accentuated. The strategic space of the informants was not necessarily formed by one extensive whole, since school and hobbies for their part also defined the creation of areas that were experienced as safe. At the same time, the strategic and tactical areas have merged and created passages within each other.

George Simmel has described the relation of people in big cities to their environment using the term *blasé*. A blasé reaction arises when the multitude of actions, which is part of urban life, provides too many impulses for the urban dwellers to process, and as a result, they become bored and indifferent (Simmel 1967, 413–414). However, these precise impulses have also been the starting point for the informants in their exploration of their environment and creation of a strategic area. In an urban environment, the children's strategic area was formed by an environment which combined the physical familiarity of the place and the expected surprising impulses that could be followed.

*[handwritten: Captful + Fulsome indication of methodology]*

## NOTES

[1] Most of these respondents to the questionnaire are born in the 1930's and 1940's. A total of 182 people responded to the questionnaire. Most responses were received from the Töölö district: 35 descriptions in all. Kallio, described in 14 responses, was also a popular object of reminiscence. The informants both from Töölö and Kallio mainly represent the middle classes. Women formed a small majority among the informants, at about 60 per cent. The most popular decade described in the material is the 1950's (112 responses) as well as the decades following. This period is strongly present in the descriptions of Töölö and Kallio. The informants describing both Töölö and Kallio are approximately 60 years old on average. Thus they were children in the 1940's and 1950's. According to Anna-Maria Åström it is understandable that the responses are concentrated on this period of time, since the respondents have experienced these decades as an important point of reference as they strive to communicate an image of a Helsinki they regard as already lost (Åström 1998, 9).

[2] A total of about 40 interviews were conducted in the Töölö and Kallio districts. The interviewees largely represent the same generations as those who responded to the questionnaires. The interviewees were mainly identified through district associations and district newspapers. Thus both the respondents to the questionnaire and the interviewees represent a group for whom the relation to their own district is important, at least to a certain extent: they have opinions about the subject and they find it important to express these opinions. Consequently the results cannot be totally generalised, but the material does reveal which factors influence the forming of a significant feeling for native place in an urban environment. The material does not reflect conscious choices of lifestyle connected to housing and environment. These are childhood memories, where the choices and opportunities of the informants' parents have affected their relationship to their environment.

[3] The names of the informants have been changed.

[4] E.g. responses I:73a (Kallio, female, b. 1941), I:74 (Kallio, male, b. 1950), I:107 (Töölö, female, b. 1942).

[5] E.g. responses I:67 (Kallio, male, b. 1943), I:73a (Kallio, female, b. 1941), I:84 (Töölö, female, b. 1930), I:88 (Töölö, male, b. 1939).

[6] The term 'a lived world' refers to the world as an everyday reality, which is directly lived and experienced (Karjalainen 1986, 114).

## SOURCES AND BIBLIOGRAPHY

### Interviews and questionnaires

Föreningen Brage, Helsinki:
Questionnaire "Helsinki elämänympäristönä" [Helsinki as living environment] (I) 1996; 49 answers.
University of Helsinki/Department of Ethnology:
Interviews conducted during the course in fieldwork "Urban memory" in 1999.

# Literature

Åström, Anna-Maria 1997. Kvarters- och hemliv i Helsingfors under 1950-talet. Minnesskildringar – med barnets blick och den vuxnes ord [Life in the neighbourhood and at home in Helsinki in the 1950's. Recollections – with the gaze of a child and the words of an adult]. In Laboratorium för folk och kultur 2/1997, 21–28.

Åström, Anna-Maria 1998. Miten 1950-luvun helsinkiläistä kaupunkikulttuuria muistetaan? [How is the urban culture of Helsinki in the 1950's remembered?]. In Elämää kaupungissa. Muistikuvia asumisesta Helsingin keskustassa. Lapsuuden- ja nuoruudenkuvauksia sotienjälkeiseltä ajalta Helsingin keskustasta, Kaartinkaupungista ja osasta Kamppia [Life in the city. Recollections of living in the centre of Helsinki. Descriptions of childhood and youth during the post-war era in the centre of Helsinki, the Kaartinkaupunki district and part of the Kamppi district]. Memoria 12. Helsinki: Helsingin kaupunginmuseo, 8–22.

Åström, Anna-Maria 1999. Ordinary People in Post-War Helsinki. Urban Popular Culture: Practices, Delimitations, and Recent Elevation. In János Kodolányi jr. (ed.): Ethnic Communities, Ethnic Studies, Ethnic Costumes Today. Hungarian Ethnographical Society: Budapest, 101–115.

Certeau, Michel de 1988. The practice of everyday life. Berkeley and Los Angeles: University of California Press.

Ekelund, Hilding 1962. Rakennustaide ja rakennustoiminta 1918–1947 [Architecture and building activities 1918–1947]. In Helsingin kaupungin historia V:1. Ajanjakso 1918–1945 [The history of the city of Helsinki 1918–1945]. Helsinki, 99–136.

Franzén, Mats 1992. Den folkliga staden. Söderkvarter i Stockholm mellan krigen [The city of the people. The Söder districts in Stockholm between the wars]. Lund: Arkiv.

Karjalainen, Tapani 1986. Paikka ja maisema elettynä ja esitettynä [Lived and presented place and landscape]. In Kotiseutu 3/1986, 113–122.

Knuuttila, Seppo 1981. Barn i stadsmiljö – en jämförande studie av lekvanor och barntradition [Children in urban environments – a comparative study of playing habits and children's traditions]. In Lauri Honko & Orvar Löfgren (eds.): Tradition och miljö. Ett kulturekologiskt perspektiv [Tradition and environment. A cultural-ecological perspective]. Skrifter utgivna av Etnologiska sällskapet i Lund. Lund: Liber Läromedel, 198–234.

Korkiakangas, Pirjo 1999. Muisti, muistelu, perinne [Memory, reminiscence, tradition]. In Bo Lönnqvist, Elina Kiuru & Eeva Uusitalo (eds.): Kulttuurin muuttuvat kasvot. Johdatusta etnologiatieteisiin [The changing face of culture. Introduction to the ethnological disciplines]. Tietolipas 155. Helsinki: Suomalaisen Kirjallisuuden Seura, 155–176.

Koskinen, Juha 1990. Kallion Historia. Kallio-Seura r.y. – Sörkan Gibat 50 v [The history of Kallio. Kallio-Seura – Sörkän Gibat 50 years]. Helsinki: Kallio-Seura r.y. & Sörkan Gibat.

Lankinen, Markku s. a. Töölö tilastojen kuvastamana [Töölö as reflected by statistics]. In Pia Bäcklund & Vivi Niemenmaa (eds.): Kirjoituksia kaupunginosasta ja paikasta nimeltä Töölö [Writings on a district and place called Töölö]. Helsinki: Helsingin kaupungin tietokeskus, 68–79.

Lappi, Tiina-Riitta 1999. Kaupunkisuunnittelu kohtaa arjen [Town planning meets the everyday]. In Elina Katainen, Anu Suoranta, Kari Teräs & Johanna Valenius (eds.): Koti kaupungin laidalla. Työväestön asumisen pitkä linja [A home at the edge of town. Long-term trends of working-class housing]. Väki voimakas 12, 56–78.

Mörck, Magnus 1998. Spel på ytan. En bok om livsstilar [Playing on the surface. A book on lifestyles]. Skrifter från Etnologiska föreningen i Västsverige 27. Göteborg: Etnologiska föreningen i Västsverige.

Nikula, Riitta 1989. Asemakaavoitus vuosisadan vaihteessa [Town planning at the turn of the century]. In Ars. Suomen taide 4 [Ars. The art of Finland 4]. Espoo: Weilin + Göös, 170–175.

Riikonen, Heikki 1997. Aluetietoisuuden sisältö paikallisyhteisössä: sukupolvet ja

101

muistinvaraiset alueet [Contents of area consciousness in a local community. Generations and remembered areas]. In Tuukka Haarni, Marko Karvinen, Hille Koskela & Sirpa Tani (eds.): *Tila, paikka ja maisema. Tutkimusretkiä uuteen maantieteeseen* [Space, place and landscape. Explorations in the new geography]. Tampere: Vastapaino, 179–189.

Roos, J. P. 1985a. Elämisen laatu ja elämäntapa [Quality of life and lifestyle]. In Keijo Rahkonen (ed.): *Elämäntapaa etsimässä* [Looking for a lifestyle]. Helsinki: Tutkijaliitto, 23–30.

Roos, J. P. 1985b. Yhteiskunnan muutos ja arkielämä [Social change and everyday life]. In Keijo Rahkonen (ed.): *Elämäntapaa etsimässä* [Looking for a lifestyle]. Helsinki: Tutkijaliitto, 59–71.

Roos, J. P. 1987. *Suomalainen elämä. Tutkimus tavallisten suomalaisten elämäkerroista* [Finnish life. A study of life stories of ordinary Finns]. Suomalaisen Kirjallisuuden Seuran Toimituksia 454. Helsinki: Suomalaisen Kirjallisuuden Seura.

Schultén, Marius af 1955. Rakennustaide [Architecture]. In *Helsingin kaupungin historia IV:1. Ajanjakso 1875–1918* [History of the city of Helsinki IV:1. 1875–1918]. Helsinki, 54–104.

Sepänmaa, Yrjö 1986. Koivu ja tähti. Kotiseutunsa lapset [The birch and the star. Children of their native place]. In *Kotiseutu* 1/1986, 6–10.

Siipi, Jouko 1962. Pääkaupunkiyhteiskunta ja sen sosiaalipolitiikka [The society of the capital and its social policy]. *In Helsingin kaupungin historia V:1. Ajanjakso 1918–1945* [History of the city of Helsinki V:1. 1918–1945]. Helsinki, 137–379.

Simmel, Georg 1967. The Metropolis and Mental Life. In *The sociology of Georg Simmel*. Translated, edited, and with an introduction by Kurt H. Wolff. New York: The Free Press.

Snellman, Hanna 1996. *Tukkilaisen tulo ja lähtö. Kansatieteellinen tutkimus Kemijoen metsä- ja uittotyöstä* [The arrival and departure of the rafters. An ethnological study of the forestry and rafting work in Kemijoki]. Scripta Historica 25. Oulun Historiaseuran julkaisuja. Oulu: Pohjoinen.

Tani, Sirpa 1995. *Kaupunki Taikapeilissä. Helsinki-elokuvien mielenmaisemat – maantieteellisiä tulkintoja* [The city in the magic mirror. Mindscapes in films on Helsinki – geographical interpretations]. Helsingin kaupungin tietokeskuksen tutkimuksia 1995:14. Helsinki: Helsingin kaupungin tietokeskus.

Tarasti, Eero 1992. Maiseman semiotiikasta [On the semiotics of landscape]. In *Johdatusta semiotiikkaan. Esseitä taiteen ja kulttuurin merkkijärjestelmistä* [Introduction to semiotics. Essays on the sign systems of art and culture]. Helsinki: Gaudeamus, 154–168.

Tuan, Yi-Fu 1979. *Space and Place. The perspective of experience*. London: Edward Arnold.

Tuan, Yi-Fu 1990. *Topophilia. A study of environmental perception, attitudes, and values*. Englewood Cliffs: Prentice-Hall.

JORMA KIVISTÖ

# Pikku Huopalahti in Helsinki

## A Place and its Appropriation

Contemporary residential areas are planned with their future inhabitants in mind, but the planners are usually knowledgeable and able enough only to consider the basic needs of the practical aspects of people's everyday life. In this article, I will explore the lived world and the adjustment of the inhabitants to such an area: their appropriation of the place. Thus, I will try to understand how the occupants actively appropriate the area and I will be looking for the factors that influence the inhabitants' well-being and their adjustment to the new housing area. By studying the ways in which the dwellers act in this planned environment, how they attach meanings to various places and how these meanings are formed I will gain insight into what the inhabitants demand of their living environment, bearing in mind their individual backgrounds.

The object of research here is the Pikku Huopalahti residential area of Helsinki, and its inhabitants. The aim is not, however, to make a particular study of the specific features of Pikku Huopalahti in the sense of regarding the area as somehow unique. This area was chosen because of the diverse opportunities for association that it offers, and the objective is primarily to gather information about the inhabitants' general ways of adjusting to their residential area. The data used in this article on the dwellers' habits in using the area are based on my 12-page questionnaire that was delivered to 600 households in Pikku Huopalahti in the summer of 2000. In this article, I will analyse the answers to one part of the questionnaire, those concerning the Tilkka neighbourhood (75 answers, return rate 43,5 % – I included only 57 of the returned questionnaires in my material, since many of them were incomplete). On the basis of these answers I will attempt to make a preliminary survey of Pikku Huopalahti as an area of activity and to place the work in the context of my continued research. Therefore this article also, on a theoretical level, deals with issues that I have not yet studied empirically.

## Pikku Huopalahti as research object

When studying the inhabitants' appropriation of place in their living environment, the special features of the area and its position in relation to the

103

surrounding urban structure must be considered. City centres offer different circumstances and opportunities for their inhabitants' adjustment to the area than suburbs situated further away from the centre. Presumably, those who have chosen either the centre or a suburb as their area of residence know what opportunities the area offers, and embrace a lifestyle in accordance with those opportunities. The inhabitants of a suburb most probably have a different way of forming a local identity than those living in the centre. Life in the city centre offers more possibilities for an individual, anonymous lifestyle, but each district also offers other distinctive lifestyle choices.

Pikku Huopalahti is a new residential area on the outskirts of the inner city of Helsinki. The reason why an area five kilometres from the centre was built this late is that building had not been considered possible before with the techniques available at that time. The approximately 3 500 flats (with just under 8 000 inhabitants) were completed during the 1990's. The district was planned to be built as four different planned areas. At the beginning of the decade, the areas of Korppaantie and Kytösuontie were built. Following these, the Tilkka area was completed and the Paciuksenkatu area was constructed during the latter half of the decade. Pikku Huopalahti is an interesting area because of the various, even contrasting, intentions that influenced its development.[1]

Firstly, it is difficult to decide whether Pikku Huopalahti should be characterised as an inner city district or a suburb.[11] The district is located on the edge of the old inner city area, but it is a new residential area and therefore its architecture displays similar features as that of suburbs situated further away from the centre. Even in the principles underlying the planning of the area, the role of the Pikku Huopalahti residential area is mentioned as twofold. The area is intended as "continuing the established city structure", which in the main streets is seen in the many business premises and relatively dense construction. The urban lifestyle is enhanced by the tramline and the quick access to the city centre. Most of the blocks are styled on the model of the closed blocks in the old inner city. Thus the houses, seen from the street, can be compared to a façade, with the implication that something hidden lies behind it. These features contribute to the creation of an urban street space.

In his analysis of the closed blocks, Mats Franzén (1992) ascribed great significance to the street and its diversity of functions in the Stockholm inner city before the Second World War. Similar kinds of inner city features have been appropriated by the Pikku Huopalahti planners, but it has yet to be explored just how the streets and the closed blocks function here, in a different historical context. While there is an exit onto the street from most of the houses, parks and other green areas are also accessible from the other side.

When considering the local inhabitants' adoption of and adaptation to the residential area, one of the ways in which the various places in Pikku Huopalahti can be categorised is according to types as described by Ina-Maria Greverus (1978, 1994). There are typically urban meeting places here, but the area also offers the opportunity to go to parks and recreational areas – to so called 'places of possibility'. The opposition between urban and local village-like features makes the area interesting.

*Pikku Huopalahti housing area consists of four different areas. In city administration these four areas belong into three different parts of the city, but most people feel Pikku Huopalahti housing area is one entity.*

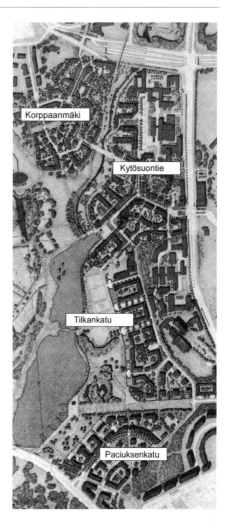

There are significant differences to be found when making a comparison between these and the closed blocks of the inner city and the centre. The centre consists of houses built at various historical periods, while all buildings in Pikku Huopalahti were built within a few years. This customarily gives an area a suburban feeling. Here however, this impression has been challenged by the planning principle for the area according to which similar houses and houses by the same architect are not built next to each other. The resulting variety of design of the houses and their bright colours give a layered effect to the structure of the block – an effect which does not necessarily appeal to everybody.

Secondly, there are various opinions as to whether Pikku Huopalahti forms an independent whole, or whether it forms part of the surrounding district. When the area was planned, the various sub-areas were left as parts of the districts of Etelä-Haaga, Ruskeasuo and Meilahti following the existing district borders, and the borders have not been changed, for example, for statistical purposes. The architecture and planning of each of the sub-areas is also partly modelled on the district it is officially a part of.

105

However, the overall aim of the planning of Pikku Huopalahti was to create an independent whole with its own central places created by town planning. The feeling of locality is increased by large parks. In addition, the Central Park of Helsinki and the seashore are nearby. The creation of social meeting-places was one of the planning principles. There is, for example an activity house for the inhabitants and a youth club at the school. Thus, the area is often thought of as a district in its own right, even by the city authorities.

A third issue to consider is the development of the inhabitants' local identity and the lively activities of the inhabitants' association during the building of the area, which also touches on the previous point. As soon as the first houses were finished, the active inhabitants founded a residents' association which quickly developed into an important channel for the occupants to express their opinions. The residents' association also initiated a wide range of hobby activities and clubs in the area.

The development of a feeling of community among the inhabitants was furthered by the principle of building premises for shared activities in the area and by the creation of channels for discussion between the residents' association, the builders and the various city authorities (particularly the social sector). The residents' influence has been greatest on the planning of the communal parks, the beaches and the shared premises. On the other hand, the activities of the residents' association have diminished since the construction of the area was finished. One might actually ask, whether this sense of community was more the result of a pioneering spirit among the first dwellers, than something more sustainable, a phenomenon which has been generally observed in the history of suburbs.

Pikku Huopalahti is also an interesting area to study in the respect that all the inhabitants of the area are new. The area as a whole has only recently been finished and the inhabitants themselves have formed several features

*The housing area has been built densely, though the bay area and big open parks offer good facilities for play and recreation, "places of possibilities". Photo: Jorma Kivistö.*

106

in it by their own activities. There was no prior "local spirit" in the area, but it had to be personally created or it was formed as a consequence of certain features of the residents' attitudes. The results of a survey conducted among the inhabitants showed that many, especially families with children, were satisfied with the environment being similar to a traditional small town and accessible social security. Some, on the other hand, disagreed and longed for a more individual lifestyle (Korhonen 1998, 98–99).

Fourthly, the heterogeneity of the population in the area can be mentioned. The land is owned by the city and therefore the area is included in the city council's programme for achieving housing targets. According to the programme, 45–50 percent of the housing should be state-subsidised rental flats, 20–25 per cent state-subsidised flats owned by the inhabitants, 10–15 per cent privately financed rental flats and 15–20 per cent privately financed flats owned by the inhabitants. The age structure differs from the age structure of Helsinki as a whole in that there is almost double the amount of children under ten years of age in the area and somewhat more 20–40-year-olds. Correspondingly, there are about 50 per cent fewer inhabitants over 45 years of age than in Helsinki as a whole.

About 8 per cent of the inhabitants in Pikku Huopalahti have another mother tongue than Finnish or Swedish. This is more than half the amount than in Helsinki on average. The answers to the questionnaire clearly show that it did not reach the occupants who speak another language.

## Perspectives on the study

The inhabitants of an area are not an undifferentiated mass of people with similar aspirations and needs, whose satisfaction is guaranteed by planning an equally good living environment with all the necessary services for everybody. Many factors influence whether the inhabitants like living in an area or not. Some of these factors are surprising ones, which do not immediately spring to mind. Therefore, in addition to the "normal" aspects connected with the comfort of living (such as the availability of services and communications) my questionnaire included questions on other issues not directly related to the present housing situation of the respondents.

The first part of the questionnaire dealt with the backgrounds of the respondents (housing situation, education, work, how long they have lived in the area). In the second part, which sought information on the adjustment to Pikku Huopalahti, the respondents were asked to describe the area and issues that have affected their adjustment. This part also included questions on what kinds of images of the area the respondent had received through the media and people who live elsewhere, as well as information on the past of the area. In addition, maps were used to identify the nice and the unpleasant places in the area.

The third part focused on the activities of the inhabitants and how they move in the area and outside of it. These questions aimed at mapping the sociability and activities of the occupants. This article will mostly deal with the material from this part of the questionnaire.

107

Michel de Certeau (1984, 34–39) uses the terms strategy and tactics to describe the forms of action people take in their everyday lives. Tactic skills are applied when moving in public areas among other people and within the framework of the rules of the environment. Using their own abilities, creative practices of everyday life, individuals make their lives more agreeable. In cities, people make choices by combining their needs, opportunities and desires when faced with external necessities.

The last part of the questionnaire asks the respondents about the childhood environment where they grew up and how they experienced that environment. In addition, I wanted to know how the inhabitants keep in touch with their former living environments. The aim of this part was to gain information on whether the environment experienced in childhood influences the perception of the present living environment and what features in it are appreciated.

The level of real space connected to social practices is somehow related to the level of ideal, mentally understood space – both of these spaces contain and presuppose each other (Lefebvre 1991, 14). In the following, I will explore the mutual correspondence of these two spatial levels.

According to Lefebvre's theory, social and economic forces, the forms of social organisation and the forms of the natural world reflect on the contents of space and the formation of people's minds. Spatial awareness and the features of place are not causal in themselves, that is, space as such does not cause people to behave in a certain way. However, the significances forming the background of space itself hold a causal force in conveying "messages" to people. Space is not just an empty field with objects in it. Spaces are charged with emotional and mythical content, as well as communal symbols and images and historical significances. In other words, I am interested in the space of social practices as a space governed by the senses including psychological and social projections, symbols and utopias of the imagination.

Lefebvre aims at exposing both the diverse whole formed by spatial comprehension and the phenomena, which in a sense are invisible, behind the habitual exploratory perspectives. As a literary or verbal method of description is usually applied to, for example, urban space, the perspective always remains at a descriptive, concrete level. When attempts are made to describe social space using the same methods, that space is reduced to 'a message' and the being in space to 'reading' – and both the history and the significance of the practices of everyday life are forgotten. (Lefebvre 1991, 4.)

The process of adjustment is perhaps not so much directly related to the physical environment (for example architecture or services), but more to the way the environment is experienced. The experience of the environment is also greatly influenced by the images of the area, which might change over time and with increased experience. In addition, factors such as profession and education may affect the way people perceive their environment. People can, for example, be divided into those who observe and experience their environment socially, those who do it rationally and those who take an aesthetic stance. All these factors must be explored and taken into account when analysing the answers of the inhabitants.

Controlling factors functioning on a larger scale must also be taken into

*[handwritten margin note: works with the Lefebvre - is the framework actually followed]*

account. When specifying spatial practices, these can be divided into spatial fields of perspectives, elements and moments of social practices. In this process, they are separated from each other, even if they are constantly subject to the control of society, such as political and economic power (Lefebvre 1992, 8–9).

## District dwellers appreciating community or urban city dwellers?

The existence of the necessary physical places and spaces has been seen as a prerequisite for the formation of community and social networks. These provide the inhabitants with the opportunity to meet each other. Joint activities strengthen the feeling of community and local identity. Shared spaces and meeting-places that are situated in the borderland between private and totally public space enable the creation of a local community.

Significances are produced constantly, but in spite of this, cultural meanings and definitions produced during a long historical development change slowly even when they have been detached from their original context. This also applies to concepts connected with the environment. For example, "suburb" is not only a term for a residential area, but also a cultural category. Places and spaces are used to create categories and hierarchies. They are levels of representation that preserve social relations (Ilmonen 1997, 21). This explains, for example, why some people call Pikku Huopalahti "suburban" or "village-like", while others define it as "an urban residential area".

There are exceptionally positive experiences in Pikku Huopalahti of co-operation between the inhabitants and the representatives of the City. One of

*The area's timber-built residents centre, previously a railway station situated elsewhere in Helsinki, is now located by Pikku Huopalahti Bay. Photo: Jorma Kivistö.*

the most noticeable achievements is the Tapanila station, the area's residents' centre, which was planned jointly by the various parties and provides a good venue for meetings, celebrations and hobbies. (Korhonen, Malin & Savola 1998, 195.) The lively co-operation between the residents' association, the city authorities and the planners of the area has helped create a dynamic image of the area. The residents' association has also discussed ideas for conducting an experiment in local administration.

Since the construction of the area was completed, the number of issues discussed by the residents' association has decreased and the character of the activities of the association has changed, even if it still is a significant channel for the opinions of the inhabitants, particularly in relation to the city administration. The many things created as a result of the co-operation among the inhabitants still exist as concrete symbols of the co-operation: the residents' centre and its activities, the annual parties, the website and the solutions in the parks.

Nearly all of the respondents to the questionnaire said they appreciate living in Pikku Huopalahti since it provides an urban lifestyle with plenty of leisure activities. The same number of respondents stated their appreciation of the opportunity to maintain privacy. Despite these answers, 27 respondents (almost half) said they value the possibility for communal activities that the area offers (e.g. through various associations), 11 respondents did not answer this question and 19 marked the alternative 'I do not value this'. In other words, those who wish to maintain their urban privacy also appreciate the opportunity for communality or *vice versa,* the defenders of communality also value the possibility for urban privacy.

A closer study of those in favour of communality and those who do not appreciate it, shows that 14 of the 18 male respondents value the opportunity for communality, while only one out of three female respondents appreciate communal activities. The answers to other questions reveal that those who do not value communality do not participate in local activities and use services in other areas to a slightly larger extent than the inhabitants of Pikku Huopalahti in average. A clear majority of those who appreciate communality also often use the city centre during their free time, that is, they seem to be active both in their residential area and in the centre.

Obviously, many are linked to the centre through their work. But also leisure activities and hobbies are important in this respect. The respondents' use of the city centre in their free time varies greatly. Approximately every fourth respondent meets their friends in the centre more frequently than once a month and a few more less frequently than that. One third of the respondents visited the city centre more than once a month for outdoor or sports activities.

The theatre, cinema and art attract about half of the respondents to the centre once a month or more frequently. The relative number of women was larger in this group than the number of men. Roughly the same number of people as above visits restaurants, but there is more balance between the number of men and women. In addition, half of the women stated that they often go shopping and spend time in the centre. Apart from one exception, those who have small children do not use the city centre at all. Children clearly keep the parents closely connected to the home.

According to Kevin Lynch (1981, 131–150), the experience of the environment is an interactive process based on the physical characteristics of the environment and the observer's prior spatial and environmental perceptions. From a cognitive perspective, the observation of space can be divided into three simultaneous levels: firstly, the *level of perception* or the level of physical reality, secondly, the *level of memory*, which is formed by the internal experience of environmental observation and is thus the level of images and emotions, and thirdly, the *level of abstraction* or presentation of the observed that is created on the basis of the observations and the internal experiences. These three levels of spatial observation influence each other and form a layered experience of space and feeling of place.

The feeling of place is, according to Lynch, influenced by the environmental elements, which are *structure*, *identity* and *symbolic significance*. These correspond to the levels of spatial observation. The environmental structure is conveyed at the physical level of space, the identity of the environment is formed at the level of memory and images, and the symbolic significance on the abstract level.

45 per cent of the inhabitants who moved to Pikku Huopalahti in 1994–1996 (the majority of them moved to the houses built in the Tilkka area) moved there from the inner city. The second largest group, 20 per cent, moved from the western suburbs. A total of 45 per cent moved from suburbs of Helsinki and the region around the capital. Less than 10 per cent moved from other parts of Finland (Korhonen 1998, 36). Thus, assumably almost half of the new dwellers in Pikku Huopalahti were familiar with a way of living typical of the inner city.

One quarter of the respondents gave the location of the area and its good traffic connections as the main reasons for moving to Pikku Huopalahti. Two aspects of the area's location were mentioned: some appreciated the fact that it is relatively close to the centre, while others valued its situation in the larger area of Munkkiniemi–Munkkivuori–Etelä-Haaga. The latter group had lived in the nearby district and thus knew the area. For these inhabitants, the feeling of place presented above did not change compared to their earlier living environment because of the move.

The closeness of the centre and the perception of the area as part of the inner city are two of the most positive features the inhabitants ascribe to their residential area. Also those who do not travel daily to the centre, for example, to work, appreciate its geographical proximity. The distance between the centre and the residential area is interpreted in relation to distances that are seen as normal within this culture.

In the Helsinki region, a distance of about five kilometres to the city centre is interpreted as short and the residential area is thus seen as located close to the centre, particularly since there are only districts built in closed blocks on the way there. The geographical distance is transformed into a conceptual connection between one's own residential area and the centre. This interpreted information becomes part of the significance of the area.

From then on, the knowledge of the closeness of the centre is always present in Pikku Huopalahti, even if the inhabitants would never visit it (Stenros 1994, 34–35).

Similarly, the knowledge that Pikku Huopalahti is situated close to their prior place of living or the environment of their early adulthood is important for those who have moved there from nearby areas (according to various studies, this applies to more than half of the inhabitants of Pikku Huopalahti). The proportion of those who have lived in nearby areas is even higher among those of the inhabitants who are born in Helsinki. Outdoor activities in the nearby areas and presumably also in the earlier residential areas were common according to the answers.

## The borders of the private area

Considering environmental structures, a house is a simple spatial archetype, while a city is the most complicated of archetypes. A central function within the archetype of the house is to create a spatial order, to understand the spatial elements and link them to each other. In the city, the central action is the marking of places. Here, the significance of borders is accentuated, that is, being inside or outside of those borders, which is part of the collective or communal identity (Stenros 1994, 34–35).

One of the inner city features that the town planners wanted to implement in Pikku Huopalahti were business premises at street level in the buildings lining the larger streets. This feature has had a great impact on the identity of the area, and the shops for their part facilitate the creation of a spatial order. However, it has not been possible to apply this principle to all parts of Pikku Huopalahti. The Tilkka area, which is my present object of study,

*A small supermarket, post office, office for social security and few small shops make everyday life easier and also offer opportunities for inhabitants to meet other people socially. Photo: Jorma Kivistö.*

is a long strip situated on the east side of the bay and bordered by one busy street. The location of the other areas on the north and south sides of the bay allows for better shop premises at street level.

Most of the shops in the Tilkka area are situated in the Paletti business building on the eastern edge of the area next to the Mannerheimintie street. Originally, there were no plans for a large grocery in the building, since the planner of the area feared that it would attract customers away from the smaller shops in the area. However, contrary to the plans, a large grocery shop was established in the Paletti building. Presumably, financial considerations were the main motivation for this initiative. In the same building, there is also a post office (which no longer provides services of the former Post Bank), a cashpoint, a large stationary shop, a Chinese restaurant and, on the Mannerheimintie side, a Social Security Office. Along the Tilkankatu street, there is a grocery kiosk and a florist's shop.

At the northern end of Tilkankatu lies the Tilkantori square, which is constituted of a smaller grocery, a restaurant, two hairdressers, a branch of the local church congregation, fabric and clothes shops, and a few other small shops. These are situated in an area north of the housing area of the studied respondents, but many of them pass this northern area on their way to the bus stop or the shops.

Of all the 57 respondents, 49 (86 %) stated that they buy their groceries in Pikku Huopalahti, 13 inhabitants said they do their shopping in the centre, in nearby areas or in supermarkets. A similar number of respondents use the cashpoint and the post office. Car owners usually use the petrol stations on the outskirts of the Pikku Huopalahti area, but, if need be, they also use service stations in other areas. Every fourth respondent uses the services of the local church congregation. Two persons said they go to a congregation elsewhere. Presumably, many go to the church of the Meilahti congregation, situated 1,5 kilometres from Pikku Huopalahti, since there is no actual church in the area itself.

Most respondents frequent restaurants and hobby premises outside of Pikku Huopalahti. Approximately every sixth said they go to restaurants in the area, while almost half of the respondents visit restaurants in the city centre. Approximately the same number of inhabitants uses hairdressers in Pikku Huopalahti as elsewhere. Many obviously have a regular hairdresser who they use frequently. Surprisingly, one respondent said she goes all the way to central Finland to the hairdressers, and one goes to Hämeenlinna (80 kilometres from Helsinki).

This part of the questionnaire also provided the opportunity for the respondents to add any other services they use in Pikku Huopalahti. About every other respondent had added something. The kiosks in the area were mentioned most frequently. In addition, the children's library at the school, the pharmacy, the veterinary clinic, the florist's shop and the drapery were each listed by a few respondents. Some of these services or shops are situated in the northern part of Pikku Huopalahti, about a kilometre from the respondents' housing area. My impression is that if all possible services had been listed in the questionnaire, more of them would have been mentioned.

113

All the activities and services mentioned above help the occupants function and move within the area, which, in turn, aids the understanding of and adjustment to one's own living environment.

## Sociability and leisure activities

Social space is both a field for various purposes and plans, and a basis for actions, a place where energies flow. It is also potentially a place of possibility. At the same time, social space in itself contains a collection of material objects and means which enable the social use of the space. The symbolism and practice of social spaces cannot be separated from each other (Lefebvre 1991, 191–193).

The inhabitants' social activities and hobbies outside the home usually take place in public premises. Some of these social spaces are situated in close vicinity to the home – even in the same building, while other premises may be located further away. For their part, the places used by the inhabitants for their social activities reflect the inhabitants' commitment to their own residential area or their preference of activities that are not dependent on a physical place.

Of the 57 inhabitants of Pikku Huopalahti who answered my questionnaire, 41 stated they know (by knowing I mean chatting to people even if one does not necessarily know their name) their neighbours. The second most common form of social interaction – almost half of the respondents marked this alternative – between the occupants takes place through using the services of the area. Almost all the respondents with children – men as well as women – also knew other residents through them. About every sixth respondent said they know people in the area through their hobbies. One quarter of the female respondents stated that they know other occupants of Pikku Huopalahti through their work, while only one male respondent marked this alternative.

About half of the respondents stated they interact with their neighbours through exchanging small services with them. The number of times this occurs varied from a few times per year to weekly occurrences; there are no significant variations according to gender in this case. Shared activities, most likely things connected to the housing companies, brought together roughly the same number of inhabitants. 16 of the 39 female respondents said they go walking or do other sports together with a neighbour, while none of the male respondents do this.

Approximately the same numbers apply to shared entertainment activities. On the other hand, five out of 18 men said they socialise with their neighbours through their hobbies. Around half of the parents with small children meet other inhabitants through childcare. One fifth of the respondents said they have no social contact with their neighbours.

Most of the respondents felt that the extent of social interaction with their neighbours was suitable. Only one person thought that there is too much interaction (even if this person does not have any contact with the neighbours as it is). 12 respondents would like to have more social contact with their neighbours. However, five of these had stated that they do not appreciate the opportunity for communality in the area. Obviously, they would want to socialise only with certain persons among their neighbours.

A preliminary study of the answers to other parts of the questionnaire, which are not analysed in this article, reveal tendencies to separate between "good" inhabitants who own their flats and "bad" tenants in the rental flats. Similarly, some respondents express their dislike of the foreign inhabitants and their "inappropriate" habits.

According to Pierre Bourdieu (1985, 88–89), members of different social classes tend to create a distance to each other using taste. When choosing objects and buildings, people classify them socially, and the socially classified buildings, in turn, classify the people themselves. In his study on the reception of the architecture in Pikku Huopalahti, Timo Kalanti (1993, 7) discusses these differences in the judgement of taste.

Approximately every third of the dwellers in Pikku Huopalahti held a positive attitude to the area's inhabitants of foreign origin. One out of ten regarded them as a negative feature. Educated women over 35 years of age took the most positive stance to foreigners (Korhonen 1998, 66–69).

Places that enable social interaction contribute to people's attachment to their living environment. Local interaction, getting to know one's neighbours, shopping in the area or visiting the local pub all increase the lived experience in the area. Additionally, in the case of Pikku Huopalahti, there are no such alienating factors as big department stores or supermarkets nearby, and the centre does not attract shoppers by car.

The question regarding leisure activities (in addition to actual hobbies, any moving in the area or cultural activities) that the inhabitants carry out in Pikku Huopalahti gave the following results. Two out of three respondents listed at least one activity, which means that every third did not mention any activity at all. Over one third of the respondents listed outdoor activities or walking. There are probably more inhabitants who carry out this kind of activities, since those who have an actual hobby in the area usually did not mention activities of a more unorganised kind. People spend time outdoors on their own or with friends. Every tenth respondent daily walks their dog and many said they thus meet other dog owners.

Every tenth respondent carries out more advanced outdoor sports, such as jogging, roller-skating or cycling. There is an allotment area in the Tilkka district and one tenth of the respondents stated that they do gardening there in the summer. Three (out of 57) go to keep-fit classes organised by the area's sports club Pihaus, two go to the arts club and one is a member of the boating club (there is a small marina at the bay).

The lively activities among the inhabitants in the construction phase of the area has, above all, resulted in social activities, which have been supported by the physical building of the area, including premises for joint activities. The environment offers a framework for various kinds of activities. The spaces for hobbies offered in Pikku Huopalahti are mostly general club premises, therefore the inhabitants must seek hobbies that require special

115

*Residents of the Tilkankatu area run an association for gardening, with dozens of kitchen gardens close to the houses and park area of Pikku Huopalahti Bay. Photo: Jorma Kivistö.* = allotments ( ? )

equipment or specific hobby groups elsewhere. Every sixth respondent said they use hobby premises in Pikku Huopalahti, and every third that they go to the centre for their hobbies.

17 respondents (30 %) stated that they have used the joint club premises and the residents' centre in Pikku Huopalahti. Half of these have attended meetings there, mostly organised by the housing companies or the house committees. The club premises were also used for sports and other hobbies, and for organising children's parties. A few respondents mentioned the art exhibitions and café in the residents' centre. Surprisingly, almost all of the respondents thought that the shared club premises are needed in the area, even if their own lifestyle was oriented outside of the area. Only one respondent, who obviously was staying temporarily in student housing, did not consider the shared club premises necessary.

According to a study of shared club premises in Helsinki carried out in 1996 (Korhonen, Malin & Savola 1998, 138–140), about half of the inhabitants of Pikku Huopalahti had used the shared club premises at least once and half of these used the premises fairly often. The school with its sports premises and the youth centre that have been built since 1996 have diminished the need for using the club premises for sports and youth activities. The same study showed that the most active users of the club premises were families with children, inhabitants with a higher level of education, inhabitants who owned their flats, inhabitants with employment and female inhabitants. These results correspond to the results of my questionnaire.

The shared club premises in Pikku Huopalahti were among those most actively used in all Helsinki according to the study of 1996. After this, the large residents' centre was built in the area, which diversified the hobbies offered in the area. On the other hand, the frequency of using the clubrooms in the individual houses was below the average of the whole city, which is probably

116

explained by the fact that there are less of those, while there are more larger shared premises in the area. (Korhonen, Malin & Savola 1998, 152.)

In the conclusion of their study, the authors observe that the residents' centres are expected to bring not only opportunities for activities to an area, but also safety and communality. However, mass entertainment and commercial alternatives form a counter-force to communality. The interviewees emphasised that the maintenance of privacy is important also in residents' centres and club premises. At their best, these spaces have increased new kinds of joint activities that allow privacy and difference, and promoted the interaction between various social and ethnic groups. (Korhonen, Malin & Savola 1998, 192–193.)

In the questionnaires, almost three out of four say they carry out leisure activities outside Pikku Huopalahti. Cultural activities such as film and theatre are concentrated in the city centre. Only slightly less that one quarter of the respondents said they go to the cinema or the theatre. However, a question in another part of the questionnaire, on the frequency of and reasons for visits to the centre revealed that about half of the respondents go to the centre for cultural activities once a month or more often. Perhaps people have varying views on what constitutes a regular leisure activity and what is an occasional event.

More than a third of the respondents have a sports hobby (e.g. swimming, gymnastics, ball sports) which requires special premises. These sports halls are usually situated on the outskirts of the inner city. Outdoor activities are also carried out in the neighbouring areas by the sea in Meilahti, Seurasaari and Munkkiniemi, and in the Central Park. It is not clear from the questionnaire how many inhabitants do this, but the number of those who spend time outdoors in the nearby areas is probably similar to those who also do it in Pikku Huopalahti. Every tenth of the respondents said they spend time at their summer cottage or go boating further away from the area.

## Primary and transitory spots

The questionnaire also included a map, on which the respondents were asked to mark the areas of Pikku Huopalahti that they are familiar with or that they use at least occasionally. A third of the respondents know the whole area very well, that is, they marked the streets, footpaths and parks of the area, also those further away from the immediate surroundings of their home. Every fifth respondent knows the area relatively well according to their marking of areas within most parts of Pikku Huopalahti. Also around one fifth of the respondents only marked the main street of the area or a few parks, thus, they only know a small part of the area.

One fourth of the respondents had not marked the map at all. However, the rest of their answers indicate that about half of them are somewhat or relatively familiar with the area. The overall impression is that there is an even spread of level of familiarity with the area among the inhabitants between the extremes of knowing it very well and not at all.

117

The spatial environment consists of focal points or primary spaces and the distances between these or structured spatial series, and significant places. The primary spaces give the environment a structural significance. Often these are symbolic and possess several layers of meaning. They are of a public or private nature, centres or shelters. The house, the market and the square are examples of institutionalised primary spaces. Usually, they have a halting effect; they function as resting places and they affect identification and identity, that is, belonging to a certain place.

Between the focal points there are transitory spaces which give the spatial structure a sense of continuity. They also influence people's willingness to choose objects and their enthusiasm to move in the spaces. These transitory spaces are everyday spaces, roads and bridges, that link the observer to the environment and bring together the individual places to a whole (Stenros 1994, 34–35).

There are primary and transitory places in Pikku Huopalahti and several of these had been marked on the maps. The inhabitants experience the design of the parks and the streets in the area as relatively positive with their variety of detail. Obviously, the planners have been successful in using a style that appeals to the inhabitants. According to Lefebvre, people experience space not only through the senses, but also through acquired language, signs and abstractions. People retreat from their physical body outside of it, words and signs enable or stimulate this (Lefebvre 1991, 203).

Only a small number of the respondents said they use their car in the area or for going to work. Only three (of 57) stated they use their car within Pikku

*Many precincts are built for pedestrians only, which together with club premises offer possibilities to organize various happenings. Flea markets have been popular especially among families with children. Photo: Jorma Kivistö.*

Huopalahti. Every sixth respondent drives to work, the same number walks. Three out of four said they take the bus or tram to work in the winter. In the summer, their proportion drops to half of the respondents, and correspondingly, the number who cycles grows. Every third said they cycle to work at least occasionally.

There are many different kinds of organisation in Pikku Huopalahti, for example, sports and hobby clubs, the congregation and the residents' association. Every fifth respondent said they participate in the activities of at least one organisation. Of these, about half are members of two or more associations. The most popular were the residents' association (5 mentions) and the allotment association.

Also the arts club, the Pihaus sports club, the parents' association and the local branch of the Mannerheim child protection organisation were mentioned. Those who are members of organisations in the area have also earlier been slightly more active than others in working for their environment or residential area.

According to Lefebvre, successfully created spaces are filled with meaning for the users; they have a distinct character. They renew themselves for their users through their lived lives. An occasional outside visitor cannot experience these same places to the same degree. Space acquires its full meaning through (spatial and signifying) social practice. A successful space also enables a creative process of signification, which gives places a personal meaning. (Lefebvre 1991, 137–138.)

## Meanings of place

In my article, I have primarily dealt with the ways in which the inhabitants of Pikku Huopalahti move within their residential area and outside of it in their everyday lives and during their leisure. In the following, I will briefly, and mainly from a theoretical perspective, explore the different levels of meaning of space. The character and formation of these have only been referred to above, but the meanings of space for the inhabitants are important for the understanding of the area as a whole.

In addition to the questionnaire, I will have to conduct theme interviews for my further research, which will assumably help me investigate the issue in more depth than using the questionnaire alone. This questionnaire distributed to a larger group of inhabitants has provided a preliminary view of various ways of understanding one's living environment.

Above, I discussed environmental elements and corresponding levels of spatial observation using the ideas of Kevin Lynch. The structure of the environment appears on the physical level of space, the identity of the environment is formed on the level of memory and images, and the symbolic meaning of the environment on the abstract level (Lefebvre 1991, 75–76).

The force of our image of an area is often surprising. One of the most interesting responses to my questionnaire came from an inhabitant who did not answer any of its questions, but still wanted to explain why. A close rela-

119

tive to this respondent had participated in filling the Pikku Huopalahti area with refuse after the Second World War, and he therefore felt that he lived in the area against his will, since he had been appointed a flat on top of an old rubbish dump. We perceive our environment on the basis of what kind of relation we have to it.

The highest level of spatial perception is, according to Lynch, the awareness of spatial observation at the level of abstract presentation. Human beings have the capacity to create inner, mental performances of the surrounding world, and to manipulate these. These presentations are subjective, personal perspectives on the environment. Individuals observe the structure of their spatial surroundings through their senses. Using the level of memory (images, emotions), people combine, classify and form contexts on the abstract level of presentation. These, in turn, inform new observations. (Stenros 1994, 39–41.)

Sometimes images and significances do not originate in a person's own experience, but new buildings are interpreted according to prior models. In his study of Pikku Huopalahti, Timo Kalanti (1993) found instances of this in the statements of some of the inhabitants. Since there are no old, existing buildings, the inhabitants soon attach new or old significances to the new places.

> It's important for me that when one moves into an area, that the area has a history, it has a spirit, it's got some kind of atmosphere. Here this didn't exist. A new area can't have that, yet. And that's why it's so difficult to know what to think of the new houses. And especially, if they are totally impersonal. And here they have kind of fooled me by putting up this tower, that gives a feeling as if there was something old about the place. And I willingly let myself be fooled. (Male, 43 years. Kalanti 1993.)

The history and principles of town planning also influence, among other things, social functions, hobbies and everyday activities. Experiences of various urban structures and their activities gathered in different places and at different times form the framework for the inhabitants' memories. Presumably, memories are strongly connected to place, but new places can also stimulate associations to old places through their details, for examples smells.

The relation of space to time differs from the temporal relation of historians. In history, a certain period is detached from the larger context, while historical periods and the generating past have left their eternal marks on space. Space is always actual and synchronic; its components are bound to each other by internal links that have developed over time (Lefebvre 1991, 110).

Models from older urban structures have been used in the planning of Pikku Huopalahti. Both the inhabitants and the planning of the area have their own history and their own past. It still remains to be studied how people experience their new living environment considering their various housing histories and backgrounds. How do the childhood living environments of the inhabitants and their experiences of them, their lifestyle during that period, their social and cultural background and their memories influence and connect with the inhabitants' opinions of their present residential area, Pikku Huopalahti?

*A port for small boats gives the bay area a maritime atmosphere. Photo: Jorma Kivistö.*

Does somebody who has spent his or her childhood in the inner city choose the streets of the area as his or her favourite place and, in doing so, does he or she attach old memories to the present environment? Does the generation born in the concrete suburbs see fewer disadvantages in the prefabricated houses in the area? On the other hand, these significances linked to place are often also collective and tied to the values of the community of the area, the social class, etc. The structural change of Finnish society, and the changes in social interaction and cultural habits also affect people's relation to place.

An earlier study of four residential areas conducted among people who have moved to or from the areas (Korhonen 1998, 52), provide indications of the inhabitants' opinions and images. For those who moved to Pikku Huopalahti in 1996, the closeness of the outdoor museum on the Seurasaari island, the sea and the Central Park was seen as positive. The look and services of the residential area were the most important reason for moving there only for every tenth inhabitant. The modern architecture and atmosphere of the area were fascinating to many. However, the most common reason for moving to Pikku Huopalahti was simply that the respondent had been offered a flat in the area; one third quoted this as their reason. The second most common reason was the location of and communications to the area, and the third was a change in one's life situation. (Korhonen 1998, 52.)

Those who moved to the area saw many pleasant features in Pikku Huopalahti. The most popular feature was its architecture, 85 per cent of the inhabitants liked it; only every tenth was irritated by its distinctive style. Two thirds of the respondents were also pleased with the built environment as a whole. On the other hand, every fourth complained about the density and disorder of the area, the poor quality of the flats and their high prices.

121

Surprisingly, when compared to two areas, Kallahti and Meri-Rastila, which are located further away from the city centre and closer to undeveloped nature, there are much fewer complaints about the built environment in Pikku Huopalahti. Obviously there is a higher tolerance for dense building in areas on the outskirts of the inner city. The inhabitants were mostly satisfied with their living environment in 1996, apart from the fact that the ongoing building of new parts of the area then constituted a considerable drawback for the environment (Korhonen 1998, 53–60).

The above issues provide important perspectives, which often receive little attention, but greatly affect the functioning of residential areas and the lives of their inhabitants. The aspects that form the object of my research should be given more emphasis when new residential areas are being planned. Well functioning areas promote the inhabitants' quality of life and indirectly decrease the social problems in cities. Thus, my work also has a further dimension, that is, the aim of achieving an understanding of how the housing of the past is conveyed and formed in a new environment in general. This information is important pertaining to the accumulating migration into cities.

## NOTES

[1]  I have explored this issue by studying the history of the area and the forms of communication between the inhabitants and the authorities during the Pikku Huopalahti local building project. The study was initiated by the Pikku Huopalahti Inhabitants Association and I carried out the research work at the Urban Research Unit of the Helsinki City Information Centre. This book project and my own research within it primarily focused on the encounter between and matching of the physical building of the new planned area and the practical life of its inhabitants.

## BIBLIOGRAPHY

Bourdieu, Pierre 1985. *Sosiologian kysymyksiä* [Issues of sociology]. Tampere: Vastapaino.

Certeau, Michel de 1984. *The practice of everyday life.* Berkeley and Los Angeles: University of California Press.

Franzén, Mats 1992. *Den folkliga staden* [The people's city]. Lund: Arkiv förlag.

Greverus, Ina-Maria 1978. *Kultur und Alltagswelt.* Eine Einführung in Fragen der Kulturantropologie. München: Beck.

Greverus, Ina-Maria, Moser, Johannes & Salein, Krister (eds.) 1994. *Stadtgedanken, aus und über Frankfurt am Main: Der stadt Frankfurt am Main zum 1200. Geburtstag.* Frankfurt am Main: Institut für Kulturanthropologie und Europäeische Ethnologie der Johann Wolfgang Goethe-Universität Frankfurt am Main.

Ilmonen, Mervi 1997. Viisi näkökulmaa alueiden erilaistumiseen [Five perspectives on the differentiation of areas]. In Mervi Ilmonen et al. (eds.): *Mitä osoite osoittaa? Asuinalueiden erilaistuminen Helsingin seudulla* [What does an address tell? The differentiation of housing areas in the Helsinki region]. Pääkaupunkiseudun julkaisusarja B, 1997:2. Helsinki: Pääkaupunkiseudun yhteistyövaltuuskunta.

Kalanti, Timo 1993. *Arkkitehtuurin vastaanotto Pikku Huopalahdessa* [The reception of the architecture in Pikku Huopalahti]. Helsingin kaupungin tietokeskuksen tutkimuksia 10. Helsinki: Helsingin kaupunki.

Korhonen, Erkki 1998. *Ruoholahti, Pikku Huopalahti, Meri-Rastila ja Kallahti muuttaneiden silmin* [Ruoholahti, Pikku Huopalahti, Meri-Rastila and Kallahti with the eyes of those who have moved to or from the area]. Helsingin kaupungin tietokeskus. Tutkimuksia 8. Helsinki: Helsingin kaupungin tietokeskus.

Korhonen, Erkki, Malin, Liisa & Savola, Kaarina 1998. *Helsingin asukastalot ja yhteiskerhotilat* [The residents' centres and joint club premises in Helsinki]. Helsingin kaupungin tietokeskus. Tutkimuksia. Helsinki: Helsingin kaupungin tietokeskus.

— Lefebvre, Henri 1991. *The production of space*. Oxford and Cambridge: Blackwell.

— Lynch, Kevin 1981. *A theory of good city form*. Cambridge, Mass. & London: The MIT Press.

Stenros, Anne 1994. Paikka ja identiteetti [Place and identity]. In Knuutti, Liisa (ed.): *Ympäristö – taide – identiteetti* [Environment – art – identity]. Espoo: Teknillinen korkeakoulu.

This article, like others earlier, is written about the data generated in a survey, but is not a dispmation on the data itself. Not tables, no maps.

Discourses of Space – Planning Practices

TIINA-RIITTA LAPPI

# Narratives of the Town

## Everyday Knowledge and Planning Discourses in Jyväskylä

*[handwritten: sub title doesn't necessarily connect to main title?]*

Cities are narrative objects. The city is not a subject that can represent itself. Rather, cities are objects of representation. People must describe their natures, document their pasts, and predict their futures. (Robert A. Beauregard 1993.)

### Lived life, presented future

From the viewpoint of ethnology, the city is not a whole, but consists of various fragments. By exploring the tension between, on the one hand urban politics and planning and on the other, everyday knowledge, I am looking for a satisfactory description of this fragmentary nature of the city. When a researcher goes about studying a city by means of focusing on a clear area which has been locally or socially limited by him or herself, the city naturally appears to be a quite harmonious whole. Its actual fragmentary nature is often obscured as research activity instinctively imposes such limitations on itself as to achieve harmony. By their very nature, maps and statistics make the city appear to be organised in terms of a coherent whole. Of course, research must always be limited in some way and a city can never be described or explained in its totality.

Jyväskylä, at least when seen from the outside, appears to be quite homogenous as a town, when it comes both to its population and its physical environment. Therefore it offers the opportunity to study differences and deviances in a seeming sameness. The German ethnologist Ina-Maria Greverus (1994) calls for an anthropology of "discrete differences". She also advocates the study of the lived world and social structures of such communities that at first glance appear as completely familiar and unsurprising. According to Greverus, even the community of the researcher is highly diversified culturally and socially. In the familiarity of one's own culture and community, it is possible to find endless realities and dimensions of "difference", which, Greverus thinks, have so far not been given enough attention (Greverus 1994, 14–16). By unravelling the harmonious appearance, differences that make visible the variations in the town dwellers' worlds of experience can be brought to the fore. The differences are linked to the way in which the

127

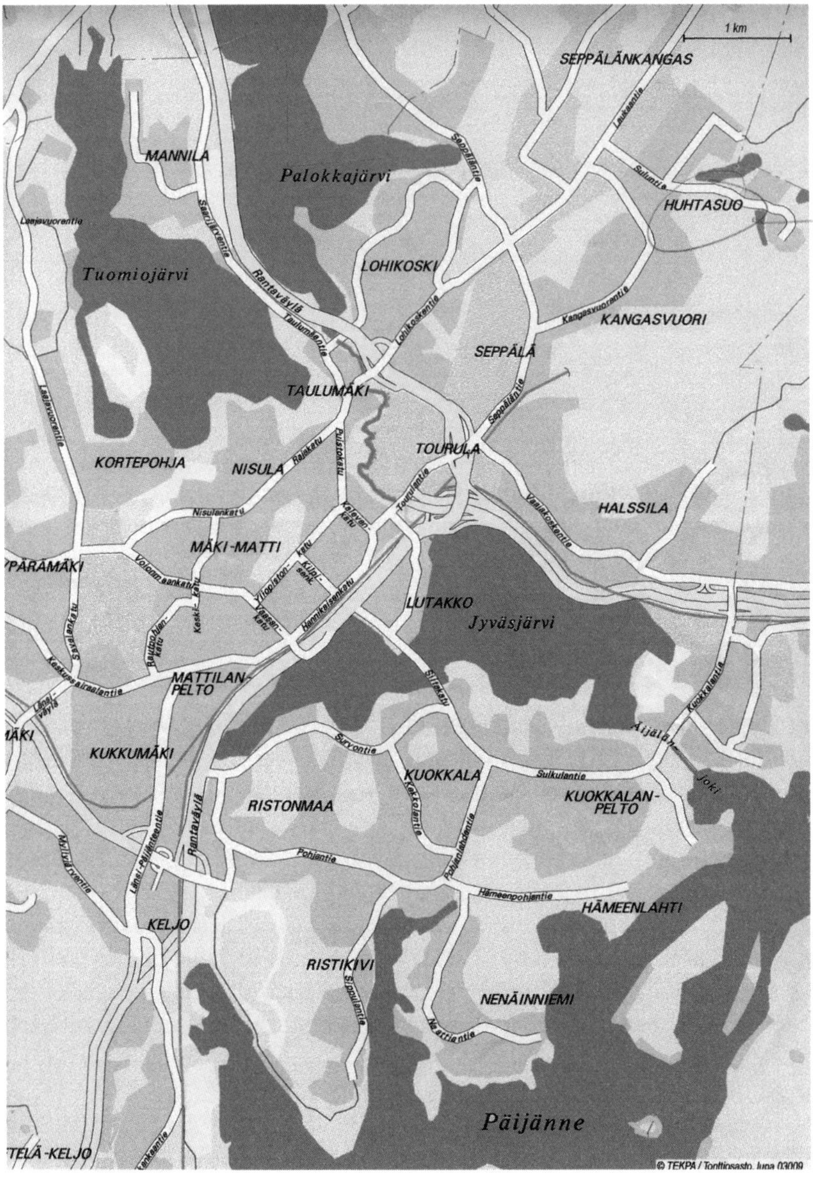


*The central part of Jyväskylä is situated between two lakes, namely Lake Jyväsjärvi and Lake Tuomiojärvi. Names written in capital letters on the map point out residential areas around the city.*

inhabitants understand the town and what significances they attach to it. These issues also include the question of how the town is planned and on whose terms this is done.

The cultural dimension of the city and its urban lifestyle are emphasised in ethnological urban research. The concept of culture refers, above all, to the way in which people, various groups and organisations map and code their activities and environment and attach meanings to the city and its places (cf. Schulman, Karkama, Karisto & Ilmonen 1995, 8). The aim is to try to understand and interpret the collective representations of culture, where the role of language – text, speech and pictures – is crucial. In this article, I will explore some representations of the urban reality in Jyväskylä and discuss the nature and significance of these representations as descriptions of the town and its urban culture.

I am particularly interested in the ways in which the everyday and lived life of the town dwellers relates to its framework: the physical environment as it has been developed by the town planners. I base my work on the concept of culture, where culture is seen as a kind of deep structure, a way of understanding and signifying things. Thus the everyday life and activities of the town and different decisions concerning it, for example, in urban planning and politics, are grounded in deeply rooted cultural structures, which people are often not aware of, but upon which their actions are, all the same, based (Immonen & Terho 1999, 108). These integral cultural structures can be thought to exist at varying "depths" or "levels". By this, I mean that even if, for example, planners and town dwellers have, largely speaking, the same cultural background, various structures and ways of thinking have nevertheless been laid down with respect to this ground, and these form the perception of the town and the nature and significance of its places.

In my case study of the district Kuokkala in Jyväskylä, I explored the planning of this new district, built in the 1980's and 1990's, as well as the relation of its inhabitants to their new living environment (Lappi 1997). The study of Kuokkala gave rise to questions that form the basis for my further development and deepening of the perspective of the study. Instead of a concrete juxtaposition of planning ideals and experiences of everyday life, I have decided to overlay an ethnological viewpoint on these issues using another approach. I do not investigate urban politics, planning and decision-making connected with these as primarily concrete activities, but, above all, I want to expose the ideas, thoughts and points of departure that inform the development and construction of the town *in the background*. I will reflect the planning as it is expressed in the experiences and perceptions of the town's inhabitants, that is, in the everyday knowledge of the town, so that these two perspectives arising from different points of departure run parallel to each other.

At the turn of the millennium, cities in which the urban spaces and places are built in blocks and according to functional patterns, are in the midst of a process of continuous change and fragmentation. The present urban structure can be characterised as a functional mega-city, where places of consumption (e.g. supermarkets and the associated functions concentrated around these) govern the development and change of the city. This development has resulted in the disintegration of the traditional urban structure and, at the same time, in the change of urban lifestyle and urban culture. However, the urban researchers Robert A. Beauregard and Anne Haila, among others, criticize the conception which is held by many theoreticians of urban studies that a new, post-modern city has replaced the modern city. According to Beauregard and Haila, the process is actually characterised by a much more complex intertwining of new and old; by an interaction between continuity and change. The modern city is never completed; neither is it completely

129

freed from its predecessors. The historical sustainability and the ever-present incompleteness of the city are both consequences of the layered and simultaneous nature of its past and present influences (Beauregard & Haila 1997). Thus, the disintegration of the traditional urban structure does not mean that the city as a whole has changed into something other than it was before, but it has become temporally layered, both physically, functionally and mentally. The lifestyles of city dwellers or rather, its many and various urban identities, are always temporally layered. By this I mean that the inhabitants live their everyday lives in cities or places of historically "different periods" within one and the same city. In different situations, activities and routines, they make use of the opportunities offered by these cities of different periods.

In my study, I emphasise the historical dimension of the change and development of the city, the temporal continuum from the past through the present and into the future. In a society saturated in information technology, there is often a feeling that everything only exists in the here and now. The past is always assessed as inferior in relation to the present and the future. However, things that might seem old-fashioned today have at some point been new and revolutionary. What is interesting about this is to observe how these things have been defended in their own time and favourably compared to things even older than themselves. For example, the activities of trading, buying and selling have always moulded the structure of cities and governed the way people move around them. When these activities change the sense of novelty is often very superficial and relative, since their fundamental character remains the same. Similar cycles of development and effect are repeated time and time again, but their expression varies at different periods. Planning can be regarded as an activity that always looks to the future, but the building of the future is always affected by various historically specific incidents and developments. Planning has also made use of history in different ways at different times, selectively emphasising certain issues and overlooking others. In ethnological research however, a historical perspective can function as an analytical tool that questions the present and opens new opportunities for understanding cultural phenomena and processes (Löfgren 2001, 181).

## The narrativity of the city

By using three examples, I will investigate how various narratives and stories associated with the town and its places mould the perception of the town and create meanings associated with its different places. My first example is the autobiographical narrative of the places in his life by a man, born in 1937, who lives in the suburb Huhtasuo in Jyväskylä. The second narrative is an excerpt from the Town Planning Programme of Jyväskylä. For my third example of the creation of significances for the town, I will explore the relation between the development of the town centre and the identity of the "town dwellers". These three narratives are not mutually comparable, but their primary purpose is rather to unfold various perspectives on the discussion concerning the town.

## "I have walked and roamed the woods here…"

The first narrative can be characterised as a private urban story, the point of departure and perspective of which are clearly different from the "public" stories of the town. The narrative is linked to a certain place or places and it is characterised by its specific setting in terms of time, place and narrator: by the narrator's personal and individual experience of the town. The private nature of a narrative is, for example, reflected in its temporal structure. All narratives comprise some kind of temporal framework, but the temporality is not necessarily presented as a chronological continuum. In the narratives by the inhabitants of the English town Milton Keynes studied by Ruth Finnegan (1998, 89), for example, the most typical temporal structure is based on the progress of the narrator's personal and his or her family's life. Another temporal framework is constructed around movements between various places.

The private or individual nature of a story does not exclude collective features and perceptions of the town, or points of contact with other private narratives. Here, the privacy of a story refers to the fact that the narrative's point of departure is the view of an individual town dweller of his or her life in the town. The places of one's everyday life are not experienced as separate, clearly defined entities that can be explained solely on the basis of their location or appearance (Relph 1976, 29). Rather, they form an intertwined complex of adjustment in space, landscape, rituals, routines, other people, personal experiences, caring for the home, and other relations to place.

The narrator of the first story moved to the rural district outside Jyväskylä in 1949 and later to Jyväskylä proper, having previously lived in Ostrobothnia and spent two years as a child evacuee in Sweden during the war. At the beginning of the narrative, its temporality is linked to the progress of the narrator's life and to certain events, but as the story continues, its temporal structure is based on the narrator's moves to various places and his experience of these places. The first experience of the town centre was memorable:

> And I will always remember how the centre of town was something wonderful to see, when one comes into it for the first time. - - It was as if there in the Kyparämäki area, that's where one noticed that one was entering the town. Then one's eyes opened wide and one stared and looked at everything.

The story continues with descriptions of the childhood dwelling places, first in the rural district outside Jyväskylä and then in the Seppälänkangas area in town. After entering working life, the narrator travelled around Finland building roads and railways, but his permanent place of residence always remained in Jyväskylä. The family moved to the Seppälänkangas area in 1951 and the narrator lived there with his mother until 1977.

> But we ended up in a crow's nest, oh my. I suppose originally it was warm enough, but over time when there were those rats and mice and I tried to catch them in all kinds of ways. - - And then it simply became so rickety, I remember once when my Ma sat on the edge of her bed with slippers on

131

her feet and said to me, look at the draught in here, and held up a piece of string like this, and we saw how it swung. Well, sometimes it was so cold in the morning it was only ten degrees in there.

Even if the flat was quite dilapidated and life was financially hard, it is recalled as a nice living place and environment. The narrator describes the places of childhood and youth and the memories connected with these clearly and in great detail. A child could, in a certain sense, be thought of as being "closer" to some concrete places than an adult. The range of the life of an adult is often both physically and socially wider than that of a child, and therefore descriptions of the environments or places experienced as an adult are less detailed. For many people, the places of childhood constitute particular focal points through which personal narratives and memories emerge (Relph 1976, 37).

> I'll always remember what we got up to during the school days, that there wasn't any kind of problem, that there wouldn't have been anything to do. Ma always said that when we romped there sometimes, me and my schoolmates, there in the yard, that sometimes when we got really wild and noisy, she thought that it would rain again. And I don't know, I think that the weather always somehow influenced the young, because then we would always run wild. And it was true that then it would rain. Yes, Ma always wondered about that too. Well, that's the way we were, we always left later so that we wouldn't make too much of a racket in the yard, so that the older people would calm down there.

Apart from the neighbourhood, the boys got to know many other places around the town as they made outings to various locations. They gradually got to know the town and appropriated various places by roaming around them:

> We went there [to the town centre]: every now and then we would cycle there, or walk. We could get ourselves bikes when we started taking jobs, but when we were younger we didn't yet have bikes, so we went there on foot. It wasn't much of a distance from Seppälänkangas into town. We went there and walked around and looked at places so that we would get to know them. I still remember at that time, when the war had left its marks, when one came along Kauppakatu street and up Puistokatu street onto the Taulumäki hill, there at the old cemetery, there was still a house which was badly, well, one end of it was, as a bomb had hit it, it was in ruins. The other end was a bit better. That stayed in my mind.

In the following, the narrator reminisces about his move to the suburb built in the 1970's where he still lives:

> Yes, then they started building them [the Huhtasuo residential area], then so many houses were erected. And this was a bit strange, this, that one felt that they just built more and more densely here. First one felt that if they at least left a bit there, that if they at least… one thought at first that why on earth must they build so densely. That it won't be nicer to live there since all the nice things had gone. Since I also had learnt, when we lived there in Seppälänkangas in that kind of, of course there was the main road,

132

*The residential area of Huhtasuo in 1970's with a newly built shopping centre and more housing rising in the forest. Photo: Risto Raittila, Museum of Central Finland, Picture Archives 1979, Jyväskylä.*

see map p 128

it wasn't more than a hundred metres from the road to the building, but one somehow, since I have lived in the countryside a lot it felt when one moved into this kind of… To begin with I always just longed to be back in Seppälänkangas. But it wasn't more than a few years after we moved here, it was somebody from Leppävesi who came and took it down [the house in Seppälänkangas] and used it as firewood. Then when we had lived here for about five years, then we too somehow learnt, got a better feeling for this as a living area. But at first, the old places were always more attractive.

In his narrative, the interviewee mentioned his present place of residence as a suburb only sporadically and in passing, even if he had moved there as long as 23 years ago. The focal point of his story is the dwelling place preceding the present one, which geographically is located only a few kilometers away. However, the "mental distance" between these two places is considerably larger. The particular significance of the previous place of residence might partly also relate to the fact that because of his job, the man had to travel around Finland and live in temporary accommodation on the work sites. In the mindscape of the interviewee, even the perception of his present living place is largely influenced by what the place was like before the residential area was built there. The significance of the place is linked to the narrator's experience of it as an exciting place where adventures happened, where the young boys spent a lot of their time. The house in which the interviewee lives is situated in a place which previously was part of the army's depot area. However, the present-day housing area called Varikko (the Depot) is located in a slightly different direction.

133

If we're really precise, then the Varikko area does belong to the Depot area too, since the fence was down there and then that tower block too, it ran around there, on this side of the house, along the edge and then in a straight line there. They have made a kind of break here, since there is the Kangaslammentie road here, so they first of all cut away here and then they levelled a bit like this, so that they would be able to build the blocks of flats. So this actually is, if we're really precise – this name, I don't know why they gave it. It should be more like a part of Huhtasuo, even if this is part of Kangaslampi, since the Kangaslampi lake is so close by. Well, then of course then there is that part of the Depot and this is left like this, it belongs to the same area. When I remember all these places, how I wandered here when I was around fifteen, so I remember, there were lots, there were those ammunition storages, there were hand grenades and all sorts of ammunition. There were storage spaces and there were those paths there, where the storage spaces were, then they were given all sorts of strange names, Puolukkakuja [Lingonberry alley] and the like, so the names are given like this. Since they are … well, even if this upper part is called the Varikko area, then they too should have their own names, for example Ammustie [Ammunition road] or something that would kind of fit better here, since they are up there. Then there on the south side, there was that guardhouse. Then there was also that, sort of, workshop, I remember there next to it. Then it was taken down when we had lived here for about two years perhaps, it was taken down. So they could have called that Pajatie [Workshop road] for example. It would have been of an older heritage, since it was long before the war that it was built, since it was in use then during the wars. This was very strictly guarded, this here area. Yes they start coming, when one reminisces, things start coming to mind. As a kid one roams and wanders an awful lot, pokes around in all sorts of places.

The style of the narrative here does not recall the past nostalgically: the past and the present are not assessed in comparison to each other as worse or better. As the new area was built, the narrator and his mother acquired a new, comfortable place to live in a familiar environment. The narrator does not primarily criticize the building of the suburb or the changes in the landscapes of his childhood and youth, but directs his criticism against the fact that the earlier history of the area seems to have been forgotten; it has been removed to give way to new things. He holds a positive attitude to most changes and the town's development, especially since they have made his life easier. Past times are not, then, romanticized, but the narrator moves along with change as he describes places and his relation to place.

When I found out that the Prisma supermarket was coming, I thought, good, then one doesn't need to go into town. Even if I always went by bus, but the stuff. Yes, I thought, good that that Prisma is coming, there will be good shopping there, they have a wider selection. It made things a lot easier. But then I still went into town by bus more often, but then of course by bike to Prisma. It did help things a lot that they had a wider selection. And then things got easier still when we got the information that in this Huhtasuo area, there by the shopping centre, they would build some shops there, then I really breathed a sigh of relief.

Quotes + comment; quotes + comment.

In his story, the narrator opens a view of the temporally and spatially layered structure of his local environment in a fine way. His present place of residence does not appear as much as a suburb in what he says, but as a place of various temporal layers and of memories linked to these different layers. The experience of the place is not only connected to its existing structure and nature; the present is explored through the past and the past as part of the present.

> I remember the time when we heard that they would now start building blocks of flats in this area, then I said to Ma, now we could even get a flat, this is a nice area. One wouldn't really want to go into the town centre, there are so many fumes from the cars and the like, that one has got used to living here on the sidelines. - - A familiar area. We were all here before, I have walked and roamed the woods here, with the boys – we always hung around together and we used to pick berries in these areas. They're such familiar places and in quite a large area. It's large, if one walks around it it's rather there to the north, let's say it's at least 20 kilometres in that direction, yes, at least. And then to the west, I have roamed there since that there Hiidenlinna was there and there are those dancing places, then when we were of that age that we went around to dances, so these areas; so one does remember them. There is Vääräjärvi lake there and there, a bit further still, there's that Ankeriasjärvi lake, when Vääräjärvi is just there where there's a housing area, it's directly behind there. Yes, we fished in those lakes then. They're that kind of place. Now there's that Kangaslampi there, but these are those sorts of nice familiar places.

According to Barbara Johnstone (1990, 5), who has studied narratives from the American town of Fort Wayne, people build experiences of the past and give it meaning through narration. Similarly, the origins of knowing and understanding a place and its community lie in narration. A person feels at home in a place that creates stories and, at the same time, stories create places. Private urban narratives expose a temporally and spatially manifold view of life in the town, of the significances of places and of their nature. The importance of these narratives also lies in the fact that they make visible the individual as a dynamic actor. The narrator is an "I", who actively lives and acts in the town, observes, bestows significances and creates perceptions. This observation is important since usually, for example in scientific writing, the identity of an individual is defined through his or her belonging to a certain group (Finnegan 1998, 106). Listening to private narratives could open up new perspectives and trigger questions about how towns and urban identity is studied and constructed, and what significance the personal narrative has for the formation of relations to a place.

## The commodification of the city – through the creation of "image stories"

In exploring the discourse of urban politics and city planning, I direct my focus on cultural perceptions of the city and of its built environment. I do not study the planning as such, but the ways in which reality is being represented by the planners. By the discourse of city planning I refer to the public "stories" and "narratives" that planners, authorities and the media collectively create and develop to symbolise the city (cf. Johnstone 1990, 6). The city's "meta-narrative" has also been different at various times. In this context, I understand the relation between urban politics and city planning as being such that urban politics are used to create general outlines for the development of the city, and these are made visible and concrete for the inhabitants primarily through city planning. City planning, urban politics and urban reforms are closely linked to each other and it is impossible, on a practical level, to explore each of them in total separation from the others (Jauhiainen 1995, 48).

The wish of the planners to create and control large wholes is still strong, although the structure of cities has been fragmented and is therefore difficult to control. Thus, the object of planning is no longer concerned primarily with the whole city, as was the case before, but with smaller, controllable areas which are delimited within the city. Such sites in Jyväskylä are, for example, the shore of the Jyväsjärvi lake, which extends via the areas Ainola and Lutakko[1] on to the Tourula former industrial area, and into the town centre. The basic idea of the plan for the Jyväsjärvi shore is to turn it "from backyard to façade":

In Jyväskylä, at least, it is possible to realise the Finnish dream of a house of one's own in the middle of town by a lake. If housing dreams are realised near a lake, would not work also fit into the same environment? The Jyväsjärvi lake, which lies at the gateway to the Päijänne lake and in the heart of the town of Jyväskylä, has offered the town both an opportunity and constituted a risk factor. In the 1970s, the lake was still the waste basin for both the paper mill and local inhabitants. There were effluents from the Lutakko veneer factory entering both the lake and the local air. The refuse dump at the end of the Mattilanniemi cape had already been closed. The extension of the railway yard further isolated the lake from the residential environments. It was hardly anybody's dream, but developments in the area were inevitably turning it into a backyard.

Now, at the end of the 1990's, the water of the Jyväsjärvi is clean enough for swimming, the veneer factory has closed down and on the site of the former refuse dump there is a splendid park, an extension of the university and a popular beach. The dream has not been realised yet, but it is now a real possibility, achievable within a short period of time. Although the development of the area as a whole has so far only burned in the minds of visionaries, workshops in the various parts of the area are already teeming with activity. In a Finnish setting, the shores of Jyväsjärvi offer an almost unique opportunity to build attractive working areas in the middle of town, by a lake, to bridge the gap between the university campus and the commercial town centre and to create new life in the environment of the old veneer factory by new housing and modern office solutions and by also creating regional and international networks. The shores of Jyväsjärvi offer an excellent environment for enhancing Jyväskylä's status as a vital town both visually and symbolically. As Jyväskylä continues to seek innovations at the interface between technology and human beings, it is only natural that the symbol for the whole Jyväsjärvi shore will be a building called Agora – a Greek word, meaning interaction, encounters, a meeting-place and a market. In the shelter of this building, top psychologists together with experts in information technology will produce knowledge for the new millennium. As expertise is sought in global growth areas, its impacts will, understandably, be extensive.

The above text is a quote from the new Town Planning Programme for Jyväskylä: "From felt to advanced physics – Jyväsjärvi shore from backyard to façade" (1999). It is a story, the plot of which is very like that of the fairy tale about Cinderella – the only difference being that the moral at the end, where evil is punished, is lacking in this narrative. In the story, the Jyväsjärvi lake and its shores, situated close to the town centre, are a symbol for the change which will turn a languishing industrial town into a centre for new knowledge and information technology. The Town Planning Programme creates a new narrative for Jyväskylä, and this narrative is used to justify the planning initiatives within its framework. The characterisation of the environment of Jyväsjärvi before the change includes only the negative aspects of the history of the area. The backyard is characterised as an area dominated by waste and pollution, which is not regarded as belonging to the town. This image is strengthened by talking about a waste basin, the effluents of the former veneer factory in the Lutakko area, a refuse dump, and about housing and living moving steadily further away from the shore. Through the change, the backyard will be transformed into a façade, the dirt will be eradicated. The water that permits swimming, and the popular beach and splendid park on its shore symbolise cleanliness. The progress of the narrative follows a tradition in an almost exemplary manner which forms the basis of modern planning. According to James Holston (1998), its objective is to change an unpleasant past and present using an imagined future. The explanation for the change always includes a dichotomy, where the old unambiguously represents something bad and undesired, and the new is the absolute opposite to this. The future is moulded by referring to its forerunners, who invalidate the significance of the prevailing circumstances.

*The former Lutakko industrial area with the Schaumann veneer factory in the foreground. The city centre can be seen in the background. Photo: Museum of Central Finland, Picture Archives 1963/1964, Jyväskylä.*

137

*Industrial buildings in Lutakko are being demolished in order to make space for new housing and office buildings. Photo: Tiina-Riitta Lappi 1999.*

The writing of town planning programmes is a consequence of a development where the balanced European town system is changing and a new kind of hierarchy of towns is arising. The aim of the programmes is, above all, to strengthen the role of the towns and define the position of the town in the new global economy. A reputation is created for the town: it is made known in order to attract investors and businesses. A new and essential feature of strategic plans and town planning programmes is that urban building is directed by programmes and agreements. The programmes can also be read as narratives, as the above example from the Jyväskylä Town Planning Programme shows. These narratives take the form of fairy tale like structures with a beginning, a crisis or threat, an action strategy and finally rescue. When carrying out a narrative analysis, it should be noted that the narrative and reality are actually two different things. The town does not necessarily possess the resources needed to realise the programme. Secondly, regardless of whether the resources exist or not, the programme as a story might influence the future development of the town. (Haila 1999, 40–41, 43–44.)

The Jyväskylä Town Planning Programme is a central part of a larger narrative that the town authorities and the media publicly create as a symbol for the town. The development of the Jyväsjärvi environment as a concrete object is chosen to illustrate the change where the industrial town of past decades is transformed into a town of information technology and higher education. The town narrative functions, above all, as a creator of an "image town". The creation of a new image is based on the idea of the town as a product, which is marketed to companies and investors. "Jyväskylä has turned into a brand well worth marketing", read a headline in the newspaper *Keskisuomalainen* in spring 2000 (KSML 23.4.2000). However, the commodification of the town requires that it be "compressed" so that this product can be presented in programmes, strategies and planning as a manageable whole.

These public narratives also include some kind of temporal framework (cf. Finnegan 1998, 15). The temporality of public stories however is considerably more linear than that of private narratives. In the above excerpt from the Jyväskylä Town Planning Programme, the past is perceived as the polar opposite of the future. Development and change are not presented so much through continuity, but rather as a break with past development. This break is regarded as necessary in order to detach the future from the past. Thus the public narrative differs from the private one, where new experiences and temporal layers are in dialogue with the existing ones. In the private story, the past is always with the narrator in one form or another.

### The centre and "urban identity"

Urban development has, at various times, been guided by different views of what constitutes a good city. In the 1960's and 1970's, Finnish towns were also fragmented according to the ideas of functionalism by situating different activities in separate areas. Work places, shops and housing were kept apart from each other. Currently, we are living in a kind of partial renaissance of the traditional urban structure, which has placed an emphasis of the centre and the urban nature of towns, for example by favouring dense building again. However, the construction of supermarkets and the transfer of consumption further and further outside the actual inner city have the effect of breaking up the urban structure, which seems to be an inevitable outcome of development. By contrast, the idea behind the current efforts to enliven the centres seems to be motivated by a desire to create a space for a new urban elite, which, in contradistinction to the masses, consumes at the centre and wants to be distinguished from the "common people at the supermarkets".

Since competition on the same terms as the supermarkets is impossible, new ways of attracting consumers to the centre as well must be created. One example of this is the wish to build a new kind of "inner city" identity: that of a cultural, civilised, urban town dweller. I here refer to the perception based on the idea that life in the city is differently organised, charged and signified than life, for example, in the countryside (Immonen & Terho 1999, 107). This urban culture is usually placed at the centre of towns – especially large cities – since these are the only places where it is perceived to be possible to lead a lifestyle associated with real urban culture. In the discussion on Finnish urbanity, the lack and under-development of a "real" urban culture is often explained by the relatively late emergence of the trend of urbanisation in our country. Issues that, however, have not been explored in any great detail are the unique features of Finnish towns or urban lifestyle from their own points of departure or from the perspective of the experience of the town dwellers.

In western culture, the city has traditionally been regarded as the cradle of civilisation and a symbol for the wealth of the nation. The culture of large cities is seen as an expression of a new kind of life rhythm. Cities fragment and expand in quite uncontrolled ways, primarily as a consequence of the continued building of new car and mega markets. Consumption increasingly moves to the peripheral areas of the traditional urban structure. The creation of the new town story of Jyväskylä is also being informed by a wish to rid the town of its former rural image and, instead, emphasise the urban nature of the town, urbanity being understood to be associated with large cities. An article published in the paper *Keskisuomalainen* at the end of 1999 (1.12.1999), states that "the plan compresses the centre, which so far has been unnecessarily spacious and almost village-like. The standard of the services will rise. Jyväskylä will come to increasingly resemble a Finnish large city. Superfluous space and inefficiency will disappear."

There is a desire to develop the centre in a controlled manner, following western urban ideals as a counterbalance to the supermarket areas that seem to spread uncontrollably around the town. The centre should be clean and tidy in order to be better suited as a consumption paradise for those who are better off. Civilisation is emphasised by placing art institutions close to the centre; the Kirkkopuisto park[2] will be tidied to fit the dignity of the new urban consumer. The polyphony and also diversity of the post-modern city is invoked, according to the spirit of the time, but in passing only, and as long as this is not visible where the 'image town' is being built. Sharon Zukin (1995, 271), talks about the various "culture strategies" of economic development, which can be directed at, for example, cultural institutions, the preservation of architectural landmarks, or the development of culture production. The common feature of this strategy is, according to Zukin, that they force the multidimensional and contradictory character of culture into a uniform visual representation. In Jyväskylä, this requirement of uniformity appears, for example, in the force of attitudes such as that the gathering of young people on the steps of the Jyväskeskus shopping centre in the pedestrian district in the centre of Jyväskylä constitutes a disturbance and that the groups gathering in the Kirkkopuisto park should be removed, or that the Lutakko Youth Dance Hall[3] is not a suitable neighbour for Paviljonki[4], but it should not be placed at Seminaarinmäki, either, to blemish the image of the area situated next to the university campus[5]. The impression is that the "Nokia employees"[6] working on the shores of Jyväsjärvi are welcome to come and consume at the centre, while the "common people of the suburbs" should confine their shopping to the supermarkets. The area on the shore of Jyväsjärvi is carefully planned, but the supermarket areas mainly expand following individual building permits.

The importance of image is more pronounced than before in contemporary town planning. The main objective of planning, for example in Jyväskylä, seems to be primarily that which promotes the strengthening of the 'image town'. At the same time, the 'image town' causes the rest of the town to fade into obscurity. Imagined identities are used to define what a desired town-identity and a real urban lifestyle are like. The imagined identity associated with the 'Nokia employees' is perceived as representing real urban identity, while the 'common people', from this perspective, are seen as deviant. A paradoxical situation arises here, since the businesses that strongly influence the change of towns, and, above all, the activities of the large chain stores are based on standardization: everybody should act in the same way, consume in a uniform manner. The planning of the development of the centres, on the other hand, seems to be informed by an idea of a different kind of town dweller, who consumes individually and shops in the boutiques in the centres. Thus, there is a constant competition between two very different lifestyles and urban phenomena.

The debate concerning the centres of towns and their development is linked to a larger question about the centre and the concept of a central position in general. The issue of centrality comprises all perspectives on the problem of space. Centrality – be it psychological or social by nature – is primarily defined as an encounter between all the things and phenomena simultaneously present in the space in question. So, centrality is the concentration of things and phenomena in space. In itself, it is an empty form, but it attracts contents: objects, natural and artificial beings, things, products, signs and symbols, people, acts, situations. As a form, centrality expresses the simultaneity of all that is prone both to connection and accumulation either in thought or in social activity. Each era, each production method, each community has produced its own centrality: religious, political, commercial, cultural, industrial or some other kind. The relation between mental and social centrality must always be defined separately case by case. The same applies to a situation where the existing defined centre ceases to be or transforms into something else. (Lefebvre 1991, 331–332.)

Following the ideas of Henri Lefebvre (1991), the significance of town centres has diminished as towns have changed and their structure has broken up; commercial activities and consumption have increasingly moved to super-markets and other large stores outside the centre. The concentration of as many functions as possible, which is essential for the significance of centres, started to turn into fragmentation at the end of the last millennium. From the viewpoint of the use of power and planning, the development that was leading to the dilapidation of centres has had to be stopped so that the centre could regain the role that it is regarded as having in the hierarchy of places within the city. The talk of a more urban living environment and the concentration of the town could thus be interpreted as a "re-signification" of centrality. From the perspective of the authorities and those in power, it is important that centrality, in this case the town centre, remains visible despite the fragmentation of the town structure. In a fragmented town, more effort than before must be focused on the strengthening and signification of centrality. In Jyväskylä this has been realised by placing new art and cultural institutions in the centre, and by concentrating commercial activities into a more limited area, for example, by planning an underground shopping area. Through planning, the shore of Jyväsjärvi and the Lutakko area have been redefined as part of the commercial centre, and thus the information technology expertise situated in the areas has been appropriated to serve the increased visibility of centrality.

*The Innova Tower built for information technology businesses is the highest building in Jyväskylä. The old chimney is a reminder of the industrial era of Lutakko. Photo: Tiina-Riitta Lappi 2002.*

*The invisible in the city* *lengthy systematic discussion but not about Jyväskylä.*

Geographer Jouni Häkli (1997, 48–49) has noted that in modern town planning the aim is to constantly operate with the visible city. The whole idea of rationalistic planning has been based on the avoidance of the unknown. That, which cannot be seen has been excluded from rational planning. According to Häkli, the principle of visibility has aimed at simplifying the city of the planning discourses into a number of elements in the physical infrastructure: buildings, roads, bridges and parks. The invisible urban experience, on the other hand, has not succeeded in being included in the issues dealt with in town planning. However, planning based on perceptions and images suggests that the modern planning tradition is about to be broken. Despite this, the legitimacy of the planning expertise is still strongly tied to the view that only information based on sense and rationality is of any importance for town planning. Therefore non-rational aspects of planning are also often motivated by, for example, financial perspectives.

The tension between expert planning information and the everyday knowledge of the inhabitants can be seen as linked, at least partly, to the fact that experts are perceived as representing rationality and the inhabitants stand for emotional views. The obstacle for finding an agreement between these differing views seems to be the notion that the perspectives of experts and those of town dwellers or laymen on town planning and on solutions of the contradictions connected to it, already by definition result in a clear state of opposition. The struggle between the various views for the right to participate in the definition of the contents of the town and its spaces has, also in Jyväskylä, appeared in various contexts (e.g. the extension of the Teacher Training School, the Laajavuori rally course, the planning of the Lutakko area and the supplementary building in the town).

> When preparing the general plan for the supplementary building in Jyväskylä, the inhabitants have been heard two times, at which points they have been able to express their opinions and motivations for these. The planners and the inhabitants have held and still hold different views. From Huhtasuo, for example, complaints have been filed both by individuals, housing companies, inhabitants' associations, the social welfare office, the day-care office and by companies. All of these have expressed well-founded reservations and expressed an authentic concern for the future of the area. Who knows the area better than the population that lives there and uses its services? It is patronizing towards those who express their opinions to claim that the inhabitants of the neighbourhood are simply complaining and to arrogantly ignore the points presented. The residents of the Huhtasuo area have been really active in contacting the planners; in our view, we have carried out constructive co-operation by presenting alternative building sites. These suggestions have been welcomed, but despite numerous submissions of alternatives, not even the worst spots have been removed from the plan.
>
> One may well ask who makes the decisions here? The planning authorities stubbornly stick to their own views (this is the plan and it will not be changed). We wonder why the planning board did not consider our – the inhabitants' – opinions when making their decisions. The final

143

plan followed the planners' suggestion in every detail. We can only note that the hearing of the residents was just a formality, which had to be organised.

We support the extension of the existing housing in our area, but one which takes into consideration the social structure of the area, the traffic problems as well as environmental values for the well-being of us all. The recreational areas in our neighbourhood are not of lesser value than those in other parts of town. We want them to remain intact.

We inhabitants are once again disappointed in the opportunities we have been given, which turn out to be non-existent, to influence issues closely related to us and our lives. We are, after all, the best experts on our residential area. (KSML 13.9.1999, Letter to the editor.)

The expertise of the planners often legitimises, in the first place, the subjects that are discussed. The discourse of urban politics and town planning comprises only those themes and the arguments linked to these, which are seen as essential from the viewpoint of experts. The world of planners is reflected in the planning practices both as an established style of expression and a body of knowledge, which define what issues might prove to be a problem and what the solutions to these can be (Häkli 1997, 47 [Lehtinen 1993, 65]). The viewpoints taken up by inhabitants are often belittled or ignored precisely because they are not regarded as belonging to the field of town planning. The conventions, contents and borders of the town planning discourse have been implicitly defined within the "ring" of expertise as seemingly self-evident and unquestionable. The ring of expertise is a strong signifier of the urban debate and usually it excludes the perspectives of the town dwellers.

The difference between the various views of the inhabitants and the planning/administration could be conceptualised using a theoretical construction concerning spatial phenomena which has been presented by Henri Lefebvre (1991). 'Spatial practices' are formed both by the routines of an individual and the systematic creation of areas. Spaces are produced and renewed through lived practices and they are concretised in the built environment and landscapes. 'Presented space' is produced by the forms and practices of information that organise space, particularly within the conventions of planning and the capitalist state.

'Lived space' is the third spatial dimension, which is to say, the collective experience of space, including, among other things, the symbolic differentiation of space and collective images, the opposition of the prevailing practices, and the consequent private and collective "splits". For Lefebvre, space is not neutral, but is constantly being produced and renewed, and therefore it is also the arena for constant battle. Both inhabitants and planners participate in the creation and maintenance of spatial practices through their own routines and concrete actions. The expertise of town planners and administrators is primarily based on the conventions and modes of expression of presented space, whilst the inhabitants' everyday knowledge of their town is mainly connected to lived space. Considering and presenting knowledge pertaining to lived space in planning is problematic, since it does not fit easily into the techniques governed by rational thinking, which are used in planning to represent reality.

Presented space is saturated with information that relies on understanding and ideology. This information is, however, relative and constantly changing. Although represented space is abstract by nature, it has its own role in social and political practices. Lived spaces, on the other hand, do not need to abide by the rules of uniformity or community. Their sources lie in history – in the history of groups as well as in that of the individuals belonging to those groups. Lived space is alive and has an affective centre such as "self", room, dwelling, square or even cemetery. (Lefebvre 1991, 41.) The affective centre of lived space is connected to the observation of places originating in the "self" in private urban narratives so that both of these define the way in which the individual ascribes significances to the town and its places. In planning and the conventions of represented space the city is observed by moving the gaze outwards from the centre of town. Individuals, for their part, observe space and places with their "self" as a starting point, and so the direction of the gaze diverges from the established perspective of planning. The signification of spaces and places is thus also connected to these differing positions of experts and town dwellers in relation to the town and changes within it.

According to Patsy Healey (1997, 60), conflicts concerning spaces and places are not only caused by the different interests and advantages of individuals, but, above all, by people with different cultures of action, different ways of doing, seeing and knowing. This means that they use different ways to construct their views of the things that cause the conflict. So, the subject of debate in conflicts pertaining to the environment is not only certain concrete issues, but also the views of what generally are perceived as problems and how the solution of these should be organised. The conflicts between different views are also often influenced by various kinds of power relations that privilege certain persons, certain forms of debate and certain ways of organisation. Therefore, I see a narrative study of the town as important in that it enables an exploration of what views the various actors hold of the town, of its places and the changes in these.

The basic difference between the knowledge of the experts and that of laypersons could be studied, for example, in the light of the following comment: "The participation of the residents is usually promoted in order to get an extensive survey of opinions and a common view that takes into consideration the interests of various parties. This aim results in tedious processes that might even give rise to conflicts. And the devilish thing is that there is no one common opinion among the inhabitants!" (KSML 22.8.1999.) Expertise usually appears uniform, without conflicts, while the viewpoints and opinions expressed by the inhabitants are seen as problematic particularly because they might stand in conflict to each other. If there is just one expert opinion, there should also be one single lay opinion in order for that to be taken into consideration. Modern planning has been unable to include the conflicts, lack of clarity and uncertainty of real social life as part of its planning programme (Holston 1998, 46), which is illustrated by the comment quoted above.

The viewpoint of laypersons has usually been assumed to be a primitive or distorted version of the expert viewpoint. The differences between the

views have been interpreted as delusions. It has not been considered necessary to investigate whether the models used by laypersons might consist of
completely different beliefs and whether they aim at different goals than the
experts' models. Thus behaviour and thinking conforming to the ideal has
been explained using other principles than behaviour deviating from it. The
behaviour of experts has been explained as guided by true beliefs towards
sensible objectives, while the activities of inhabitants have been explained
by circumstances resulting in a wrong kind of behaviour. The task of the
decision-makers and the experts assisting them is seen as guiding the social system according to familiar rules. For this task, the viewpoint of the
layperson, the understanding of the actor's own perceptions, is not essential
(Jokinen, Kamppinen & Raivola 1995, 174).

The Swedish researcher Elisabeth Lilja refers to the existence of the invisible in her comment that each planning commission reflects some kind
of notion of the people who will use the area or the places. This outlook on
people expresses both a view of the inhabitants and their present needs, and
a view of their imagined future (Lilja 1995). The view of humans incorporated in planning is often presented as "imagined identities" associated
with places, which are used to define the town and its various places as well
as the differences of places, and even differences in the value hierarchy of
the places in town. The imagined identities are usually constructed without
taking into account the historical layers of the town. The nature of the view
of human beings inherent in planning has hardly ever been contemplated or
problematised in the theoretical discussion on planning, even if its existence is
a prerequisite for all planning work (Lilja 1995). The view of humans incorporated in planning, imagined identities, as well as the aim for an imagined
future in town planning all reveal the existence of the invisible in parallel
with the rationality that is made visible with maps and statistics.


## Do the narratives meet?

Town planning is an activity oriented towards the future, but functioning
plans are not formulated in a temporal void; the past and the present must be
considered when planning the future. Therefore, it would be desirable that
the planners would, already in their plans, take into account the community's
experience of the past, the changes that the community has undergone, and
the prevailing social and economic circumstances. The traditional method of
getting the material needed for planning is to gather quantitatively expressible
information, which can be used to present probable courses of development
and formulate a number of different action strategies. In this process, the
role of the planner is often understood as that of a technical trouble-shooter
who applies scientific principles to control the direction, pace and objectives
of change. (Bridger 1997, 1.) This planning tradition dedicated to scientific
method and freedom of values has been criticized, above all, since it de-le-
gitimises other forms of knowledge and often functions as a tool for the elites
to exercise their power (Healey 1993, according to Bridger).

Jeffrey C. Bridger (1997) suggests that stories or narratives hold a key role in the changes and stability of communities. They function as mediators between the past, present and future and are of crucial importance for the continuity of the collective identity that separates community from a mere accumulation of individuals. What might be even more important, is the role these narratives play as a frame of reference for people's interpretation of change and the planned future. Understanding this process of intcrprctation might help planners predict the reactions that their suggestions might cause.

Applying Bridger's view, in Jyväskylä too, the tensions between planners and town dwellers concerning the town planning might partly be a question of an attempt to change the "narrative" symbolizing the town so fast that the inhabitants feel they are being completely disregarded. The frame of reference that the inhabitants use to interpret change is different from the one on which the planners base the change. The model and frame of reference used by the town dwellers thus diverges from that on which the planners assess the change. The individual and collective urban narratives of the inhabitants, which form the frame of reference for the interpretation of change are built and can be seen in the discussions about individual planning objects.

## NOTES

[1] The aim of the town is to turn the Lutakko industrial site into an area comprising town centre amenities. The area is planned to be an extension of the town centre with an emphasis on housing (Lutakko general plan 1994, 21).

[2] Kirkkopuisto (the Church Park) is one of the oldest parks in Jyväskylä: its construction was started at the beginning of the 1880's. At the time of the founding of the town (1837) there was a market square at this central location of the town plan. The appearance of the square changed when a brick church was erected in the middle of it in 1880. In 1899, the Town Hall was built at the edge of the Kirkkopuisto park; the highest echelons of the town administration still work in this building. After the market moved elsewhere, the park plan of the architect Kerttu Tamminen was realised in Kirkkopuisto in 1933-1934. The appearance of the park is more or less the same today as it was in the 1930's. Kirkkopuisto is one of the most popular outdoor public spaces in the town centre. The "parade square" in front of the Town Hall is still used for celebrations and larger gatherings. In September 2000, a project for the restoration of Kirkkopuisto was started, which has given rise to lively debate among the town dwellers (Kydén & Salmela 2000).

[3] The Jyväskylä association for live music, Jelmu, has organised concerts in the Lutakko Dance Hall, which has been renovated in the old premises of a bakery, since 1990. The building will be demolished within the next few years to give way to new buildings. Jelmu has negotiated with the town to obtain other premises, but this issue is yet to be resolved.

[4] A fair and congress centre opened in 1999.

[5] A former beverage factory in the area was, for a while, suggested as new premises for Jelmu, but the project stranded and the building was rented to the university.

[6] 'Nokia employees' here refers to a wider group of experts within the IT field, who form the basis of the planned new growth and image of the town.

# BIBLIOGRPAHY

Beauregard, Robert A. 1993. *The voices of decline. The post-war fate of US cities.* Oxford: Blackwell.

Beauregard, Robert A. & Haila, Anne 1997. The unavoidable incompleteness of the city. *American Behavioral Scientist* 41 (3), 327–341.

Bridger, Jeffrey C. 1997. Community stories and their relevance to planning. *Applied Behavioral Science Review* 5 (1), 67–80.

Finnegan, Ruth 1998. *Tales of the city. A study of narrative and urban life.* Cambridge: Cambridge University Press.

Greverus, Ina-Maria 1994. Kulturtexte. In Ina-Maria Greverus et al. (eds.): *Kulturtexte: 20 Jahre Institut für Kulturanthropologie und Europeische Ethnologie.* Frankfurt am Main. Kulturanthropolgie-Notizen, 46, 9–28.

Haila, Anne 1999. Kaupunkiohjelmat: uudenlainen tapa rakentaa kaupunkeja [Town programmes: a new way of building towns]. In Mari Kortesoja & Tarja Pyöriä (eds.): *Näkökulmia kaupunkitutkimukseen.* [Perspectives on urban studies] Kaupunkitutkimusforum 1999. Kaupunkipolitiikan yhteistyöryhmän julkaisu 5/99, 39–47.

Healey, Patsy 1997. *Collaborative planning. Shaping places in fragmented societies.* Basingstoke: Macmillan.

Holston, James 1998. Spaces of insurgent citizenship. In Leonie Sandercock (ed.): *Making the invisible visible. A multicultural planning history.* Berkeley, Los Angeles & London: University of California Press, 37–56.

*Huovasta hiukkaskiihdyttimeen – Jyväsjärven ranta takapihasta julkisivuksi* [From felt to advanced physics – The Jyväsjärvi shore from backyard to façade]. Jyväskylän kaupungin ehdotus kansalliseen kaupunkiohjelmaan [Suggestion of the town of Jyväskylä for the national urban programme] 25.05.1999.

Häkli, Jouni 1997. Näkyvä yhteiskunta: kansalaiset ja kaupunkisuunnittelun logiikka [Visible society: citizens and the logics of town planning]. In Tuukka Haarni, Marko Karvinen, Hille Koskela & Sirpa Tani (eds.): *Tila, paikka ja maisema. Tutkimusretkiä uuteen maantieteeseen* [Space, place and landscape. Explorations in the new geography] Tampere: Vastapaino, 37–52.

Immonen, Kari & Terho, Henri 1999. Kaupunkitutkimus ja kulttuuri [Urban studies and culture]. In Mari Kortesoja & Tarja Pyöriä (eds.): *Näkökulmia kaupunkitutkimukseen* [Perspectives on urban studies]. Kaupunkitutkimusforum 1999. Kaupunkipolitiikan yhteistyöryhmän julkaisu 5/99, 107–122.

Jauhiainen, Jussi S. 1995. *Kaupunkisuunnittelu, kaupunkiuudistus ja kaupunkipolitiikka: kolme eurooppalaista esimerkkiä* [Town planning, town reform and urban politics: three European examples]. Turun yliopiston maantieteen laitoksen julkaisuja 146. Turku: Turun yliopisto, maantieteen laitos.

Johnstone, Barbara 1990. *Stories, community, and place. Narratives from Middle America.* Bloomington & Indianapolis: Indiana University Press.

Jokinen, Pekka, Kamppinen, Matti & Raivola, Petri 1995. Riskit yhteiskunnassa ja kulttuurissa [Risks in society and culture]. In Matti Kamppinen, Petri Raivola, Pekka Jokinen & Hasse Karlsson (eds.): *Riskit yhteiskunnassa. Maallikot ja asiantuntijat päätösten tekijöinä* [Risks in society. Laypersons and experts as decision-makers]. Helsinki: Gaudeamus, 126–180.

KSML = Newspaper *Keskisuomalainen*

Kydén, Tarja & Salmela, Ulla (eds.) 2000. *Kaupungin sydämessä. Jyväskylän Kirkkopuiston rakennettu ympäristö 1837–2000* [In the heart of town. The built environment of the Kirkkopuisto park in Jyväskylä 1837–2000]. Jyväskylä: Kopijyvä.

Lappi, Tiina-Riitta 1997. *Mielikuvia kaupungista. Ympäristösuhteen etnologista tarkastelua Jyväskylän Kuokkalassa* [Images of the town. Ethnological study of environmental relations in Kuokkala in Jyväskylä]. Jyväskylän yliopisto, etnologian laitos. Tutkimuksia 32. Jyväskylä.

Lefebvre, Henri 1991. *The Production of Space.* Oxford: Blackwell.

Lehtinen, Ari Akusti 1993. Kansalaisyhteiskunta ja ympäristöliikkeet – käsitesekaannuksia uudessa yhteiskuntamaantieteessä [Citizens' society and environmental movements – confusion of ideas in the new human geography]. *Alue ja Ympäristö* 22:2, 62–70.

Lilja, Elisabeth 1995. *Människosyn och samhällsplanering* [View of humans and town planning]. Nordiska institutet för samhällsplanering. Rapport 1995:1. Stockholm.

*Lutakon osayleiskaava* [The Lutakko general plan]. 16.5.1994. Architects Harris-Kjisik. Jyväskylän kaupungin yleiskaavatoimisto. Julkaisu 2/1994, 32.

Löfgren, Orvar 2001. European Ethnology in the Jungles of the "New Economy". In Pirjo Korkiakangas & Elina Kiuru (eds.): *An Adventurer in European Ethnology*. Jyväskylä: Atena, 179–193.

Relph, E. 1976. *Place and Placelessness*. London: Pion Limited.

Schulman, Harry, Karkama, Pertti, Karisto, Antti & Ilmonen Mervi 1995. Johdanto. Kulttuurisen kaupunkitutkimuksen näkökulmista [Introduction. On the perspectives of cultural urban studies]. In Harry Schulman & Vesa Kanninen (eds.): *Kaupunki kohtauspaikkana. Näkökulmia kulttuuriseen kaupunkitutkimukseen* [City as meeting place. Perspectives on cultural urban studies]. Yhdyskuntasuunnittelun täydennysko ulutuskeskuksen julkaisuja C 33. Teknillinen korkeakoulu. Espoo, 7–12.

Zukin, Sharon 1995. *The Cultures of Cities*. Cambridge & Oxford: Blackwell Publishers.

PIRJO KORKIAKANGAS

# Memories and the Identity of Place

## Strategies of Town Residents in Jyväskylä

*[handwritten marginalia: titles don't necessarily connect?]*

*[handwritten marginalia: Maybe the approach is one of strategies to build self-conscious identities of place, but such identity is arrived at sub. consciously often it is recognized rather than intentionally formed. So a major qn arises about intentions of identity formation in the modern urban world small scale of Finland maybe makes this easier?]*

S paces, places and buildings acquire their significance from the actions that take place "within" them. Spaces and places also have a physical form, which defines their being and seems to attract specific actions that create meanings. The actions that create meanings strengthen the characteristics we attach to space or place; these, as a whole, form our notion of what a certain space or place is, what it is like, what should be included in it, and what cannot be removed from it.

Urban space can be studied as the continuous interaction of three different perspectives (Lefebvre 1994). Spaces are used for various purposes, according to which people behave within them in various ways; these everyday routines refer to spatial practices. Experts, such as architects, understand spaces from their own points of departure. Representations of space achieve their form and are seen in plans and in the built environment, but they also contain aspects connected with ideology and conditions of production. Life in spaces gains significance for the users as lived spaces and as the experiences and memories attached to these. *[handwritten marginalia: Between bldgs or well. Lefebvre again]*

The significance of a space varies according to the people who use and experience it: conceptions and images can, on a certain level, be shared, but clearly differ from each other in another respect. Since space is always socially produced, it is formed through its users. Thus, for example, the images, hopes and expectations regarding the function of a certain space held by planners on one side and by town dwellers on the other, do not necessarily always meet. However, the conflicts arising from such differing views must not be an obstacle to the arrival at an agreement; in fact, the resolving of disputes may rather produce totally new, even innovative perspectives on problematic situations. At the same time, the Lefebvreian thought that space or place develops a being, an identity, as well as its own lifecycle and history through functionality, is realised.

In this article, I will analyse the reactions and writings against the plans for the new building of the Jyväskylä University Teacher Training Elementary School (1999–2000) as a case study of the way town dwellers construct spaces, places and buildings and turn these into a part of a shared, or sometimes very individual, narrative. It can actually be claimed that spaces and places are created in narratives and as narratives. The town itself, too, is a

150

*See previous chapter;*

narrative, which can be collectively familiar and collectively narrated. However, commonly shared narratives also include many different and differing individual narrative parts – depending on who the narrator is. The various narratives can even stand in conflict, particularly when the interests of the town dwellers and those of the town planners are not in agreement.

The events and public writings related to the building plans of the Teacher Training Elementary School include both private and collective emotions and memories connected with the creation of the identity of the town dwellers. The materials and events are a very good illustration of how the conflicts between town dwellers and planners and experts, when reaching an acute stage, can be the basis for finding an agreement. I have analysed my material as a description of how the opposition of the town dwellers, forming a united front, can result in a solution which is seen as more suitable – expressly by the town dwellers themselves.

The means and motives of the town dwellers' opposition in my sample case varied. One common feature was, however, that they appealed to memories, which, in turn, seemed to be upheld by nostalgia. I interpret this case as reflecting how nostalgia in its various forms and meanings can be part of the way in which the town dwellers experience the plans in relation to their own perceptions of the unique and comfortable character of their hometown. People evaluate changes specifically from the perspective of memories, not only in relation to the experiences and opportunities for action here and now. Nostalgia as imprinting memories and as a process for constructing and strengthening relations to space and place (Knuuttila 1998, 205) seemed to be one of the tactics taken on by the inhabitants of Jyväskylä in the defence of things they perceived as unique and associated to the identity of their town. In a Certeauan sense (de Certeau 1988, xix; 34–39), the issues could be described as a clash between strategies and tactics, and attempts at reconciling these. De Certeau uses the term strategy to describe a dichotomy that arises when institutions or political decision-makers use their power in, for example, town planning. The town dwellers, who do not have the opportunity for such exercise of power, resort to various tactics in order to, at least temporarily, take possession of places in their town. One tactic in my examples was the use of memory and nostalgia. Nostalgia thus functions as a resource which not only strengthens the identity of a place, but also creates a kind of "legalised" moral claims against those in power (see Mitchell 1998).

## The school building plans as trigger of memories

School children have been part of the Jyväskylä University campus from the very beginning of its history, which spans over a century. The first were the pupils of the Model Schools for Boys and Girls of the Teacher Training College founded in 1863 and the present children on campus are the pupils of the Jyväskylä University Teacher Training Elementary School. The school is situated in the central university campus, where it has been since 1954. This school building, designed by the architect Alvar Aalto and regarded as

*Also Toronto City Hall?*

151

very modern and functional at its time, according to Jyväskylä University no longer fulfils the needs of modern primary education and teacher training. In spring 1999, Jyväskylä University, the Town of Jyväskylä and the State Property Board published a plan, according to which the school and the pupils would have been moved away from the campus. The plan was to construct a new school building adjacent to the Teacher Training Lower and Upper Secondary Schools outside the campus, partly on the site of the Mäki-Matti Family Park. This park is the first of its kind in Finland and it has developed into a popular meeting place for town dwellers of all ages.

The plan gave rise to plenty of protest both at its presentation meetings and in the letters-to-the editor columns in the newspapers. In addition, 4 400 people signed a petition for the protection of the Mäki-Matti Family Park and the Town Planning Office received over sixty notes, each signed by one or several people, criticising the plan. The town dwellers' resistance bore fruit: the original plan was abandoned and an investigation into the placing of the new school on campus or in its immediate vicinity was started. According to the new plan published in spring 2000, the new school building will be constructed on campus, close to the present elementary school.[1] The solution clearly reflects the wishes and emotions of the town dwellers: the university campus as well as the Mäki-Matti Family Park has developed into a part of the history and townscape of Jyväskylä, the various temporal layers of which are elements in the attitudes of the inhabitants of Jyväskylä to changes that potentially break down the identity of their town.

Using my material, I will explore the process of resistance which emerged from the town dwellers' concern about the future of the children on campus and of the Mäki-Matti Family Park. My material samples consist of letters to the editor published in the Jyväskylä-based newspaper *Keskisuomalainen* and comments submitted to the Town Planning Office. I relate these to the significance of memory and reminiscence for the images that people create of places as well as to the ways of "appropriating places" through these recollection and images. The object of my analysis is not the plan itself or the phases of the planning process, but people's expression of their opinions after the plan had been publicised. I will explicitly focus on expressions where reminiscence and nostalgia can be interpreted as a central argument against the plan.

I will also explore the defended places as reflections of times past and present by analysing photographs of them. A significant recorder of the university campus and certain of its phases was professor Ahti Rytkönen who was lecturer in the Finnish language at the Jyväskylä College of Education (predecessor of the University of Jyväskylä) during the years 1938–1965.[2] His extensive collection of photographs contains numerous pictures of the life and activities of the college; one subject is the school children on campus during lessons and breaks. Photographing children and their play was not very common in Finland during the 1940's and 1950's. Ahti Rytkönen, however, possessed the skill of finding subjects, the value of which was realised only decades later. By means of his pictures, he has unconsciously supported the creation of the identity of the university campus as a place including children.

In connection with the debate concerning the Teacher Training Elementary School, the pictures have attained an added value related to present events alongside their historical significance. Walter Benjamin (1986, 14–22) introduced the concept of unconscious memory that, in turn, is based on the thoughts of Marcel Proust and Sigmund Freud on the characteristics and potentials of memory. Photographs represent a typical example of unconscious memory; in them, many details which are unobserved and even unintended at the moment when the picture is taken, are recorded. Thus, the photograph, as a kind of encapsulated "piece of the past" awaits the observer and seeker of the past (Peltonen 1999, 91). The "now" of the photograph is a bridge between two time levels: as a memory of the past, the photograph functions as a mirror for the present through the past. Apart from time, a photograph also contains space, which, like time, is limited and frozen, and only waits for the moment and an observer in that moment who will give it life and movement.

## The places of the children on campus

The main campus of the University of Jyväskylä is, above all, known for its buildings, designed by architect Alvar Aalto, and its lush vegetation. The location of the campus on this site, slightly outside the present town centre, goes back to the latter half of the 19th century and the establishment and development of Finland's first Finnish-speaking teacher training seminary. The Jyväskylä Teacher Training College was founded in 1863 (from 1934 it was Jyväskylä College of Education and from 1966 the University of Jyväskylä) and the Model Schools for Girls and Boys, established in 1866 to provide practical placements for the teacher candidates, brought children onto the campus (Tommila 1973, 425).

The Seminary and its Model Schools were first located in a rented building in the town centre. The planning of separate buildings for the institution started in 1866. Uno Cygnaeus, the first Director of the College, thought that the best place for the buildings would have been a site parcelled out from the Tourula crown estate close to the town. According to him, the site would have been well suited for the College's needs and its pedagogical ideology "to work through work" thanks to its "natural beauty" and "size big enough for farming". However, this plan was abandoned, and in 1874 the then Director K. G. Leinberg suggested the present central campus as a location for the College. One of his motivations was that Tourula would have been too far from town for the pupils of the Model Schools (Brummer 1916, 704–705; Raitio 1913, 105–111, 258).

The buildings were completed by 1882 and by then "a total of six stone buildings had been erected on this beautiful, magnificent site - -. Next to the houses is an extensive garden, and in addition to this, a grove of tall pine trees, sports grounds and an artificial lake provide the area with a variation that has turned it into a unique district adjacent to Jyväskylä. From the windows of the houses there opens up a beautiful view of the Jyväsjärvi lake or the town, and of the surrounding dark forests" (Brummer 1916, 708). The present campus of the Jyväskylä University is still characterised by the same features: its location is next to the town centre in the midst of beautiful, lush nature and overlooking the lake. The original red-brick buildings still dominate the central campus and are in harmony with the hilly terrain of the area. At the time of their completion, the buildings had a "lifting" effect on the townscape of Jyväskylä: their silhouette slightly above the other buildings gave the whole inner town a more urban appearance than before. The area of the Jyväskylä College could already at that time be characterised as the first university campus in Finland – actually before the term campus was generally used (Tommila 1972, 129).

The Model Schools (called Teacher Training Schools from the academic year 1900–1901 onwards) moved from their premises in town to the campus in 1881 (the girls' model school) and 1883 (the boys' model school). As the Seminary was turned into the Jyväskylä College of Education and further to the University of Jyväskylä, the pupils followed along with the changes and stayed on campus.

*At the end of a break, pupils of the Teacher Training School wait for entering on the steps of the older school building in May 1953. Nowadays the Unit of History of the Department of History and Ethnology, Jyväskylä University is situated in the building. Photo: Ahti Rytkönen, Memory Archives of Central Finland, Ahti Rytkönen Collection, Jyväskylä.*

*Pupils with their parents outside the new Teacher Training School in spring 1957. Photo: Ahti Rytkönen, Memory Archives of Central Finland, Ahti Rytkönen Collection, Jyväskylä.*

Up until around the Second World War, the Jyväskylä College of Education fitted into the building it had inherited from the College. After the war, the expansion of its activities and the increasing number of students caused considerable lack of space. In December 1950, the "Planning Competition of the Jyväskylä College of Education" for the use of the college grounds and new buildings to be constructed there was inaugurated. Of the proposals submitted by the tree architects who had been invited to participate in the competition, the plan of Alvar Aalto was considered the best one; his sub-mission was praised by the jury for its town planning merits, and particularly for its suggested design for the public part of the main building, the training school and the sports building. The whole complex was built in two stages, the first one of which included the construction of the training school. The school moved into its new premises class by class during 1954. The training school – the present elementary training school – was located in a peaceful environment which was safe for the pupils: the four wings placed at various angles enclosed the school yard which is connected to the campus garden (Lukkarinen 1994, 11–17, 66). The functionality of the school complex is supplemented by the gymnastics building, the swimming hall and the sports

155

field next to it. However, after forty years of use, the school building, which was originally considered very modern and functional, was in need of both expansion and renewal.

## Layers of the identity onion    *Children + The university.*

Human beings build their identity throughout their lives, as they adapt to changes and new life situations by modifying their environment and purposefully aiming both to change and to remain unchanged. Identity may be compared to an onion, where one layer encloses another (e.g. Lönnqvist 1997, 57). Can the same metaphor be used for the identity of place, for the attitudes to the changes of a place? Can the identity of place be peeled like an onion? What would happen if the school children who have been part of the campus of Jyväskylä University for more than one hundred years were removed from the campus as a result of the realisation of building plans? Would the campus still be the same, would something be missing, could the possible lack be replaced by something else? These kinds of question were in the minds of the town dwellers and others who criticised the building plans:

> What would happen to the university campus without schoolchildren, the scaled down people who for decades have reminded the students of their actual target group? In the 1950's, Alvar Aalto designed an extension for the Seminaarinmäki hill of the 1880's, for the Educational College. The university area, which has been widely presented in international architectural literature, forms the only real campus area in Finland. One essential feature of the area, apart from its red-brick architecture, has been the presence of children and the sound of play on campus. Finnish university areas are usually quiet, the students sneak to their lectures or their desks in the library. In Jyväskylä, children bring life to the campus. Regularly, throughout the academic year, the patter of running feet, the chime of names called, children screaming, snowballs whizzing, puddles splashed, the sounds of spring streams being dammed and redirected can be heard on the campus. (KSML 21.4.1999.)

The author is worried about the identity of the campus: it would suffer if the layers of "running feet", "children screaming" and "chime of names called" in the identity onion were turned into mere memories. The disappearance of the children who bring life to the campus would also deprive the future teachers of the opportunity to see and experience the authentic contents of children's, their "scaled down people's", school days in their own study environment.

The problem of preserving an identity has, for example, been illustrated by the metaphor of a ship, all parts of which, one by one, have been replaced with similar ones. Finally, there is not one single original part in the ship, but at the level of experience, the ship is still perceived as having remained the same ship (Kaunismaa 1997, 48). Pertaining to the identity of place, the issue is more complex: even small changes cause a blurring of the features that we associate with the place and think of as genuine – the elements of

*Pupils of the Teacher Training Elementary School playing the game kirkkis (or kirkonrotta, 'church rat') during a break. Photo: Pirjo Korkiakangas 1999, Memory Archives of Central Finland, Jyväskylä.*

the place that produce experiences, memories and mental images change. Space and place do not only occur as physically understandable, nor are the significances associated with them generally applicable, but individually experienced, layered by personal and collective history (see Saarikangas 1996, 312). However, identity and memories are not items that we only think something about, but also items that we use for thinking (Gillis 1994, 5). They, for their part, define our thinking and our actions. So, referring to the above, is it possible for the "real" identity of a place to totally disappear as a result of changes, as the writer I quoted rhetorically assumed, or is just another new layer added to the identity onion characterising the place? Does the place also carry with it as memories the earlier layers of its identity? Those who worry about the disappearance of children from the campus think that at least the character of the place will change totally, if the spaces that for decades have been used by children and that were designed for them were to be taken over by mature students, as has been planned:

> When the Training School is filled with mature students of education, those who at the moment study in rented premises scattered around town, the whole nature of the Jyväskylä University campus will change (KSML 21.4.1999).

> To hand over a building designed in detail for the use of children, to be used by mature students is a waste and scorn of the beautiful thoughts of the significance of the environment and the holistic view of education (KSML 19.9.1999).

If we assume that the identity of place includes social relations and interaction, changes pertaining to place naturally also require adaptation. New buildings or new users of a building produce new kinds of social relations, which do not necessarily have very much in common with the previous ones. So, is the wish to defend, for example, a building and its perceived original users only a way of seeking to hold on to the past for a strengthening of one's own identity and personal memories? The environment, and particularly the built environment, always includes layers of various levels and times. This is also a conscious aim in the conservation of parts of the environment as authentic and unchanged. Often the objects for this are buildings that we want preserved to remind us of something past – even if those supporting preservation nowadays usually have to struggle against arguments of efficiency and market forces. However, fragments bearing witness of the life of times past help people of today find their own place in the flow of time. Seeing a reminder of the past can give pleasure; it might awaken forgotten memories and images, stories of the past. A return to the past – even to times prior to one's own life – can also have a therapeutic effect in stopping the reminiscing person at least for a moment in the midst of the hectic pace of modern life (Boyer 1998, 19).

A return in time to one's own childhood experiences is one of the issues appealed to as an argument for keeping the Teacher Training Elementary School at its old location. The return might entail various emotions, atmospheres, smells and visual images which in retrospect are given a positive tone. The experience of place through reminiscence is sensory and consists of moving in space, touching, smells, shades of light and colour, as a kind of "cartography of the body" (Kristeva 1980; Saarikangas 1996, 314–315) and an expression of unconscious memory. The production of spatial significances and the interpretation of these happen simultaneously through reminiscence; the reminiscing person organises and moulds his or her spatial experiences by mirroring them in his or her childhood memories.

> I joined the Training School in the third grade. I do not remember if I then knew who had designed the school building or that it and the whole campus are somehow significant. But my direct experiences of the school itself and the area around it are still strongly preserved today. I remember as images, smells and feelings the hilly landscape, the tall trees with their brown bark and the buildings embedded on the slopes as well as the feeling of slightly worn brick floors of the corridors (such are not to be found anywhere!) and the faint smell of clay and wax that rose from them. And the winding and the light and the strange secret passage from the arts class wing to the main building. And the amazing top windows, which in an obscure but lasting way questioned the everyday naturalness of things. Perhaps the finest thing of all, however, was the roof terrace between the school and the assembly room – which I later learned is the main building of the university; the views, the strange white pillars supporting the corner of the building and the wonderful, surprising, child-sized stairs down to the assembly room side. Therefore I want to claim that the building itself is a very essential part of the education of and growing in the Training School. Aalto's school building and its surroundings aid

158

learning, thinking, feeling – even sentimentality. I do not doubt that a
new school could be good, too, but there will never be one like the old
school. (KSML 19.9.1999.)

Often – particularly when an old building is threatened – the layered structure
of a town is referred to. This usually means that the town is built by different temporal layers, building and spaces from different periods of time. And
if some portion of the layers is interfered with, it is felt that this part of the
narrative of the town is threatened; a part of the town's built history is left
to rely for its existence on memory alone. We usually assume that all things
past disappear and nothing new can replace them. On the other hand, we
cannot prevent the fact that our environment changes and that it is changed
and moulded to fit various purposes. In such situations the human ability to
remember and tendency to reminisce is valuable. Our mental recollections,
independent of time and place, help us understand our place in the present
and use the past as a resource.

The desire to keep something unchanged, for its part, also reflects the aim
to attach and strengthen the identity of a place by maintaining old features.
Being is always inseparably connected to place: place does not exist as place
unless it contains being, various experiences and events and actions creating
memories. Thus, place is created through its signifying relations, by life in
the place (Karjalainen 1997, 231; Lefebvre 1994, 33–36). The writer I quoted
earlier is convinced that a distinct atmosphere has developed in the building
of the elementary training school, which it is impossible to transmit as such
– as the authentic training school atmosphere – to another building. A building is not a mere building, but a distinct and "personified" individual, the
life-story of which is upheld expressly by the memories, beings and experiences of actors of various ages. These have been formed and developed over
the years through life in the place and have been crystallised for the persons
experiencing them as important memories, the effect of which they, like the
person reminiscing above, feel they carry throughout their lives and which
are a part of their self and their identity.

The children's place on the campus of the University of Jyväskylä is historical as a phenomenon and changes regarding it have caused reactions among
the town dwellers. The presence of school children in an academic environment is not very common, which in itself makes the issue more interesting
and relevant as a cultural and historical phenomenon. The children on their
way to or from school have become such a self-evident part of the people
moving about on campus, that they have not attracted any specific attention
until their situation has been threatened. The change in attitude towards these
children can be described as a kind of anticipatory nostalgia. Usually nostalgia is connected with the reminiscence of something already lost or past,
which is marked by melancholy, sometimes romanticising, sometimes even
bittersweet longing to reach that which is past or lost (Korkiakangas 1999,
171–173). On the other hand, the feeling of nostalgia, as a rule, is awakened
precisely in situations containing a threat of future loss: nostalgia then functions as a kind of mental preparation for a disappointment to be expected. In

159

my sample case, nostalgia was awakened by a feeling that history is being unnecessarily disturbed and its continuity obstructed. The significance of place consists of both memories of the past and experiences of the present: we interpret the significances associated with a place and those we attach to a place, on one hand, according to what we have inherited from the past and, on the other, to what we experience in the present (Rotenberg 1993, xiv). The meandering between past and present experiences appear in several of the writings in reaction against the plans for a new building for the Teacher Training Elementary School. The arguments for the preservation of the school in its current location refer both to the architecture of the university campus and to a "violent" break with the seminary tradition:

> The alternative to preserve and expand the school on its present site on the basis of Alvar Aalto's plans should still be investigated. There are well-motivated reasons for this, even if the campus area is protected against additional constructions. The training school is an essential part of the 1950's building complex of the College of Education, which at its completion received a lot of praise from experts in the field for its progressive nature. The school, situated in a green environment, connected through playgrounds to the park and the sports field, is still a beautiful and safe milieu for its small pupils. Aalto's design for the buildings of the College of Education included a suggestion for an extension of the training school. - - The College tried to obtain state funding for the extension throughout the 1960's. However, this was never realised and the main reason was probably the new building projects of the recently established university. Aalto himself considered the building of the extension for the College that he had sketched as "very desirable from the perspective of the area". (KSML 27.4.1999.)

> Why move away the pupils from this campus where they have been from its establishment? That would mean the disappearance of yet another tradition. Can the old building of the Training School not be renovated and extended to fulfil the current requirements? However, if a new school must be built, it should implement new architecture and encourage the imagination of the pupils and not be a box crammed with several floors. Is the area next to the swimming pool in Pitkäkatu street [the area were the new building actually will be situated] and its environment such a more valuable whole than the completed and well functioning Family Park, that the new building cannot be placed there? - - At the information meeting held at the Training School, additional alternatives to the four models planned on the site of the family park were requested. Therefore, I finally want to inquire why the town of Jyväskylä does not appreciate and is not able to preserve anything old? (KSML 25.10.1999.)

> There are many schools in the world with a history that goes back one or two centuries. Why is the University of Jyväskylä not interested in its past, why does it not appreciate its world-famous architecture, why are financial interests more important than values of cultural history? Jyväskylä is full of buildings, to the names of which the term "former" is appended. Do we have to add yet another to that list, "the Former Training School"? (KSML 1.4.1999.)

## *The Mäki-Matti Family Park – an example of successful town planning*

The history of a totally new residential area or another space or area that "contains something new", is created by living and acting. In this process, the significance of earlier living environments and of memories associated with these might be accentuated and help in the adaptation to a new space. Place and space are formed by being lived in and significances from earlier experienced and lived places are attached to them. Living also creates totally new spatial and mental meanings and symbols for a place, characteristic for that very place. On the other hand, the history of a town with its events and features from various periods form an essential part of the present, past and future lives of the town dwellers. So, history is alive and in this respect it also defines the present, since people give life to it through their lives and activities. Thus a town's structure of temporal layers, just like the formation of its spaces and places, needs to be interpreted explicitly by a person who experiences it.

The history of the children on the Jyväskylä University campus stretches over more than one hundred years and in the course of their history, they have become part of the identity of the campus. Many town dwellers also feel that from a cultural historical perspective the proper place for the school is precisely the university campus. This connects to the Lefebvrean idea of lived space and the social production of space. The children, who have been part of the campus from its very beginning, have helped mould it into a certain kind of space and place through their living and being. A similar course of development can be discerned in the case of the Mäki-Matti Family Park, although the history of the park in its present form is considerably shorter. The Family Park was established in 1979 in honour of the UN International Year of Children. Some of the ideas included in the national target programme for the Year of Children directly influenced the development of the Mäki-Matti Family Park:

> An environment favourable to children is a positive environment for everybody. - - For the child, an environment is always a learning environment. The child's local environment should be filled with the active lives of various people of various ages. It should include enough and suitable premises and equipment for playing and other activities. It should form the framework for people's natural social activity. - - Children are still too often forgotten in town planning, land purchase policy and housing production. Better and more diverse opportunities are granted for driving and parking cars than for the play, activities and adventures of children. - - The increasing uniformity of the environment deprives children of the opportunity to learn to know life and nature. (Mannila 1994, 47.)

Concern about the increasing uniformity and limitation of the living environment of children in cities was expressed in many contexts in the 1970's. It was felt that children in cities lacked the opportunity to freely play and find adventures in their local environment. This concern was also felt in Jyväskylä and the Day Care Department of the town's Social Affairs Office suggested in 1977 that a kind of "children's town" should be established; in the preparation process the name changed to family park. A working group was appointed for the development of the project with representatives of the town's offices for social affairs, building, culture, town planning, and parks. The inhabitants of the Mäki-Matti area were also engaged in the planning of the park through an inhabitants' council that was set up especially for this project. Originally, the family park was planned to be part of the day care activities, which would include supervised playgroups and other activities for children. The park was also intended to serve as an afternoon club for school children, as a place for leisure activities for families and children and as a common meeting place for the inhabitants in the surrounding area (Mannila 1994, 46–48).

A suitable location for the family park was found in the Mäki-Matti district, which is situated on the outskirts of the town centre behind the Harju area (see map, p. 128). The area was originally included in the land of the Syrjälä farm, which during the 19<sup>th</sup> century developed into the site for cottages built by the poorer town dwellers thanks to its cheap leases and lack of town planning, and thus to a separate suburban district. The border between the town and the rural district was the Mäki-Matinkatu street, which still runs as a cycle lane through the family park. In 1908, the town bought the area and a town plan was made for it. The maze-like neighbourhood gradually began to turn into a district regulated by the new town plan (Brummer 1916, 422–426). In 1924, the Oikokatu street was built through the western end of the Harju district to the Mäki-Matti area. This street with its flea markets is today included in the Family Park complex. Over the decades, the Mäki-Matti area has developed into an oasis resembling a garden district almost in the middle of town (Mannila 1994, 51).

The Family Park was constructed on both sides of the Mäki-Matinkatu street so that it is bordered by the streets Oikokatu, Voionmaankatu and the sites of its houses, Pitkäkatu, and the area of the Jyväskylä Teacher Training Secondary School. Before the Family Park was established there was still some of the old cottages and buildings of the Syrjälä farm left in the area. In fact, the area had quite a dubious reputation at the end of the 19<sup>th</sup> century: life in Mäkimatti during that period was described thus: "- - in the so-called Mäkimatti cottage and other shacks that were situated next to the town on the lands of the Syrjälä farm, people who got their living by fraud and theft in town lived and were sheltered" (Brummer 1916, 422). However, over time the area developed into a cosy district of craftsmen and workers. That era is still symbolised by two preserved old buildings. The café of the Family Park, a former shop, has been situated in one of them. The red cottages in the Park seem to be a clear link to the past; they also connect the urban space to a rural landscape and "granny's cottage", to a lifestyle which is experienced as harmonious and human. One writer offers the following as a defence of the Family Park:

How would this change affect the urban culture and cultural heritage which is now passed on by the red cottages to the users of the park? There should be free meeting places in town, green spaces and a connection to the past. The change would mean that the activities of the Family Park in their present form would come to an end since there would be no opportunities left for this kind of function (for example, meeting opportunities for inhabitants of various ages). It is crucial that the oasis of the town centre, "the green lane" (Harju – Mäki-Matti – the University campus – Hippos) is preserved as an area for the diverse outdoor activities of the town dwellers. Thus the images of Jyväskylä as a "green town" would be maintained. It is absolutely necessary that the historic and unique townscape be protected. We do not want old Jyväskylä further destroyed than is already the case. (K: 29.9.1999.)

Some writers have also used their own memories from past decades of the area where the present Family Park is located. Thus, recollections from a period prior to the actual park are connected to the idea of a family park; the park and its significance for the town dwellers is constructed through memories:

My first memories from the neighbourhood of the present Family Park date back to the early 1950's when I was a secondary school pupil and we went to the Mäki-Matti area to draw and paint the wooden houses during the lessons with our art teacher. Most of the buildings from that period have been torn down and new ones built instead and the Harju district has been muddled several times. What is left of the old houses is an important link to the past. I have lived in the Mäki-Matti district since 1961. Some of the most positive things that have happened in my local environment during these years is the development of the Family Park and the Mäkitupa area preserving old buildings and old trees and gradually

*One of the red cottages in the Family Park. Photo: Tiina-Riitta Lappi.*

163

adding new plants, playgrounds and other constructions. The Oikokatu street with its flea markets is an essential part of this complex. Even if I do not use the park very actively, like other older inhabitants of Mäki-Matti, I enjoy the peaceful pedestrian path to the town centre and the beauty of the park and watching the children play. - - I believe that the children and youth of today also need something permanent in their environment as a basis for their memories. There are already a lot of teenagers and young adults who have memories of playing in the Family Park. As one of the employees at the Family Park said, a child who has played in the park will most certainly not come back as a teenager to smash and scribble. But what happens if adults act as an example by destroying the playground with chain saws and bulldozers? (K: 15.10.1999.)

The Family Park is situated in a very suitable location: it is close to the town centre and accessible from all directions, it is also protected from the busiest nearby streets and borders on a pedestrian street (Oikokatu). The area is also of cultural historical value regarding its old environment with its diverse vegetation: there are, among others, Norway maples, downy birches, apple trees, cherry trees, bird cherry trees, Siberian pea-shrubs, burnet roses, Ural false spirea, lilacs, red currents and gooseberries (Mannila 1994, 51–52, 64).

The plans to remove the Teacher Training Elementary School from the university campus caused the clearest reactions amongst those who opposed the project. They mainly represented two perspectives: those who defended the children on campus and those who wanted to preserve the Mäki-Matti Family Park. The plans to place the new school building on the site of the park – an area which many town dwellers perceive as being personally important to them – seemed to affect a larger group of people and to be a more sensitive issue and a harsher break with the historical continuum than the possible removal of the children from the main campus. The defenders of the Family Park consisted of users of the park who are of very varying ages: families with small children, young people, senior citizens. The Park seems to have developed into a diverse meeting place for town dwellers of all ages, an environment that brings together different generations and supports parenthood. For example, the various supervised activities in the park in 1998 attracted 28 492 participants of various ages. (K: 14.10.1999; Statement from the Jyväskylä Town Technical Service Centre.)

Over the years, the Family Park has become one of the symbols for the identity of Jyväskylä. In addition, it seems to be part of the identity and everyday life of its users: socialisation processes of both children and adults develop in the park. Like the University campus, the park is perceived as a part of the history and townscape of Jyväskylä: to intrude on it would cut and destroy the roots of experiencing a shared history and townscape and lessen the well-being of the town dwellers:

> The Mäki-Matti Family Park is the oldest family park in Finland and the like of it is hard to find. Over the years and also through the rebuilding carried out a few years ago, the park fits exceptionally well into its environment. Together with the Harju area, the Family Park has been a symbol of Jyväskylä, an indication that people like living here. The park

and its old buildings help the inhabitants of Mäki-Matti and the town dwellers at large to trace the roots of the residential area and the town to the history of Mäki-Matti and the town as a whole. The park provides an excellent opportunity for town dwellers of all ages to participate in various activities and meet each other. The urban culture in a town that respects its inhabitants and functions well should include not only the preservation of traditions but also open spaces that offer places for socialising and encounters. The Family Park had found its place in the usage of the town dwellers. The Family Park as a built playground is a paradise for the children in Jyväskylä and a space to breath for parents who take care of their children at home. The activities of the Family Park support families and create everyday networks. These activities are important even from a financial perspective. (KSML 22.4.1999.) *Beams of praise*

The writer identifies part of his argument in defence of the park with its function and significance as a preserver and transmitter of traditions and as interpreter of the town's history. Many others who wrote in favour of the Family Park emphasised these same things. Apart from being a place for town dwellers of various ages to spend their free time, the park has developed into a kind of showcase of a place in Jyväskylä which is particularly suitable and functioning for socialising, playing and creating everyday networks. So the park is a socially produced, lived space, and it illustrates how the ideals and ideologies behind its establishment have turned into a practical reality. The park can be characterised as a place of possibility (see Greverus 1994, 33), which has been realised through the people who use and experience it. The identity of the place is attached explicitly to the place in its present form, that is, the park. The identity onion of the place has obtained a totally new layer, which the users of the park perceive as so "final" that no opportunities for any fundamental changes are provided. For its users, the park seems to hold a personal, social, functional and emotional significance. The place has met the expectations with which it has been charged, which in turn have created new activities to supplement the established patterns of action. Thus, the stability of the activities on one hand, and their flexibility on the other, have increased the park's significance as a place that creates shared and individual experiences and memories. As a semi-public environment it has also clearly lowered the threshold for social activities and encounters.

Throughout this year the media has been full of articles on parenthood and coping with the strains of this. One good reference is, for example, the article "Children need time, parents support" in *Keskisuomalainen* on 4 October [1999]. This article frees parents from the feeling of insufficiency: "when one does not have the time nor the energy to provide one's child with experiences" – being together and doing things together is enough for the child. The Mäki-Matti Family Park is being together and doing together. Here, the children and their parents or minders play in the fresh air, train the skills of their hands and feet, learn the difficult art of socialising with other people. In addition, it is a place where one's own parenthood gets support from other parents – everybody is familiar with the discussions on child rearing and sorting out problematic relations on the bench by the playground. - - Why ruin something so valuable and well-functioning, which is so highly and unconditionally appreciated by the town dwellers? The inhabitants of Jyväskylä are proud of the Family Park; it is the first of its kind in Finland, built in honour of the UN's Year of the Family in 1979. (KSML 10.10.1999.)

The Mäki-Matti Park and its various events is already a foundation of the cultural environment in Jyväskylä. People come here from further afield than just Jyväskylä. The place provides a space to breathe for several tens of families. Without it, the social problems in the area will increase significantly. The park is a meeting place for mothers and if this chance to see other grown-ups disappears, the loneliness and isolation of the mothers will grow. This, in turn, will increase social problems. For example, post-natal depression will certainly become more common. As a result of the isolation of families, the maltreatment of children, among other things, will increase. (K: 1.10.1999.)

The majority of my material of letters to the editor and the comments sent to the Town Planning Office can be interpreted as speeches for the defence of the Mäki-Matti Family Park. The future disappearance of children from the University campus, for its part, seemed to mostly worry those who have personal experience from the Training School or, like myself, nostalgically followed the fate of school children on campus. On the other hand, the actual need for a new school building was hardly criticised at all, with the exception of a few letters to the editor that were in favour of a renovation of the present building to suit modern requirements. So, in principle everybody defended a common cause, even of the motives for the criticism of the plans varied. However, the changes will most directly affect the pupils themselves, who obviously have hardly been heard at all in the case, as is common when taking decisions concerning children. The placing of the new building next to the Teacher Training Secondary School would have meant that about one thousand pupils of very different ages would have been crammed into a relatively small area, and would also have led to a change in the conditions of the Family Park activities. In particular, changes to established habits easily give rise to criticism and cause indignation. The criticism has condemned the plan for its massiveness which is assumed to cause various kinds of problems.

Is the Training School intended to be a mammoth complex where elementary school pupils who have only just started their education study alongside grown-up secondary school pupils? There is evidence that the disorder among pupils in mammoth school multiplies. Drug abuse has also entered the picture in large school complexes. (KSML 11.10.1999.)

Finally, I cannot but express my horror of the "complex benefiting the children and the teaching" that the university envisages. Should we not try to get rid of all kinds of complexes? It is a pure advantage that there is also a physical distance between elementary and primary school. I remember that starting secondary school was frightening, but to move from the sheltered forest to the town and from a soft environment to a hard classical school was also part of the change in school levels and of the adulthood looming ahead. (KSML 19.9.1999.)

Also observe, that I do not at all believe that the elementary school and the secondary school could function in the same premises or around the same yard, particularly if also the pre-school children were to be placed in the same building. I remember from elementary school how frightening the sixth-graders seemed to a small pupil in the first grade, but how would a 6-year-old experience students in the third grade of upper secondary school? What about increased bullying? Drug problems? Increased drinking? Smoking? All these will be everyday things to younger and younger age groups, since learning from the model provided by older pupils will be inevitable if the schoolyard is realised as is rumoured – shared by all pupils. Does this kind of education provide a good example? You probably do not know what kind of stress and problems bullying in school causes a person for the rest of his life. This problem should absolutely not be underestimated. (K: 1.10.1999.)

It is incredible that you can even suggest such a change of the town plan! How do you think we who take care of children react to the issue? I have a younger sister whom I have taken to playgrounds and looked after since she was little and therefore I very well understand why the parents of my godson are very upset about the plan. There is no sense in placing all schools in one complex, since it has always been a big and exciting moment to start secondary school – it is a sign of approaching adulthood and a step towards being a grown-up. Is the intention now to put 6-year-olds on the path towards adulthood? Madness! Let's keep the elementary school where it belongs – on campus. (K: 26.9.1999.)

A mammoth complex is perceived as a threat that would cause disorderly conduct among the children, even drug abuse. The thoughts of the writers also reveal a kind of emergency call for the right of the elementary school children to a protected childhood, which the cramming of pupils of varying ages into the same complex would destroy. It is remarkable that not one advocate of small village schools which are perceived as ideal has published their opinion on the plan for the Teacher Training Elementary School. At least some schools in rural communities continuously implement a system where the aim obviously is to remove the border between the primary and secondary level within the comprehensive school. However, the situation in village schools is completely different from the one in mammoth schools with a thousand pupils. The existence of small rural village schools is defended to the very last as ideal learning environments, while the pupils in large urban schools must manage in totally different circumstances. The case might be, that the opportunities of schools in cities and those of small village schools to function as successful learning environments and places for the pupils' social growth are different despite the fact that both should train their pupils to survive the same kinds of challenges found in "the big world" and the unknown future.

## Place and the "borders" of place – nostalgia as strategy

Places contain many kinds of significance and connotation that connect them

167

to various situations and aspects of life. Place has often conceptually been associated with "localised" time, and thus place has mainly been regarded as a "frozen stage" for people's physical activities which is linked to time (Pred 1985, 337). However, place, the positionalising of space, and time both gain their significance as a framework for human life, above all, as producers of experiences and memory. In order for us to be able to understand time and place at all (as space) we must humanise them, link them as places and times to a historical continuum or to the course of our own life. Thus, place and time are usually experienced very personally. On the other hand, individual experiences and the birth of personal memories also require some kind of social context, a social sharing of experiences and recollections (Fentress & Wickham 1992). When experiencing and reminiscing we are bound to and socialised in our own culture and habits, and the community surrounding us implicitly creates the basis for what we as individuals perceive as worth reminiscing about and what we think of as a valuable experience or historical features worth preserving. Yet, if historical experience of place and time vary individually; place and time are also interpreted differently according to the positions of the interpreters as part of space and time (Halbwachs 1992 [1941/1952]; Massey 1996, 3; Karjalainen 1998, 95–101).

Human beings typically understand space as a certain place that is delimited in some way – nationally, regionally, locally. The limits are attempts at attaching meanings to spaces, to enclose them, supply them with a given identity and claim them as one's own. This kind of definition of place is a type of strategy, the place is "appropriated" and at the same time one is, in a way, granted the right to the place and the right to make decisions, "use power", concerning the place (cf. de Certeau 1984, 35–36; Greverus 1994, 28–33, places of possibilities). Nostalgia is often attached to places that are perceived in this way and through nostalgia one's own history of experiences is mirrored in connection to the place and its history. However, assuming that space becomes place not only through personal experiences but also through social relations, networks and social communication, the experience of place cannot remain static and unchanged. Neither can a place be unambiguously limited and thus have a "closed" identity, since it is also connected to the world outside of it through social networks. Thus the identity of a place also consists of various relations and links that it has outside its seeming borders (Massey 1996, 4–5). Since the character and identity of a place are created through its significances, apart from its physical features, the place is perceived in terms of the experiences, images and memories connected to it. Spatially, place can always be situated somewhere, but in images and memories places are detached from their spatial connections.

Reminiscence of mental places involves the layers of the life stories both of the person experiencing and reminiscing and of the place itself, as well as the manifold significances of nostalgic reminiscence. In people's everyday lives and experiences places "function" and remain "in place" unnoticed, but when they are perceived to be threatened, nostalgic emotions and memories are activated. It could be assumed, that these same emotions and memories would also be brought to the fore in people whose working environment is threatened by change. However, hardly any of the teachers at the Teacher Training Elementary School have reacted – at least publicly – to the building plans. It seems that the school has not yet developed into an object for nostalgic reminiscence for them, but it is more clearly understood as a space for everyday work where the functionability of the space is more important than memories attached to it. Space and places appear to be more functional to those who work in them than to those who mirror their experiences through nostalgic constructions of the past. The planning of new spaces usually focuses on finding and realising functional solutions, even if also significances originating in memories should be considered for the various aspects and functionability of place and space. The plans must live and be realised in the sphere of all the significances through which people experience and use spaces. My case study of the writings in reaction to the building plans of the Teacher Training School reflects the various ways in which people construct spaces and places, create mental borders around them, and how memories and nostalgia emerged as strategies for the defence of the Teacher Training Elementary School and the Mäki-Matti Family Park that were connected by the building plans. This strategy proved to be so effective that the whole planning process took on a new direction and a solution that satisfied all parties was reached.

NOTES

[1]   The winning entry of the architectural competition, the *Syli* building (the name translates into English as 'embrace'), was seen as harmonising with the campus architecture of Alvar Aalto. The new school building was completed in 2002.
[2]   Ahti Rytkönen (1899–1989) was one of the most industrious photographers of Finnish everyday life and he can be regarded both as a researcher-recorder and a documenter of his own time. He took up photography in 1924 and continued more or less throughout his life. His pictures from Jyväskylä recorded and documented events, people and environments in a small rural town. These urban pictures also show Rytkönen as a popular photographer: he was interested in people's everyday life and subjects that others ignored. His pictures of children are one example of this. (Korkiakangas 1998, 28–35.)

## SOURCES AND BIBLIOGRAPHY

### Material

K = Comments on the plan for a new building for the Jyväskylä Teacher Training Elementary School submitted to the Town Planning Office in September and October 1999.

KSML = Newspaper *Keskisuomalainen*. Entries published in the columns 'Letters to the editor' and 'People's voice' 21 April – 19 November 1999.

169

## Literature

Benjamin, Walter 1986. *Silmä väkijoukossa: huomioita eräistä motiiveista Baudelairen tuotannossa* [Orig. Über einige Motive bei Baudelaire]. Helsinki: Odessa.

Boyer, M. Christine 1998. *The city of collective memory: its historical imagery and architectural entertainments.* Cambridge, MA: MIT Press.

Brummer O. J. 1916. *Jyväskylän kaupungin historia vv. 1837–1912* [The history of the town of Jyväskylä 1837–1912]. Jyväskylä.

Certeau, Michel de 1984. *The practice of everyday life.* Berkley and Los Angeles: University of California Press.

Fentress, James & Wickham, Chris 1992. *Social memory.* Oxford: Blackwell.

Gillis, John R. (ed.) 1994. *Commemorations: The politics of national identity.* Princeton, NJ: Princeton University Press.

Greverus, Ina-Maria 1994. Was sucht der Anthropologe in der Stadt? Eine Collage. In Ina-Maria Greverus, Johannes Moser & Kirstein Salein (eds.): *Stadtgedanken, aus und über Frankfurt am Main.* Frankfurt am Main: Institut für Kulturanthropologie und Europäische Ethnologie der Johann Wolfgang Goethe-Universität Frankfurt am Main, 11–74.

Halbwachs, Maurice 1992 [1941/1952]. *On collective memory.* Chicago: The University of Chicago Press.

Karjalainen, Pauli Tapani 1997. Aika, paikka ja muistin maantiede [Time, place and the geography of memory]. In Tuukka Harni, Marko Karvinen, Hille Koskela & Sirpa Tani (eds.): *Tila, paikka ja maisema. Tutkimusretkiä uuteen maantieteeseen* [Space, place and landscape. Explorations in the new geography]. Tampere: Vastapaino, 227–241.

Karjalainen, Pauli Tapani 1998. Real place images. In Arto Haapala (ed.): *The city as cultural metaphor: Studies in urban aesthetics.* International Institute of Applied Aesthetics Series vol. 4, Lahti: International Institute of Applied Aesthetics, 94–107.

Kaunismaa, Pekka 1997. Mitä on kollektiivinen identiteetti? [What is collective identity?]. In Kalle Virtapohja (ed.): *Puheenvuoroja identiteetistä. Johdatusta yhteisöllisyyden ymmärtämiseen* [Comments on identity. Introduction to the understanding of communality]. Jyväskylä: Atena, 37–54.

Knuuttila, Seppo 1998. Paikan synty suomalaisena ilmiönä [The birth of place as a Finnish phenomenon]. In Pertti Alasuutari & Petri Ruuska (eds.): *Elävänä Euroopassa. Muuttuva suomalainen identiteetti* [Alive in Europe. The Changing Finnish Identity]. Tampere: Vastapaino, 191–214.

Korkiakangas, Pirjo 1998. Ahti Rytkönen – sanojen "sieppaaja", valokuvaaja, tutkija, opettaja [Ahti Rytkönen – "catcher" of words, photographer, researcher, teacher]. *Villa Rana* 1/1998. Jyväskylä: Jyväskylän yliopisto, Etnologian laitos.

Korkiakangas, Pirjo 1999. Muisti, muistelu, perinne [Memory, reminiscence, tradition]. In Bo Lönnqvist, Elina Kiuru & Eeva Uusitalo (eds.): *Kulttuurin muuttuvat kasvot. Johdatusta etnolgiatieteisiin* [The changing face of culture. Introduction to the ethnological disciplines]. Tietolipas 155. Helsinki: Suomalaisen Kirjallisuuden Seura, 155–176.

Kristeva, Julia 1982. *Powers of horror: an essay on abjection.* New York: Columbia University Press.

Lefebvre, Henri 1994. *The production of space.* Oxford: Blackwell.

Lukkarinen, Päivi 1994. *Alvar Aallon kasvatusopillinen korkeakoulu. Menneittein motiivien kiteytymä* [Alvar Aalto's College of Education. A crystallisation of past motives]. Jyväskylä: Jyväskylän yliopisto.

Lönnqvist, Bo 1997. Suomenruotsalaisten etninen identiteetti [The ethnic identity of Finland-Swedes]. In Kalle Virtapohja (ed.): *Puheenvuoroja identiteetistä. Johdatusta yhteisöllisyyden ymmärtämiseen* [Comments on identity. Introduction to the understanding of communality]. Jyväskylä: Atena, 55–62.

Mannila, Helena 1994. *Kolme puistoa sosiaalisina ja fyysisinä kaupunkiympäristöinä.*

*Mäki-Matin ja Yrttisuon perhepuistot sekä Lounaispuiston leikkipuisto Jyväskylässä vuosina 1991–1992* [Three parks as social and physical urban environments. The Mäki-Matti and Yrttisuo Family Parks and the Lounaispuisto Playground in Jyväskylä in 1991–1992]. Unpublished Master's thesis in Ethnology. University of Jyväskylä, Department of Ethnology.

Massey, Doreen 1996. *Space, place and gender.* Cambridge: Polity Press.

Mitchell, Jon P. 1998. The nostalgic construction of community: Memory and social identity in Urban Malta. *Ethnos* 63 (1), 81–101.

Peltonen, Matti 1999. *Mikrohistoriasta* [On micro history]. Hanki ja jää publication series. Helsinki: Gaudeamus.

Pred, Allan 1985. The social becomes the spatial, the spatial becomes the social: Enclosures, social change and the becoming of places in Skåne. In Derek Gregory & John Urry (eds.): *Social relations and spatial structures.* Basingstone: Macmillan, 337–365.

Raitio, K. 1913. *Jyväskylän Seminaarin 50-vuotinen toiminta. Katsaus sen syntyyn ja vaiheisiin* [The 50 years of the Jyväskylä Teacher Training College. An overview of its establishment and development]. Jyväskylä: Gummerus.

Rotenberg, Robert 1993. Introduction. In Robert Rotenberg & Gary McDonogh (eds.): *The cultural meaning of urban space.* Westport: Bergin & Garvery, xi–xix.

Saarikangas, Kirsi 1996. Katseita, kohtaamisia, kosketuksia. Tilassa muodustuvat merkitykset [Gazes, encounters, touches. Significances formed in space]. *Tiede ja edistys* (4), 306–318.

Tommila, Päiviö 1972. *Jyväskylän kaupungin historia 1837–1965* [The history of the town of Jyväskylä 1837–1965]. Jyväskylä: Jyväskylän kaupunki.

171

Everyday Knowledge and Remembrances
– The Town Dwellers' Views

PIRJO KORKIAKANGAS

# Steps to the Past

## The Town of Jyväskylä From the Perspective of Autobiographical Memory[1]

*[handwritten annotations: "title annotations ok"; "This paper takes the auto-biographical statements of people (15) + then constructs a sort of collective understanding of the town as a place. but leaning upon the experience of individuals to do so."]*

Memory is like an anti-museum: it cannot be delimited or located and only fragments of it emerge through reminiscence. In reminiscence there are also gaps, in which the past dozes. Memory awakens through narratives, and although the places that are reminisced about are present as images and memories, they are also gone. The memories bind the reminiscing person to the places that are a part of his/her personal history and meaningful to him/her in particular. The place-specific individual memories are some kind of mental histories, which unfold to others only through the narratives of the person those memories belong to. (de Certeau 1984, 108.)

When beginning to reminisce about our lives, we tend to construct them into chronological continua that we conceive as being real and having actually happened as such. The memory is not as straightforward as this, however; the life that is being reminisced about is composed and constructed of different recollections and images of events, sometimes strong and vivid, sometimes merely passing through our minds. As humans, however, we prefer organisation to chaos, and when reminiscing, we perceive our lives as coherent entities composed of individual details and temporal organisation, following narrative logic. Janina Bauman (2000, 338) has given the following outline of the characteristics of reminiscence from the point of view of an autobiographer:

> Writing an autobiography involves inventing, or even creating, a significant pattern of one's own personal history. It requires a selection of memories in accordance with this pattern. The selection is the first task but by no means the only one. Memories emerge as tiny pieces, with smaller or larger gaps always left in between. Tiny pieces do not constitute a narrative. In order to create a narrative, the author must fill in the gaps and smoothly and credibly join the individual pieces together. This is where imagination enters the picture, imagination with an idea of authenticity to it: this could have happened. No autobiography can ever be written without this fictive touch.

In her text, Bauman discusses authors and their ways to prepare an autobiographical work, but her thoughts can be more generally applied to both the study of reminiscence and the reminiscence of one's own life without literary pressure. A person's life and life narrative consist of the endless flow of individual events, personal event memories. The events are biographically connected: the focus of the reminiscence has thus widened from the "self" to the entire event and to its consideration from an autobiographical perspective. This, of course, raises the question: what determines which individual events are preserved as memories which are consciously reminisced about and which may later affect our lives, us not even being aware of it. An essential feature of these kind of memories is that they are conceived as some kind of milestones or turning points in one's own course of life, and they help the reminiscing person to understand and interpret him/herself as well as his/her whole life. (Pillemer 1998, 1–4.)

In the following, I shall look at the town of Jyväskylä as a discourse of steps, as it were, a mental landscape reminisced about by the town dwellers.[2] The discussion does not focus on the monuments or monumental locations generally recognised by the town's residents but on the lived spaces of individual people (cf. Lefebvre 1994 [1974]; Lynch 1968, 1–4), which have (or have had) meaning as monuments of their individual course of life. As places of individual autobiographical reminiscence, these monuments could, in principle, be situated anywhere. What binds them to a certain location, and to a certain time, is the life environment of the narrator and the identification with a place that wells forth from it; the identification consists of both individual and shared mental images which characterise the place in question. The ideas, memories and experiences of identity which are connected with the place also involve locating oneself; the question "where am I?" raises the question "who am I?". Thus, the place identities, as well as the process of locating oneself, are produced through experience and reminiscence. (See Vilkuna 1996, 8.)

The tripartition of social space by Lefebvre (1994 [1974]) has been examined as interrelationships between spatiality and temporality. According to Simonsen (1991, 427–430), spatiality manifests itself in three dimensions: as institutional spatiality, which refers to the structural and communal level of the social production of space; as lived space, that is, the meanings that individuals and groups attach to the space; and as individual spatial practices, in which the spatiality refers to the physical presence of individuals and groups and their spatial interaction. The interaction between an individual and the community culminates temporally and spatially in the individual biographies and life stories. Individual conceptions and experiences of temporality and spatiality are associated with conceptions of generations, spatiality and identity. Simonsen's (1991, 429) concept of a situated life story illustrates the temporal-spatial contextualisation of an individual person; the analysis of a situated life story focuses on examining chains of events, causing the significance of individual events to be conceived as dependent on the entire "life project".

*Place memories in the perspective of individual and shared history*

This article is based on material constituted of what could be called situated life stories. Different places are reminisced about autobiographically, as belonging to the different events of life. Individual situated memories are bound to a time in the narrator's life that he/she considers important and besides that, to a common, collectively experienced time and history. Individual and collective history intertwine in a way which causes the individual spatial experience to expand in reminiscence past the individual or even a family's shared experience.

When the time being reminisced about is at a long temporal distance, as is the case when an elderly person reminisces about his/her childhood, for example, the reminiscing person finds situating him/herself very important. It is a different time and a different place, the reminiscence is very reflective and the reminiscing person situates him/herself both temporally and spatially. Although reminiscence is very individual and autobiographical, situating oneself becomes easier if the reminiscence can be joined with a collectively shared experience and history. Thus, the historical, collectively recognised and historically verifiable event frames the individual experience and its memory.

> Well, we moved then to Jyväskylä and my father was, the parliament in Helsinki used to assemble in the Heimola hotel at the time, and Helsinki was back then, there was also the war going on the war you call either the war of independence or the civil war whichever way you prefer. - - Helsinki was under a red command. You couldn't get out. My father was in hiding and they had to, they had to hide him a little there was an MP that was murdered even. So then, my father couldn't come home, I hadn't seen him. As a baby we had moved to Jyväskylä and I hadn't seen my father in maybe sixteen months. And then when there was this man who came to visit from Karstula who was about the same size and, - - a small slender man who wore glasses like my father. I thought it was him I ran towards him and shouted dad is here. First the joy, and and then the disappointment and then the shame that I had thought a strange man was my father, and this these strong emotions made it stick in my mind it's the first memory the first thing I can remember myself. (Woman 1916; the narrator was about two years old at the time of the incident.)

This excerpt can be characterised as a personal event memory. It describes an event which took place in a certain place at a certain time and which concerns the narrator's own personal environment at the time of the event. The memory also covers a spectrum of distinct emotions, ranging from joy to disappointment and further to a strong feeling of shame. The narrator herself believes that her recollection is real, and quite special even: she thinks of it as her first childhood memory. Rather typically, she makes use of her emotional experience as evidence for the reality of the event. (See Pillemer 1998, 50–52.) On the other hand, the personal event memory is part of a more general chain of events – the independence war of 1918 and its effects on a family in Jyväskylä.

The First and the Second World War act as important watersheds and means of outlining joint memories, especially for the Europeans (Connerton 1989, 20; Passerini 1992). Experienced individually, the historical turning points intertwine naturally with the different stages of life, different times and different places. Time, or a strictly determinate moment in time, thus turns into a secondary concept. It has significance only when included in the frame of individual or collective history, where it has a sense or a position from the point of view of experience. When experienced, time grows multilayered: the past point of time is part of our past, which we look at from the present time. Time gives perspective for the way we interpret our individual and collective past and present. For individual memories, however, the period of life is essential in which the individually touching event, which can also be associated with the experience of collective history, has taken place. The memories of childhood experiences, in particular, are completely different and have completely different effects than the memories of other stages of life. (Korkiakangas 1996, 34; Korkiakangas 1997; Elder et al. 1993.)

Furthermore, it is understandable that upsetting childhood experiences may intermix with things that the person hears about later, like in the following citation, where the narrator reminisces about the Second World War. He was three years old at the time of the incident. In fact, Jyväskylä was bombed only during the Winter War, in the last days of 1939. In the Continuation War of 1941–1944, Jyväskylä was spared from actual enemy bombings but there were frequent air-raid alerts, especially in 1944 (Tommila 1972, 567–570), the year the narrator reminisces about. One particular air-raid alert has stuck in his mind as a traumatic memory, his only memory of the war. As regards location, the memory is mainly anchored to the working-class neighbourhood of Halssila. In spite of its traumatic nature, the memory also incorporates many features of a vivid memory (Conway 1995; see Korkiakangas 1996), that is, auditory images and strong emotions, in particular – the howling sirens of air surveillance, the thunder of the bombings assumed by the narrator, the crying children. The entire memory is characterised by anxiety and fear of death:

> Of the war I remember clearly this one stage when in forty-four Jyväskylä was bombed, and my mother grabbed my brother put a blanket around him and took my hand and... cried that now we're going to the woods, we could hear the sirens, the sirens howling. Every woman from Halssilanmäki hill ran with their children down to the woods. And then there was the booming noise.- - Of course there was other bombings too but that one was, we got into a real panic - - the planes they got so, right above us - - and that crying when, the children were lugged into the woods. That's the only memory I have of the war. (Man 1941.)

The traumatic emotions remain when the narrator reminisces about the life after the war, a time when the family was lacking even in food. Their home was still in Halssila (on the Halssilanmäki hill), and the narrator went to a school that was two miles away from their house. The narrator's school years were overshadowed by the shame he felt for his family's straits and for his own "defects". He had poor eyesight and was therefore the first person in his school to wear glasses: "They really made me suffer for that so I always came home crying. They called me four-eyes. Then little by little, they gave it up." The narrator has fond memories of his teacher, however. Apparently she was aware of the situation in the boy's family and gave him little tasks to do after school to help them: he held the skeins of yarn while the teacher coiled them, he shook the carpets, etc. This gave yet another reason for the other children to bully him: "They bullied me about that too. Teacher's pet and that sort of thing. But I did it to get milk and buns and biscuits afterwards." However, the most tormenting shame, still bothering him as an adult, was caused by the family's poverty and their need to resort to the post-war social security:

> But this one thing that I will also remember for the rest of my life is - - after the war they gave out food at Halssila school. And I was the eldest child so I always had to go get it, with a milk churn. In the winter they always warned me don't slip, that is the family's main meal for the day. Or all there was. They gave me a two-three litre churn and a few plates of crisp bread. Halssila school was about one and a half miles away from Halssilanmäki hill. And I carry the churn and I'm scared of falling and then it happened once that, I fell and the churn flew from my hand and, it all ran to the ground. I couldn't go back home. I sat there by the side of the road cried and ate the crisp bread. Then, I remember it was getting dark and I was really scared - -. Then my father came walking, he had guessed. - - He saw me I'm crying it's not my fault I... He said it's okay we have some bread at home, don't cry now. All that has kind of stuck in my mind, - - I still remember how the churn flew from my hand and, there it went the potato soup. (Man 1941.)

A situated life story seems to follow the same kind of pattern in reminiscence as life stories in general. The reminiscence proceeds by the different stages of life, some external change or personally significant event characterising each new stage. In change, the place may act merely as a frame, as in the previous citations. On the other hand, a change in the physical environment always brings something new and different on the level of experience, too. Different places of residence within the same town usually clearly divide into periods the reminiscence of the person's own and, more generally, the town's course of life. In the foregoing citations the narrators use the historic period, the wartime and the depression that followed it, as a background for their individual childhood events. The memories are also connected with particular places that have been of significance to the person's own life history. The spatiality is thus associated with the individual time, or the events that have taken place in the person's life. The mode of life model employed by Simonsen (1991) incorporates the idea that temporality and spatiality are closely bound together and that this bond directs the choices and the time allocation of an individual or a family. Upon reminiscence, the situated life stories tend to proceed from one dwelling to the other. The memories of the living environments of different periods may give an impression of being, and partly even are, of photograph-like precision and portray the times and the common way of life as well as the individual life story. This is the case in the following excerpt, which resumes the reminiscence of the lady born in 1916 of Jyväskylä of her childhood days. Her reminiscence paints a picture of the lifestyle and goings-on of a small rural town in the early 20th century.

> Well, the first place in Jyväskylä which my father had got for us before joining the parliament, that was in 6 Kalevankatu street, a very modest flat, it was a three-family house, right next to the street, and a plank fence surrounded the rather large site, the owner of the house even had a small potato patch there and a kind of a garden. On the other side of the yard there was an outhouse, where there was a privy and a shed, each tenant had their own corner in the shed and, took care of it themselves, the house was heated with wood. And then there was a tool and coach house, because the owner of the house, he had a farm too, in Kuikka, and he had horses there too so from time to time he would come with the horses to town, and he needed a place for the cart or the sleigh, and a small stall where he put the horse. So all these were in the outhouse that was on the other side of the yard. (Woman 1916.)

Next, the family moved to a quarter by the name of Älylä. As its name – a place where intelligence abounds – suggests, the area was a conglomeration of villas and gardens owned by the lecturers and professors of the Jyväskylä Teacher Training College and later those of the College of Education. Almost the entire Älylä[3] was built in a very short period of time between 1912 and 1914. As regards its population, the area was socially very homogenous: it was the residential area of the town's then prevailing cultural elite. There are still some representatives of the old cultured families living in Älylä at present, and it is the only one of the older residential areas of Jyväskylä that still mainly consists of wooden houses. The cultural heritage of the area is further fostered by the museums that have been built there: the Museum of Central Finland in the verdant upper part of the area in 1960 and the Alvar Aalto Museum in the site of Juho Mikkola's house, the former head of the Jyväskylä Teacher Training College, in 1972–73. (Kiiski 1976, 217, 242.) The narrator, the lady born in 1916, continues her reminiscence:

> Well then, the time came that my uncles' and aunts' children got old enough for secondary school, and at that time there were no secondary schools in Karstula or in any other rural commune for that matter - -. The schools in Jyväskylä had a better reputation and you applied here of course, and, as they happened to have some relatives here the parents began bargaining that couldn't we take the children that they wouldn't have to send them to live with strangers. So our house became a boarding house. It was, we were five, our family, and then suddenly we had four school children living with us and then two young bank clerks whose homes were outside Jyväskylä so they needed a place to stay in Jyväskylä and they worked with my sister. So suddenly we were a household of twelve people. And this flat of three rooms and a kitchen where there wasn't even, well the water came in and went out. Those were the only facilities. But there were no loos, let alone bathrooms so we used a public sauna whenever we needed to use a sauna. But then we found, the Jussila house in Älylä - -.

- - Jussila[4] himself lived in a house along the street it was a kind of light greenish grey or something, and then there was, the gable facing the street - - a red house - - and he rented the red house to us. But it turned out to be too cramped, there was only, downstairs there was, a dining room, two other rooms and an alcove. And one room upstairs. So there wasn't really room for twelve people. We somehow managed to live there for a year, a little over a year. And then Ojala, the head of the seminar, he died, and he was replaced by Mikkola. [The family moved to Juho Mikkola's house.] - - There were rooms on two floors. Downstairs there was a drawing-room, a dining room, three bedrooms and a kitchen so five rooms downstairs, and upstairs there were two normal-size rooms and one smaller, like a maid's room, so there was enough room even for us. Two people were put in each room so nobody had to sleep in the drawing-room. - - I was the odd one out and I slept on the sofa in the dining room.

During the narrator's childhood years, the family moved house once again but they still stayed in Älylä:

- - we lived in three different flats, the last one was, it is still standing like the Jussila house, it was built then. I guess my mother got tired of taking care of the household for such a big lot and my sister's husband had died and my other sister had moved to Helsinki, so there was only my father, my mother and me left then. - - it made no sense us having such a big house, there was a two-storey house being built on the opposite side of the street - - and it was the first house which had, we had a bathroom and a loo. There was a loo in the two houses in Älylä but there was no bathroom instead there was a sauna in both of them. - - They also had, privies even though there were loos too both of these houses in Älylä had a privy, and when it was warm the school children [who lived at home] went in there to share their secrets. Why would have one wanted to queue for the loo, with twelve people there was always a queue. (Woman 1916.)

In a few years time (in the early 1930's), after the father of the family had died, the mother and daughter moved to Helsinki. In the 1960's, the narrator returned for a few years to Jyväskylä, her childhood home. In a way, the moves followed the development of the present-day Jyväskylä university, which the narrator finds to have had a distinct effect on the town's development. She moved with her mother to Helsinki approximately four years before the Jyväskylä Teacher Training College changed into the College of Education (in 1934), when the "secondary school graduates, the studying secondary school graduates became part of the town's life". When she returned to Jyväskylä for the first time, the college changed into a university (in 1966) and "then the town really changed". In a few years time, the narrator moved to Tampere and back to Jyväskylä again in the early 1980's when she retired. In her old age, the narrator's reminiscence seems to concentrate on her childhood days spent with her family in Jyväskylä of wooden houses, whose townscape began to change, however, in the 1920's and 1930's through the emergence of multi-storey stone and brick houses to complement the already existing population of small two-storey stone and brick houses. Before 1930, there were altogether nineteen two-storey houses made of stone or brick in central

*The centre of Jyväskylä in the 1930's and 1940's. Photo: Museum of Central Finland, Picture Archives, Jyväskylä.*

Jyväskylä; by the mid-1970's, more than one third of these houses had been demolished to give way to bigger high-rise buildings.[5] The emergence of the first multi-storey houses in the 1920's and 1930's foreshadowed the shift from a town of low wooden houses to a town of high-rise buildings made of stone and brick. (Jäppinen 1976, 103–107.)

In the reminiscence of the narrator (woman 1916), the stone and brick house tour in central Jyväskylä of the late 1920's begins from the Vaherto house which was built in that period and which is still standing in the lower end of Kauppakatu street; the building is commonly known as the old brick house:

> The last years we were here as a family they started to build those stone and brick houses [multi-storey]. The first one was the red brick house there the one they call the old brick house. And I got to know it because in our school they gave an order that everyone must go to a doctor's check-up. And the doctor we had to see, a few girls at a time, lived in the old red brick house. And it had the first lift. The house had four floors. (Woman 1916.)

The tour proceeds along Kauppakatu street from one building to another, from bank to bank, and then back again. At the same time the narrator meanders on different time levels – the past and the present:

> The Kansallispankki building or the Merita Pankki building did exist back then but it was rather lower I think they have made it higher since then. It didn't use to have any lifts. And then, after that came the Gummerus house and that was an event too, I remember it when the corner crashed down when it was under construction. That created a sensation in

*Kirkkopuisto park and Kauppakatu street in winter in the 1930's or 1940's. On the right, the building of the Säästöpankki bank, which was finished in 1930. Photo: Museum of Central Finland, Picture Archives, Jyväskylä.*

Jyväskylä there was a fault in it. The higher corner when it was still under construction it suddenly collapsed. There was a miscalculation. And then the Keskisuomalainen newspaper building was made higher an extra floor was added. And they started to build a Säästöpankki bank in the corner. But Yhdyspankki was still in the old red building. - - There were two big banks, these commercial banks. They both had their own buildings in Kauppakatu street, Kansallispankki is still in its place but where Yhdyspankki used to be there is the big Jyväskeskus shopping centre now. The bank was there but before that there was a smaller red building on that spot that was rather an elegant building. (Woman 1916.)

The narrator clearly remembers how the southern end of the five-storey commercial and residential house of the publishing company Gummerus suddenly collapsed when it was being built in the crossing of Gummeruksenkatu and Kauppakatu streets in October 1928. The building was finally completed in 1930 and, on the outside, it has remained almost the same since then. A cinema by the name of Opiksi ja Huviksi (For Education and Entertainment) – the first one in Jyväskylä designed for that specific purpose – was demolished from the site of the new building; the cinema was designed by Yrjö Blomstedt, an architect and a lecturer in the Jyväskylä Teacher Training College, and completed in 1909. (Kydén & Salmela 2000, 72–73). The informant remembers the rather peculiar-looking house from her childhood as different experiences and visual images:

*Kauppakatu street on the right, and Kirkkopuisto park on the left in summer in the 1910's. In the middle, the cinema Opiksi ja Huviksi (For Education and Entertainment). Photo: Museum of Central Finland, Picture Archives, Jyväskylä.*

> And then there was Opiksi ja Huviksi. I thought it was such a lovely name, it was there in the place of the Gummerus house. - - It was a very elegant long wooden house and at both ends there was a round gable. And circling the round gable there was a string of tiny torches, and inside the string of torches there was the name, also in a curve Opiksi ja Huviksi. I remember that I went to see at least Kalle Andersson it was one of these guttersnipe films, they had these children's films too. And then there were Chaplin films with that little boy - - who wore ragged baggy trousers and who had round brown eyes and a cap with the peak at an angle. (Woman 1916.)

Kauppakatu ("commercial street") is the oldest street name in Jyväskylä, dating back to 1838, the year following the town's foundation. As its name suggests, Kauppakatu street has been the main street for commercial activity in Jyväskylä from the very beginning, and its central position has further strengthened since the 1860's and 1870's. (Jäppinen & Fredrikson 1995, 10–13; Jäppinen 1976, 126–128.) Kauppakatu street is best known as a banking street, as the narrator recounted earlier. Of the buildings that she mentioned, the four-storey Kansallis-Osake-Pankki building was the biggest high-rise building in town when it was completed in 1915. The rivalry over the number of floors was launched by the two-storey Suomen Yhdyspankki in 1899; Pohjoismaiden Osakepankki (Pohjoismaiden Yhdyspankki since 1919) raised the number of floors by one and Kansallis-Osake-Pankki further increased it by one. A Säästöpankki bank was raised opposite the former in 1930 – higher than any of the other buildings. Finally, Pohjoismaiden Yhdyspankki won the day by having its old commercial building pulled down and replacing it with a seven-storey building in 1955. (Jäppinen & Fredrikson 1995, 24–25.)

184

## Jyväskylä of memories – an idyll of wooden houses

> Looking at the town from the lake, you could see a beautiful, leafy park with the gables and roofs of low wooden houses appearing here and there. Today these houses are – elsewhere than in the areas of Seminaarinmäki and Älylä – reduced to only a few samples of the precious cultural period that we have lost. The pleasant wooden houses that were a joy to look at, the entire integrated wooden house town has disappeared. Of the thousand oldest wooden houses from the turn of the century, only about twenty have survived. Today, faceless and stiff concrete buildings leave their cold and monotonous mark on the town. (Tissari 1987, 27.)

Usually, when reminiscing about old Jyväskylä, the narrator "walks" through the wooden house town, the town of memories, and reminisces about Jyväskylä that no longer exists. Until the beginning of the 1950's, the general appearance of Jyväskylä was that of a rather small, even sleepy, rural town, whose peacefulness was emphasised by the harmony of its low wooden houses. After the Second World War, however, at the close of the 1940's and in the 1950's, the town's unhurried lifestyle underwent a critical change of course, which was further accelerated in the 1960's and 1970's: the small wooden house town was transformed into a medium-sized town of stone and brick houses. The town's population increased from the little over ten thousand in the 1940's to the thirty thousand in the 1950's. This was mainly due to the incorporation of Tourula, Halssila, Nisula and Lohikoski, areas outside the then existing town proper that were inhabited mostly by industrial workers, into Jyväskylä in 1941 and also by the settling of 4 000 evacuees. The new town dwellers were in desperate need of housing and this is why the low wooden houses had to give way to high-rise buildings. During the following decades the rate of growth became faster and faster, and finally in the 1960's and 1970's, the town and especially its centre had undergone a complete transformation. Culturally and historically important buildings and architecturally harmonious blocks of wooden houses were systematically and mercilessly pulled down: at the close of the 1960's no more than one fifth of all residential houses dated back to the time before the Second World War. (Ojala 1999, 27–28, 66–67; Jäppinen 1997, 278–283.) Therefore, it is highly understandable that the decades of upheaval do not inspire reminiscence in the town dwellers; their memories tend to go back to earlier times.

The changes in the overall appearance of Jyväskylä during the last decades naturally also draw the narrators into comparing the lost town of memories with Jyväskylä of today. The reminiscence conveys a regret for the destruction of all things old; the old building population has had to give way to new, more urban one. The town administration and the decision-makers, however, prefer a completely different set of values in marketing the image of Jyväskylä – they portray the town as an example of dynamic development. Although the town dwellers largely accept this image, Jyväskylä of the old days appears as more genuine and real in the minds of those who still remember it. The current rate of change and development remains mainly a source of astonishment. The feelings of the town dwellers are summed up in the following

185

account of the lady introduced earlier, born in 1916, about her return to her home town after retiring:

> Well when I next came to Jyväskylä, after Tampere, then almost everything here had disappeared. Old. I'm under the impression that, of old wooden Jyväskylä they have left here the railway station and the Kaupunginhotelli hotel to show how it used to be. They are in the middle of the town, and it seems they don't tear them down while they have mercilessly pulled down everything else. Well then there is of course the Älylä end and Seminaarinmäki hill where there are these, private villas. (Woman 1916.)

Along with the wooden house town, the narrators feel that they have lost the spaciousness, tranquillity and personality of the town – these are the features that the lady who moved to Jyväskylä in 1940 misses in her written reminiscence. Although she writes in a matter-of-fact style, the sentimental tone of simple nostalgia (Davis 1979) may be detected in the writer's text about the old way of life and the past living environment:

> With Helmi, my friend from the women's auxiliary defence services, we were released from service at the end of May 1940. That was the end of my war. - - My fiancé got a job in the Kivääritehdas state rifle factory in Jyväskylä. We were married on 21 July 1940 in Punkaharju church. - - The next day we went to Jyväskylä where my husband had managed to rent a two-room flat in a single-family house in Mäki-Matti area. My mother-in-law, my sister-in-law and my brother-in-law all came there, they got a flat in the same yard. Both of our sons were born in that house - -. It had a peaceful yard and an entire area full of old wooden houses, near Cygnaeus school. I had water on the knee in 1945 and my little son wheeled me to the school to vote, for the first time. - - The town was a beautiful wooden house town. It is a shame that the old houses were pulled down and replaced by those stone monsters. Especially in Kauppakatu street they pulled down the beautiful old SYP bank building made of brick – the wooden house town disappeared and the town lost its individuality. (Woman 1918.)

Our constructed environment is in a circle of constant change; change is perceived exclusively as a feature of the modern times, despite the fact that this is not the first time the building population of a town is renewed nor the first time there is a need for it. Nevertheless, in Jyväskylä the development has been directed towards the destruction of the past, and it seems to be very difficult for many town dwellers to adapt to the rate of development. It is also felt that the new and the modern cannot possibly compensate for the losses:

> And I remember those beautiful gates there were those board gates and the wooden houses and the beautiful carvings in the window frames, and then came all the machines and fancy equipment then all they can make is straight walls with or without holes. And bland. And then those beautiful like where nowadays is Gummeruksenkatu street there used to be the old wooden houses and the old chemist's there was this lovely, I remember

186

the, there were those beautiful diamond-shaped windows and different colour glass. (Woman 1944.)

Above all, people want to remember Jyväskylä as a wooden house town, characterised by low commercial and residential houses. As such, the image is collective and unites the towndwellers who remember the time in question. In the reminiscence, one can detect a touch of nostalgia, in which the people and the way of life of a small town are joined together with a pleasant and controllable environment. Within the general framework, small details of individual buildings are also remembered – those in particular that are no longer part of the town scape. In the same way as the previous informant, many others, too, stopped in their reminiscence at the corner of the old chemist's of Jyväskylä, which was situated in Gummeruksenkatu street and built in 1861. Their attention was drawn especially to its entrance porch decorated with coloured polygon windows. The chemist's operated in the same building for a hundred years; in 1964 the building as well as the other wooden houses on the same site were pulled down to make room for a seven-storey residential house (Kydén & Salmela 2000, 67–69).

As structural details, the informants reminisced about fences, gates and peculiar tower constructions typical to wooden house towns;[6] as a sample of the latter, a tower has been preserved in the Jyväskylä City Education Department (formerly the Kaupunginhotelli hotel, cf. citation on page 186). Characteristically to autobiographical reminiscence, however, the leading role is played by an event connected with the physical object of reminiscence:

> - - the gate to which I stuck my tongue and when I wanted something from my mother. I had noticed of course how it scared my mother to see me there my tongue stuck to the gate. - - So I remember that gate and how I often used to sit on the street outside the gate, and mum said that each passer-by thought I was leaving. - - And I remember saying to this one woman I said that I will go with you and she said darling I live so far away I live there on the other side of the lake [Jyväsjärvi lake]. And you see then you went, the transportation was by boat then, there were no bridges, so I said it's okay I can go there with you. (Woman 1944.)

The narrator's reminiscence proceeds to the police station (built in 1888) which stood next to her house, and quite especially to a small workshop built in its yard in the early 20th century. The workshop was renovated in 1948 to accommodate the drunks arrested by the police. Both buildings were demolished in 1970 to give way to a car park and a new police station designed by Alvar Aalto. (Kydén & Salmela 2000, 110–113.) On the cell wall close to the ceiling there was a small barred window, under which the narrator stops in her reminiscence:

> I felt so sorry I didn't understand why those men had to be in jail in the hot summer weather because I heard sounds because the barred windows were open. So then - - you know we stood there and sang Christmas carols because we wanted to be nice to them. In the middle of the summer - - there too I remember the feeling, how it made me feel bad so I think

that my social nature is a kind of an inborn thing since I was a child, and which has continued ever since. (Woman 1944.)

Opposite the narrator's house and its iron gate was a wooden house which had a dairy in its stone foundation; the narrator recalls that her father called the shop a "maid's shop". In her reminiscence, the narrator expresses many vivid memories about the dairy, which portray the everyday routine of a little girl and the future dreams that the routine generated. In her written remi-niscence, the narrator carries her dream and the possibility of its realisation through decades, as it were, and the childhood memory thus reflects the dif-ferent stages of development in milk processing and sales:

I leaned against the counter with my hand on my cheek and marvelled the lady who tilted my steel milk jug against the side of the churn which stood on the floor, and with one graceful move of her wrist poured the milk in the churn with a long-handled measure. The steel measure made a nice clanging sound when it hit the brim of the churn. I dreamt that I would be a dairy lady when I grew up. I would wear a white coat and a starched hood on my head. My dream was dashed. First came the bottled milk, then milk bags and finally milk in cartons. Even the cream measured in a small jug with a long-handled measure changed into bottled Vuokko or Atlanta cream, and the cream made with my aunt's whirring separator wasn't real cream. That tasted of cow, too. (Woman 1944.)

The narrator grew very familiar with the centre of Jyväskylä in the 1950's: being the only child in the family, she also entertained herself by watching the life of the town – either by sitting in front of their own gate or by making journeys of exploration to the town streets:

Very often I found the spacious yard too small for me. There was a young man living in the house at the back, and he helped my mother by fetching me back from my flights. There was a chemist's in the next block.. The glass veranda of the old wooden house had different colour diamond-shaped windows. The storeroom in the stone foundation of the veranda was a real treasure trove. We used to slip in there with the son of the pharmacist every now and then. In the storeroom, there was the smell of liniment, camphor and sweet cough mixture, even though they were not stored there. But there were high stacks of beautifully coloured paper caps that were used to cover the medicine bottles. When I wanted to play at being a lady, I went into a shoe-shop [Kenkäkauppa Eira] that was in the same street. If there was nobody else in the shop, the saleswomen would attend to me. The previous time I had been there, I had been rejected. For the following time, I planned a bluff to ensure my being served. I decided to speak in a proper, elegant way. I practised a distinguished-looking walk in the street. I let my arms hang down by my sides and slowly moved my shoulders back and forth, slightly moving my hips at the same time. I stretched myself to my full five-year-old's height. I lifted my chin up and was certain that the saleswomen would take me for an adult. - - I sailed into the shop and nodded my head as a nonchalant and dignified greeting. "May I fit on the click-click shoes?" My plan worked. The high-heeled shoes clattered on my feet when I turned around in front of the mirror. I cannot remember if the saleswomen smiled at me. (Woman 1944.)

The signboards of the shops gave their own distinct flavour to the streets of the wooden house town: with their texts they were like compact advertisements. In the reminiscence of Jyväskylä of past decades, these kind of details may serve two purposes: they anchor the reminiscing person either to the concrete object of reminiscence, a building, or to personal events in the person's own life history. Proceeding from one "landmark" to another, the reminiscence creates a life story which is spatially and temporally coherent. (Pillemer 1998, 95–98.) Thus, as objects of reminiscence, these landmarks are both physical and mental. They guide the reminiscence spatially, and they also contain personal event memories which are factualised by historical reality. In other words, the impression of realness is strengthened by the fact that the memory includes collectively acceptable features. Like in the following citation, reminiscence functions in two ways: the informant remembers that she learnt the letters f and b when walking in town with her mother and asking her about the texts in the signboards, anxious to know what they meant. Decades later, in her old age, she still remembers the name of a specific shop through the memory the incident left in her mind.

> I still clearly remember how I learnt the letters f and b. My mother used to take me with her when she, went to run errands she couldn't, my father was at work and the big girls were at school and my mother went into town so she took me with her, and I always asked when there were signboards above the shops. The finest draper's shop in Jyväskylä it was there, opposite Kirkkopuisto park in Kauppakatu street in the middle, in the central lot, and there, was in big letters the name of the shop owner Lida Forsblom and that is where I learnt f and b. I asked what is that that's like an e but without the cross-line and, what is that that's a bit like a d but with two of those round things and that is how I learnt f and b. This is why I still remember Forsblom's name. (Woman 1916.)

Ellida Forsblom's boutique and draper's shop Lida Forsblom Oy operated in Kauppakatu street until the depression of the 1920's: it was the leading shop in its trade for three decades. By the latter half of the century, the building was badly deteriorated – it was one of the last spared wooden buildings – and it was demolished in 1960. (Kydén & Salmela 2000, 81–82.) The reminiscence of old Jyväskylä constructed in wood serves as an answer to the need to find something stable, especially in the midst of the development which began in the 1960's and 1970's and which still continues – the development which has caused the constant change in the town scape of Jyväskylä. Characteristically to reminiscence, the past environments, which are felt to be permanent even when they are gone, are preserved as material for both individual and collective reminiscence. They are permanent as memory traces. By reminiscing about Jyväskylä of the old days, even with a trace of nostalgia, one deliberately controls forgetting. One remembers the past as one wants to remember it, even though the positive sides of the town's current development are also acknowledged – the increased tidiness of the town centre and the facilitating effect of the pedestrian streets on walking, shopping and taking care of other errands. It seems, however, that remembering and forgetting do not go hand in hand. Instead, by remembering we emphasise the need for preservation in order to express our appreciation of the past.

## Roaming the streets

Timo Kopomaa (1997, 27–28) has described urban space as a collective commodity: it is open for many users simultaneously, an object of shared use and consumption. Each person uses the space as an individual but he/she is still dependent on the rules, norms and conventions concerning the use of the space. In Jyväskylä of the 1950's it was still the custom that the adherence to the rules was supervised by beat policemen, who used to walk in pairs, maintaining order. Gatherings in public places were strictly regulated: in the streets, for example, it was prohibited to stay in one place even with a small group. Kopomaa refers to Foucault's idea of discipline dividing people spatially. According to Foucault, the street is a totalitarian institution of society, an element of discipline. The informants remember that in Jyväskylä of the 1950s the groups of young people that gathered in the streets and wandered about were under particularly strict surveillance:

> And then you see in town there was this, walking around the block it has always been but of course it was different at that time even though we were so, young people and the youth of today, we behaved really well, thinking about it now. - - Back then we walked Asemakatu, Yliopistonkatu, Väinönkatu, Kauppakatu streets. This circle. We went round and when we started to feel dizzy we went round the other way, and you see in the Yliopistonkatu and Väinönkatu street crossing there was Oro's hardware store and where there's a chemist's now there are those broad kind of, window ledges, so when we felt tired we would sit there every now and then but at that time there was a beat policeman he did the same round all night long. Wearing a long robe and a fur cap in the winter too the policeman walked slowly, the same route all night long, and then, when we sat on the window ledge if certain policemen approached you knew they were a bit crabby, so, when we saw him coming, at the other end of the street, that's when we got up and started walking but when there was a nice policeman, we just sat and, he walked past us and said move it move it, and we took back to walking. It was fun for us. (Woman 1944.)

> We wandered about in town and. And spat and. Also the only time in my life I landed in jail was when I, we were four mates and. We just walked there the usual Kauppakatu, Asemakatu, Kilpisenkatu, Väinönkatu streets this circle round that block. In the early fifties, in fifty-five, six you were not allowed to gather like this. The police were you see, always two and they, said break up you are not allowed to gather and. We had hair pomade and these, hats on and we spat and, the first time they said now boys clear off and stop that spitting, but we didn't we were back in no time. I guess they got fed up with us then they took us into jail, they kept us in jail for three hours because we, had gathered and spat there, on Kauppakatu street. (Man 1941.)

190

*The pedestrian street in the centre of Jyväskylä in 1999. Photo: Memory Archives of Central Finland, Jyväskylä.*

Wandering the streets can be regarded as a manifestation of youth culture, to which the youth of today, asscmbling in the centre of Jyväskylä at the weekends, is an extension. The stretch of Kauppakatu street which is closed from traffic for pedestrian use and the shopping centres along it, in particular, serve as meeting points for people of all ages – and especially the young. In the same way as before, the gatherings of young people are not always looked at approvingly, and some of the youngsters themselves admit being tired of loitering in the shopping centres and on the steps in front of them. (Junkala & Sääskilahti 1999, 58–66.) It is true, however, that there are not many other places available in the town centre which would be suitable for their daily get-togethers.

The emergence of international youth culture in Finland is dated to have taken place in the 1950's when the distinctive features of youth culture, such as boys' hats and hairdos styled in a special way with hair pomade, contributed to the unification of youth fashion, dress style and behaviour. (Heiskanen & Mitchell 1985.) Even before the behavioural and dress code by the name of youth culture had become common, the young people of Jyväskylä used to take certain routes in the streets of the town. At the time, the territories were based on the level of education: those in secondary school walked on the right-hand side of Kauppakatu street, the others used the other side.

> At that time [the 1920's and 30's] the young people used to gather together in town in the evenings and at the weekends, in particular, mainly in Kauppakatu street. Then you walked back and forth all the way from Puistokatu street corner to Gummerus corner. The side of the street facing

191

the ridge, which had odd house numbers, was the "one mark side" and the side of the so-called bourgeoisie and the secondary school-goers. The side of even numbers was the "vintsa", or the fifty penny side, or at another time the 25 penny side, which was used by the working class youth. The "class division" was far from strict, however, and "dissidents" were well tolerated. - - When you got a little older you began to make eyes at an interesting girl whenever your paths crossed, walking back and forth. You would even turn right back to see that attractive girl more often. When the girl's look and behaviour suggested that she might accept you in her company, it gave you the courage to turn around straight after passing the girl, to walk beside her and to cautiously start a polite conversation. If the girl accepted your company the other girls would go their own way. Because it often happened that the girl had another fellow "in view", and then she would just lift up her nose and not join in the conversation. Then it was best to leave her alone. (Räsänen & Räsänen 1985, 37.)

The youth walking about the streets could also be described as idlers or, as Walter Benjamin (see Kopomaa 1997, 34) calls them, *flâneurs*: wandering about and observing the street life, they aim at seeing and at being seen. For adolescents, being seen, making an appearance, watching others and being the object of gazes is the main motive for gathering together. Like the youth of today, the Jyväskylä youngsters of the 1920's, 1930's and 1950's – boys with hair pomade in their hair, walking around the block – also wanted to be seen, but to stand out, too. In these examples, the streets and wandering about the streets are a part of the communication between the young, in which the meanings bound to both place and time are common to all the groups of young people roaming the streets. The police, on the other hand, have interpreted the stirring and gatherings of young people from their own frame of reference, and have acted accordingly in trying to break up the groups of young people.

The elderly town dwellers seem to think that the town centre functions quite well. The pedestrian street, almost the full length of which is kept unfrozen even in the winter by a heating system, serves as a safe passage from one shopping centre to the other. With the coming of the pedestrian street the town centre is regarded as having become tidier and better functioning in many ways. Moreover, in the summer the pedestrian street is looked upon as an oasis, which brings a breath of international atmosphere for the passers-by to enjoy.

> I was rather sceptical about the whole pedestrian street but now I have realised because there is the heating now, it stays unfrozen in the winter. So it's marvellous. I give it my blessing in that respect. What I was surprised by was that, how could they pull down all the houses along the street, make them hollow inside. They used to be full of apartments and offices. Suddenly there are no walls, just the corridor and there you zigzag your way, to the shops in different directions, it's as if they had suddenly become hollow, the old stone houses. They changed completely. (Woman 1916.)

192

It's true that it's a kind of an oasis in the summer, that you can go and sit there, there are those, what do you call those square things. Yes, seats - -. Many people sit there, and now there are those open-air bars, pubs and there's one in front of almost every house. - - It does feel nice when it's a warm day, it feels really relaxing to walk there, you don't have to wear much clothes, watch the people there's a lot of foreign tourists. (Woman 1927.)

In the reminiscences of the elderly people, in particular, the town is an organised whole, which is defined by the memories of the old wooden house town, on the one hand, and by the more vaguely conceived decades of change, the 1960's and 1970's, on the other hand. Although the town is still partly transforming into something new, all new things are not condemned on the basis of memories; instead, the current situation has to be taken under control, too. These efforts to achieve control are helped and supported by individual factors considered as having a positive effect on the town's development and general atmosphere, such as the pedestrian street.

## People and places

A town can be examined through the different images that it evokes in the town dwellers and in those who use the different areas and places of the town. These images can be physical, concerning buildings, spatial areas, borders or landmarks. The images may also accommodate more human, social and communal signs: in this case, the above street routes could be explained by social channels and points of contact, for example. (Lynch 1968, 123–139.) In reminiscence, the events and places of everyday life often also involve people who have stuck in the reminiscing person's mind particularly well: they serve as social landmarks and guide him/her through the places of his/her memories. The situated life story (Simonsen 1991, 429) is bound to time and place as narratives, the principal roles of which are played by the people who come to the mind of the reminiscing person as recollections and by their then ordinary daily lives. Upon reminiscence, however, the ordinary is transformed into extraordinary because its ordinary nature has become history. I shall illustrate this process by the mental wandering of the male informant, born in 1941, quoted above: in his mind, he wanders through the alleys of Halssila in Jyväskylä of his childhood days, and the people he "meets" guide him further in his childhood environment. The narrator's family, which in those days consisted of the parents and two sons, moved to Halssila from a single-room shack next to the Taulumäki church of Jyväskylä in 1943; they became the tenants of a Russian-born shopkeeper, and lived on the upper floor of his house in a flat of one chamber and a kitchen. The shop was downstairs. According to the narrator's recollection, the shopkeeper himself was a peculiar, superstitious man.

We lived there on Halssilanmäki hill, in Siilinkuja lane, there was Varonin's house, on the upper floor of a wooden house - - downstairs there

193

was a shop, Varonin's shop. - - And this Varonin had been Russia - - these emigrants or emigrated from there. And a very superstitious man. He had an apple garden there were apple trees and for us Halssila kids that was one heck of a place. He thought he could, with some red pieces of string, to hold us in check, he hung them and cast those, spells so that the kids wouldn't steal the apples. But he didn't scare us off. We teased him a little because he was so that he didn't really speak Finnish that well. The big boys once decided to throw a cat in that well and so they did and then there were even the police involved because, Varonin got cross with us for casting such spells on him. He reckoned that everything people do is magic and witchcraft. The apples were good, though. (Man, 1941.)

The reminiscence proceeds along Siilinkuja lane. Next to the narrator's house lived a smith, in the house after that a cupper and at the end of the street there was a ski shop. It was the end of the 1940's, and in the wooden house town life was still warm and human. The neighbours were acquainted and self-sufficient in many services. For the children in the neighbourhood, watching the activities of the adults and all the comings and goings of everyday life was a kind of a school of adversity; indeed, their reminiscence often focuses on people and their affairs.

[The smith who lived next door] ... he did everything that goes with the trade, from locks to hinges. At the time, he fixed all these, all this farm equipment because then people still used mowers and all these. And it was a pleasure to look at when, there from the doorway when the sparks flew and he forged and forged. And the old men they tell stories. The same thing was, there were these, public saunas in Halssila. Oh boy they were we sat there wide-eyed. The old men sat there and, told stories it was always about women and booze and fighting and war. They didn't use much alcohol there it was forbidden to be drunk there so, some tried but they were always banned for that. - - And going up from the smith's - - from Siilinkuja lane there was a cupper. - - there was this little sauna by the lake where she cupped. And especially in the summer they would come outside to lie on the bunks the old men with the cups, the cups on their necks and backs and we watched that in amazement. - - Then there was Oksanen's ski shop was there in the upper end of Siilinkuja lane where they made the first slatted skis. We always went there to buy skis that had a little something wrong with them and got them cheap. (Man 1941.)

Life in the working-class neighbourhood of Halssila appears very realistic in the reminiscence of the narrator. The adults had their own secrets, which they could not, however – perhaps did not even want to – completely hide from the children. The children naturally understood things in their own way but, watching the adults, they shared in the joint secrets of the community. The living environment embraced its own way of life, to which outsiders had no access: thus, the community was fortified to endure the intrusions of outsiders. In the reminiscence of the same man (1941) the self-sufficiency of the community even extended to a kind of "social security" – the community took care of its own:

When we lived there in Majavakatu street there was, I won't mention his surname but Topi, lived with his family. When people my mother and father had to use too, borrow money. Topi always lent it. I mean you could always get it from him. - - And this Topi was one of the most well-known bootleggers in Jyväskylä. - - And there used to be a lot of the city fathers came there by taxi, to get the booze and then every little while came the police cars came there, to raid the place. But the way he could keep out of being caught was, he had two sons our age. And one that was a bit younger. Every time the police came in the wife took the child and took him to this wooden bed where children used to sleep. And the police never rummaged in the child's bed. And it had a false bottom and underneath were the bottles. They found it out then. This Topi he also had a wooden leg. He had in Halssila or in Vaajakoski he had been run over by a freight-train and lost his leg. When he was drunk, he always showed it to us children told us boys to come and see how he drove a nail into his leg and the first time when you didn't know it, when he put a nail there and hit it with a hammer... He really liked children and then he kept us there and said if you hear a police car coming come and let me know straight away. - - Many a time we sat there on the fence and watched the police go through all the stores but they didn't find it. (Man 1941.)

## Reminiscence and the permanence of places

A situated life story attaches the reminiscing person to a time, a place, people and events significant to his/her course of life. The significance of events is very personal: characteristically to individual reminiscence, an event significant to the reminiscing person may be totally insignificant to an outsider. Moreover, a situated life story provides the reminiscence with coherence, which helps the reminiscing person to "move" in times and places and to tolerate the features of the present which are still unorganised, or which may even feel uncomfortable. Jyväskylä is an illustrative example of a town whose townscape has undergone more or less radical changes during the last decades. In a situation like this, coherence must be sought from the past, from what is physically gone. In the case of Jyväskylä, the elderly narrators find it in the period of wooden houses. Changes, especially when radical or clearly challenging the past, easily entice us into looking back nostalgically on the past times, which often are also lost. In a way, nostalgia is used to call something that no longer exists; the present, on the other hand, does not evoke nostalgic feelings. Change is always required for the nostalgic feeling to arise, and the present thus exists by way of its past.

Although the past is often seen in a nostalgic light, it does not exclude being content with the present at the same time; the present is regarded as having its own advantages. In fact, there is no other way of going back to the past than reminiscence; a part of the town of memories actually is only a town in the memories. If the object of reminiscence still existed, it would not have to be reminisced about as something that has been lost. On the other hand, if past times were to return, they would be familiar and satisfactory for some town dwellers only; the development of a town cannot be entirely based on memories, either. (Forty 1999.)

195

The development prospects of Jyväskylä are clearly future-oriented, a tendency which could be seen already in the upheaval of the 1960's and 1970's. It seems that during those decades the town was not considered to be something that should uphold the past, but the trend was rather to create new things, encouraged by the optimism of the economic boom. At that time, there was no room for reminiscing about the past – and people experienced no need for it, either. In Jyväskylä, the present and the past – the time of the wooden houses – are separated by the fact that the present time is constantly changing: it has not reached a similar degree of permanence as the Jyväskylä which is now reminisced about. Nevertheless, in recent years, in particular, remembering and its meaning have occasionally manifested themselves collectively: collective reminiscence has proved valuable in serving as a strategy for defending a variety of old places in the town, and in joining the town dwellers of different ages in making common cause (Korkiakangas; article on pages 150–171).


NOTES

1    This article has partly been published previously in Ethnologia Scandinavica vol. 30/2001.
2    As my material, I have both personal, biographical interviews and reminisces written by the town dwellers themselves. The material was collected during the year 2000. There are altogether eight written accounts and seven two-to-five-hour biographical interviews (one of the interviewees has also written down her recollections). All those who have provided written reminisces are women, born between 1913 and 1948. Three of the interviewees are men, who were born in the 1930's and 1940's; the four female interviewees were born between 1916 and 1944. The interviews, in particular, have proved not only extensive in size but also very versatile. The material, quantitatively somewhat scarce, is qualitatively rich and repeatedly brings forth collectively shared memories and similar features of reminiscence. However, recollection material, and quite especially autobiographical material that can be extremely personal, must not be analysed and used as the medium of "truth"; reminiscence is always meandering between the past and the present, and therefore even the "truths" change in the flow of time and adapt to the requirements of the time. The interview citations are unedited except for the occasional elimination of repetition. The names of persons, places and streets mentioned in the citations are in their original form. The interviewees and the writers of reminisces are referred to by their sex and year of birth. Any differences between the interviews and the written texts are left outside the discussion.
3    Älylä is situated in the western part of Jyväskylä, in an area bordered by Kramsunkatu, Keskussairaalantie and Seminaarinkatu streets. At its largest, Älylä has been regarded as also covering the area between Seminaarinkatu and Vapaudenkatu streets, all the way to Lounaispuisto park. (Kiiski 1976, 217.)
4    Juho Jussila was the head teacher of the Jyväskylä Teacher Training College and later a factory owner. The factory, which mainly manufactures children's toys, is still in operation in Jyväskylä.
5    The average age of the demolished stone and brick houses was no more than 55 years, whereas that of the wooden houses was 90 years. Jyväskylä has not known how to appreciate, or has not been willing to appreciate, the importance of small stone and brick houses as historical documents of an era. (Jäppinen 1976, 107.)
6    Characteristically to a wooden house town, the gardens around the houses were separated by fences. The town building regulation from the year 1872 provided that

the yards be enclosed by a fence to make the facades harmonious. However, originally the yards were fenced also to stop the domestic animals from running around town. The gates, which originally were usually made of wood, were placed between the fence and the gable of the house closest to the street. The main gateway was usually kept closed; next to, or in one half of, the main gate there used to be a smaller gate for pedestrians. (Valjakka 1971, 197–198.)

## BIBLIOGRAPHY

Bauman, Janina 2000. Muisti ja mielikuvitus. Omaelämäkerran totuus. [Memory and imagination: Autobiographical truth.]. In Maaria Linko, Tuija Saresma & Erkki Vainikkala (eds.): *Otteita kulttuurista. Kirjoituksia nykyajasta, tutkimuksesta ja elämäkerrallisuudesta.* [Cultural passages: Texts on modernity, research and biographical quality.]. Nykykulttuurin tutkimusyksikön julkaisuja 65. Jyväskylä: Jyväskylän yliopisto, 331–344.

Certeau, Michel de 1984. *The practice of everyday life.* [Origin. Arts de faire.] Berkeley and Los Angeles: University of California Press.

Connerton, Paul 1989. *How Societies Remember.* Cambridge: Cambridge University Press.

Conway, Martin A. 1996. *Flashbulb memories.* Hove: Lawrence Erlbaum Associates.

Davis, Fred 1979. *Yearning for yesterday: A sociology of nostalgia.* London: The Free Press.

Elder, Glen H. Jr., Modell, John & Parke, Ross D. (eds.): 1993. *Children in time and place: Developmental and historical insights.* Cambridge: Cambridge University Press.

Forty, Adrian 1999. Introduction. In Adrian Forty & Susanna Küchler (eds.): *The Art of Forgetting.* Oxford: Berg, 1–18.

Heiskanen, Ilkka & Mitchell, Ritva 1985. *Lättähatuista punkkareihin. Suomalaisen valtakulttuurin ja nuorisokulttuurin kohtaamisen kolme vuosikymmentä.* [From teddy-boys to punks: Three decades of interaction between mainstream and youth culture in Finland.] Helsinki: Otava.

Junkala, Pekka & Sääskilahti, Nina 1999. *Kadun risteyksessä. Etnologinen analyysi kaupunkitilasta.* [At the crossroads: An ethnological analysis of town space.] Etnografia 2. Jyväskylän yliopiston etnologian laitoksen julkaisusarja. Jyväskylä: Atena.

Jäppinen, Jussi 1976. *Kaupunkiympäristön muutos Jyväskylän keskustassa.* [The transformation of town space in the centre of Jyväskylä.] Keski-Suomi 15. Keski-Suomen Museoyhdistyksen julkaisuja 15. Jyväskylä: Keski-Suomen Museoyhdistys.

Jäppinen, Jussi 1997. Katsauksia kaupunkikuvaan. [Glances at the town space.]. In: *Jyväskylän kirja. Katsauksia kaupunkielämän vaiheisiin 1940-luvulta 1990-luvulle.* [The book of Jyväskylä: Glances at the life in town from the 1940's to the 1990's.]. JYY:n Kotiseutusarja 33. Jyväskylä: Jyväskylän kaupunki, 276–285.

Kiiski, Hannu 1976. *Jyväskylän "Älylä".* [The "Älylä" area (="Brainy Quarter") of Jyväskylä.] Keski-Suomi 15. Keski-Suomen Museoyhdistyksen julkaisuja 15. Jyväskylä: Keski-Suomen Museoyhdistys.

Korkiakangas, Pirjo 1996. *Muistoista rakentuva lapsuus. Agraarinen perintö lapsuuden työnteon ja leikkien muistelussa.* (English summary: The Childhood of Memory: The agrarian ethos in the recollection of childhood work and play.) Kansatieteellinen Arkisto 42. Helsinki: Suomen Muinaismuistoyhdistys.

Korkiakangas, Pirjo 1997. Individual, collective, time and history in reminiscence. *Ethnologia Fennica* 25, 5–16.

Kydén, Tarja & Salmela, Ulla (eds.): 2000. *Kaupungin sydämessä. Jyväskylän Kirkkopuiston rakennettu ympäristö 1837–2000.* [In the heart of the town: The constructed environment of the park surrounding Jyväskylä Town Church.] Jyväskylä: Kopijyvä.

197

Lefebvre, Henri 1994. *The Production of Space.* [Origin. La production de l'espace, 1974.] Oxford: Blackwell.

Lynch, Kevin 1968. *The Image of the City.* Cambridge, Mass. & London: The M.I.T. Press.

Ojala, Jaana 1999. *Niinikankaan kulmalta Café Eloseen. Muisteluksia Jyväskylän kahvilaelämästä 1930-luvulta 1990-luvulle.* [From the corner of Niinikangas to Café Elonen: Remembrances of the café tradition in Jyväskylä from the 1930's to the 1990's.] Etnografia 1. Jyväskylän yliopiston etnologian laitoksen julkaisusarja. Jyväskylä: Atena.

Passerini, Luisa (ed.) 1992. *Memory and Totalitarianism.* International Yearbook of Oral History and Life Stories. Volume I. Oxford: Oxford University Press.

Pillemer, David B. 1998. *Momentous Events, Vivid Memories.* Cambridge, MA: Harvard University Press.

Räsänen, Riitta & Räsänen, Matti 1985. *Älylästä Tyhmälän torille. Jyväskyläläiset muistelevat menneitä.* [From Älylä (="Brainy Quarter") to Tyhmälä (="Thick-Headed Quarter") marketplace: Jyväskylä inhabitants recall the past.] Jyväskylä: Gummerus.

Simonsen, K. 1991. Towards an understanding of the contextuality of mode of life. *Environment and Planning D: Society and Space,* 9 (4), 417–431.

Tissari, Jorma 1987. Jyväskylän puutalo- ja puutarhakaupunki. Muistikuvia ja tiedonjyväsiä yli puolen vuosisadan takaa. [The wooden houses and gardens of Jyväskylä: Remembrances and morsels of information from over half a century ago.] *Sukuviesti* 1987 (8), 24–28.

Tommila, Päiviö 1972. *Jyväskylän kaupungin historia 1837–1965 I.* [The history of the town of Jyväskylä 1837–1965 I.] Jyväskylä: Gummerus.

Valjakka, Sirkka 1971. *Jyväskylän kaupungin rakennukset ja asukkaat 1837–1880.* [The buildings and inhabitants of the town of Jyväskylä 1937–1880.] Keski-Suomi X. Keski-Suomen Museoyhdistyksen julkaisuja. Jyväskylä: Keski-Suomen Museoyhdistys.

Vilkuna, Johanna 1996. Suunnittelun ja paikallisuuden luonnot. Tulkinnan viitekehys. [The natures of planning and locality: A frame of reference for interpretation.]. *Yhteiskuntasuunnittelu* 4/1996, 4–13.

MONICA STÅHLS-HINDSBERG

# Town, Language and Place

## Language-based Strategies in Vyborg

"Four languages were spoken in old Vyborg" is the name of a collection of columns by Victor Hoving (1960). The title utilises a well-known expression, a statement made by Vyborgers and outsiders alike. All four linguistic groups concerned, the speakers of Swedish, Finnish, Russian and German, were deeply rooted in Vyborg, but the hierarchy between them changed radically over the years. In this article, my intention is to demonstrate differences in the spatial experiences of Vyborg in the 1930's as expressed by representatives of the respective language groups.

Were there differences in the way members of the linguistic groups were moving in Vyborg in the 1930's? If so, which were the areas concerned and which factors contributed to the fact that the groups were directed to the areas in question? Which factors contributed to the appropriation of these areas? Which factors influenced the choice of habitat after the evacuation and how did people adapt to it? Despite the fact that Vyborg is considered to have been a town of four languages, in this article I will refer only to speakers of Swedish, Finnish and Russian, since the German-speakers in the 1930's had to a great extent been assimilated into the Swedish-speaking group.

In contemporary urban research, space, place and identity constitute basic concepts. Space can be constructed at several levels and the experience of space is socially, individually and territorially constructed. Place as a concept is closer to the personal experiences of the individual than space is. We live in different places and through different places. Local identity is what makes one's own town a unique experience. Thus, spatial identity cannot exist without place, space and local features or without collective and individual experiences. Space, place and identity emanate from social interaction and should be seen as parts of our social universe. Together, these concepts contribute towards a deeper insight into and understanding of the individual parts that urban research is made up of. With the aid of these, it is possible to throw light on the daily life, routines and habits of the town dwellers, which in turn give us a picture of the cultural climate of the town in question (Ojankoski 1998, 225–228). The importance of space correlates with local identity and sense of community, of which a feeling of similarity between people and a feeling of continuity constitute important components (Brück 1988, 78).

## Vyborgers and space

The spatial significance of the town of Vyborg was largely a result of how one moved about, where one lived and how deeply rooted one's family was in the town. Quite naturally, one tended to settle in areas where one could feel at home, i.e. together with a group which socially, linguistically and economically was at the same level. Changing groups or areas was done only as a last resort, since a feeling of living in the wrong place would only create insecurity in the long run. Within one's own group, one obtained local knowledge of the area, of who was living where.

The opposite of similarity, sense of community and continuity is dissimilarity, alienation and disruption of everyday life. I here refer to a polarisation between "us" and "the others". The relation between linguistic groups is constructed on the basis of attitudes and knowledge about other groups. Even their historical significance in everyday life plays an important part here. For instance, one of the oldest informants mentions the City Library designed by Alvar Aalto as a terrible mistake as far as the site was concerned. The Torkkeli Esplanade, the flourishing park with the bandstand where there was always some orchestra performing, was a pleasurable place for the Vyborgers. A modern functionalist-style building definitely disturbed the overall view of the lovely park and the cathedral. The cathedral was completely destroyed by bombing in the Second World War. Of the building itself, the informants do not remember much, but the park where they were walking in the company of their parents is a cherished memory. The construction of one's self-image is often done in relation to something one is not or has not (Åström 2001). According to the anthropologist P. C. Lloyd, one's self-image is constructed in direct contact with the local environment. Regarding linguistic and ethnic distinctive features, the construction often takes place against the background of what one is not, in combination with what is experienced to be typical of one's own group. According to several anthropological studies, ethnic groups co-existing in towns rank each other hierarchically. (Lloyd 1974, 224–225.) My intention is to analyse spatial identity among Swedish, Finnish and Russian-speakers in Vyborg

The informants, arbitrarily chosen for this article, were born in the 1910's and 1920's. The number of informants is six, two from each linguistic group, each with a different social background. Socially, one of them represents the lower middle-class, as defined by the occupation of his or her parents, and the other one, the upper class. Both ethnological reminiscence material and answers to questionnaires were used as material for this article. The interviews (SLS 1881) I have carried out myself, and in addition to these, I have used the life story questionnaires of the Finnish National Board of Antiquities (MV:KEL). Within the range of possibility, I have tried to obtain representative material, in the sense that the social background should be the same for the respective language groups. Gender was not considered significant in the selection of informants. The informants left Vyborg either to study in Helsinki or in anticipation of the outbreak of the Winter War in 1939. The informants, who in this article tell about the Vyborg of their childhood, were pleased to reminisce. It meant that they, once more, could return to the streets and home of their childhood.[15]

It was difficult for the informants to structure the process of reminiscence with the aim of focussing only on memories related to Vyborg. Such a long time had passed and so much had happened since their childhood. Much of the memories of childhood are of a social character, in the sense that social and collective events hold a central place, whereas memories related to buildings and architecture have fallen into oblivion. In one's memory, an emotionally tinged spatial experience will dominate over a recollection related to a building.

As mentioned above, in Vyborg, different linguistic groups lived side by side. The linguistic boundaries were sometimes crossed, for example, in clubs and societies, but for the main part of the town dwellers, the multi-cultural environment was merely a backdrop. One was aware of it, but in everyday life it played no great role. The contacts between the language groups largely depended on where one lived, on family background and leisure interests. In the following, I will analyse the way some individual Vyborgers looked upon their town.

## Linguistic groups

In the 1930's, Vyborg was a town in a process of rapid change, as the Finnish and, more specifically, the Karelian element became more dominant. According to the last census, carried out in 1930, the number of inhabitants was 72 239. Only 5,3 per cent of them (3 868 persons) were born abroad, and the share had decreased steadily since the beginning of the 20th century, when it was 14,8 per cent. The number of inhabitants whose mother tongue was other than Finnish or Swedish was 2 527 (Viipurin kaupungin historia, IV:2).

In 1930, the following linguistic groups could be found in Vyborg:

| Speakers of | | | |
| --- | --- | --- | --- |
| Swedish | Finnish | German | Russian |
| 2,9 % | 93,6 % | 0,6 % | 2,5 % |
| 2 103 persons | 67 609 persons | 439 persons | 1 807 persons |

(SVT VI:71, 1930:1–3)

The cosmopolitan image of Vyborg is also visible in patterns of residence. In my other article in this book, the Swedish-speaking informants revealed that the "old town", i.e. the Fortress district was where one ought to live; the closer to the castle, the better. The higher social classes traditionally included Swedish, German and some Russian-speakers. In 1920, a large part of the Finnish-speakers still lived outside the town boundaries; in the Fortress, 25,8 per cent of the inhabitants spoke another language than Finnish, in Salakkalahti, 24,2 per cent and in Repola, 15,0 per cent. Thus, in the

201

central areas, the Finnish-speakers constituted approximately 75 per cent. (Viipurin kaupungin historia, IV:2.)

There were great differences in the way the respective linguistic groups related to the town, one basic reason being the fact that the Finnish-speaking group was gradually increasing as a result of migration and incorporation of suburban areas, while some of the Swedish-speaking families had lived in Vyborg for centuries. Swedish-speakers could rely on existing social networks and close contact with many people outside the nuclear family, whereas those Finnish-speakers who had recently moved into the town had often travelled a long way, and family contacts were sporadic or broken. The new inhabitants had to create new social contacts in the town to replace the old ones, which to a large extent contributed to the fact that one sought the company of people sharing a similar background; one settled among other Finnish-speakers and was content with having the same social position as other Finnish-speakers.

A large number of the Russian-speakers had moved to Vyborg as members of the Russian armed forces, or accompanying them, but this group also included free tradesmen. Some of them had arrived just before the border was closed. Out of this group, not many stayed on in Vyborg; most of them moved on after settling their finances. Most of the poor Finnish-speaking informants recollected that Russian-speakers lived primarily in the districts of Siikaniemi or in the Pietari suburb. The Swedish-speaking informants had no clear picture of where the Russian-speakers lived (SLS 1881; MV:KEL).

## Everyday symbols

The image of Vyborg before the outbreak of the Second World War has been tinged by works within the nostalgic and idealizing memoir genre. It is not always possible to consider the oldest parts of the beautiful city built in stone as an example of Finnish architecture, the design being a result of Russian building activities in the late 18th century and early 19th century, with the aim of strengthening the town as a military fortress. At the beginning of the 20th century there was a lot of construction going on, and the town was extended, but no new integrated image of Vyborg was to be seen as a result of this. As early as in the 1920's, there was an interest in protecting historical buildings, and for instance, instead of tearing down the Round Tower, the building was restored and transformed into a restaurant (Neuvonen 1994, 14–15).

The ethnologist Helge Gerndt has worked out three approaches to the city. The approaches are overlapping, but, in order to gain a deeper insight into the nature of urban culture, Gerndt uses these approaches as a basis for his theories. According to Gerndt, the question arises as to how the city can function as a forum for various cultural expressions. By this, he refers to the use of different buildings, or cultural activities. Cities work like magnets, attracting business and industry. Commercial and industrial institutions also give rise to a particular kind of culture. For instance, in the 1930's, Vyborg was a town in a state of vigorous expansion. In the previous centuries, one of

*The Round Tower that was built by orders of Gustav Vasa in 1547–1550 at one of the eastern exits. After the town wall was demolished in the mid-1800's, the tower was used only as storage for a long time. In the 1920's, the building was restored and the upper floor became a restaurant. Photo: Partanen 1940, National Board of Antiquities, Helsinki.*

the main assets of Vyborg was its geographical proximity to St. Petersburg. In the 1930's, however, the character of the town as a port and business centre was emphasized. Vyborg was also a garrison town and home to a great number of educational institutions. All institutions brought with them a particular culture, which was also reflected in everyday life, in the streets and in the homes. But at the same time, in the buildings used for commerce and industry, educational and military purposes, a particular culture was created in direct contact with everyday life. (Gerndt 1985, 11–19.)

Urban social life also involves contrasts such as tolerance versus distance, anonymity versus mobility etc. Everyday communication is influenced by the number of strangers present in the environment. The meeting places were different ones for immigrants than for the local population. Thus the town is perceived differently by different groups, it is a unity of co-operating cultural forces, and our everyday microcosm is made up of continuous processes of transmission and exchange, which are actualised in varying patterns of communication (Gerndt 1985, 11–19).

A third approach, based on whether the city can be seen as a separate space, an image with a specific meaning, is also of interest in the case of a lost city such as Vyborg. Gerndt asks himself how the individual constructs his or her own image of the city. Here we might also ask: how is this image preserved in one's memory?

Besides group affiliations and background being of great importance here, the individual's image of the city incorporates various "situational markers". Self-images of the city can be seen as a common denominator for all inhabitants of any given city. For instance, in the interviews with former Vyborgers, most answered the question on important sights by mentioning the castle, the Torkkeli Esplanade, the old town (i.e. the Fortress district) and the Monrepos park. These answers were given by informants of all linguistic groups. These self-images may be different from the images constructed by outsiders, depending on what value is attributed to the most important sights of the town. It is also possible to establish different symbolic links to the self-image of the town and its elements, as presented by the former residents. In Vyborg, for instance, the Torkkeli Park may symbolize leisure, pleasure, musical experiences or walks; Monrepos may symbolize art experiences as well as the park; and the Fortress, history, languages, tolerance or minorities.

*But interview instrument not included.*

In some way, these markers, these self-images of the town differ from outsiders' images and can function as a unifying link, even if the interpretation may not always be shared by all town dwellers. The image of the town is a living one, and changes according to the prevailing cultural environment (Gerndt 1985, 11–19, SLS 1881).

In the following, I will take a closer look at the town using three different fields which help us in the analysis of the symbolic meaning of the town:
1) urban spaces and buildings
2) markers of the social situation
3) geographical position.

*see end of chapter*

## Urban spaces and buildings

We come across descriptions of urban spaces and buildings above all in the informants' recollections of their childhood neighbourhood. According to statistical information, almost half of the Swedish-speaking and more than half of the German-speaking population of Vyborg lived in the oldest part of the town, called the Fortress.

According to my first *Swedish-speaking* informant, everyday life was characterized by a great deal of leisure activity and social time with friends. The father of the family was employed; the mother a housewife, and the informant's recollections of life at home are coloured by cosiness, freedom and a pleasurable daily life. The family had two maids who took care of the cleaning and cooking. Both Swedish-speaking informants had a very respectful attitude to the oldest parts of Vyborg. However, their answers differed, as the informant having an upper-class background had a poor local knowledge of the town as a whole. For him, Vyborg was primarily the old town, i.e. the Fortress. He would go on bicycle tours outside the town centre with his friends, but he had taken no interest in getting to know the various suburban areas. His knowledge about the town is related to historical buildings and the works of various architects, the general significance of the town centre, and leisure activities in the Esplanade park.

*Swedish*

> You might say that the neighbourhood was dominated by the Ullberg house and it had a magnificent garden where it was wonderful to play.

*In summer, concerts were given in the Torkel Esplanade. The picture shows the old stage for outdoor concerts. Photo: National Board of Antiquities, Helsinki.*

There were alleys and gateways and everything you could imagine, and there we gathered, everyone who lived in the buildings around the yard, and we played ball games and so on. [...] And opposite was the lovely park, I mean the Espilä restaurant was right opposite, so that even in early spring you could hear music when you opened the window: there was a bandstand there, it was always either a military band or the town orchestra who gave open-air concerts. And it was fantastic to sit outside or keep the window open – you could hear the loveliest music there. But later on there were more cars around, and the streets were asphalted. And soon there was bus traffic, but there were no proper bus stops. You could stop the bus anywhere – for instance, if you were going to the country, you would raise your hand and the bus stopped and you jumped in. [...] But the old town proper was in no way suitable [for bus traffic], however there were trams going round there. [...] The Regional Archive, and it was an outstanding work of architecture, up on Siikaniemi Hill, rather close to the statue of Peter the Great. And next to it was the statue of Independence, which stood out in the townscape, so to speak. In my time, the statue of Peter the Great no longer existed, we had removed it, and there was the Statue of Independence instead, the lion, or the Thessleff poodle, as it was also called. (SLS 1881, 1996:81–82, male b. 1920.)

In the interview with the Swedish-speaking lower middle-class informant, it is revealed that his home was situated in a neighbourhood outside the centre of Vyborg, which was common for the lower middle-class. The family, consisting of a mother and three children, occupied three rooms and a kitchen, but they still considered themselves to be, relatively speaking, of a lower social class. The reason was, among other things, that they did not live in the very centre or in the vicinity of the castle. They were also considered socially different because their yard was not asphalted, and instead there was a garden with lawns and apple trees. While the children were small, and the father still was alive, the family had a housemaid. In the beginning, the mother supported the family by renting out rooms to lodgers, and later on she took up employment. From an early age, the children helped out bringing in firewood and water and carrying heavy bags with goods from the grocery shop. The description of the neighbourhood focuses rather on the vegetation in the neighbourhood, not buildings, architecture or monuments. The yard outside the house was the safest and best playground, even if the lawn sometimes suffered from the rampage of the children.

> I usually say that I was a bit envious of my classmates who lived in the centre, who had asphalted yards, while we were so, well, I thought we were poor [...] We were so poor that we had apple trees and spruces and maples and lots of other things, grass in the yard. And we couldn't have a sauna bath quite in the same way as other people. Our sauna was right under our living room floor. (SLS 1881, 1996:130, male, b. 1923.)

The description by both *Russian-speakers* as regards urban spaces and buildings also differ from each other as in the case of the Swedish-speakers, but with regard to class, the linguistic groups do not differ from each other. The first Russian informant, exhibiting upper-class characteristics verging on the aristocratic, in the interview tells about how money influenced the housing conditions of the family. They had a large and elegant flat "at least 600 square metres", they had servants, governesses, cooks and maids. Modern conveniences were a matter of course. The family residence was situated in the oldest parts of Vyborg, but a new stone house, including a warehouse, was built on a site that was convenient for transports. The informant primarily moved in the oldest parts of Vyborg. He had no need to go elsewhere, since his friends lived in the neighbourhood. During the interview, the informant several times repeated that the family had lived in Vyborg for generations, and that they were rich, facts which provided him with a better start in life compared to the poor Russians who had fled to Finland before or after the border to Russia was closed. The fact that families of his kind were socially accepted also contributed to his different attitude to the town, as he had been able to move around in a much freer way than later the poor Russians from the east.

> The railway was, well, in 1908, the railway had existed for a long time already, but there was an unoccupied piece of land right by the tracks [...] From the point of view of transport and such, the site was excellent, and if you were rich enough you could live anywhere you liked. Yes, "die Angestellte", employees, they had to look for places to live which were better or worse. But those who weren't Angestellte could live anywhere they damn well pleased. (SLS 1881, 1997:113, male b. 1919.)

Russian-speakers tended to live close to others from the same linguistic group. Many Russian immigrant families lived in the district of Neitsytniemi. Saunalahti, just outside the town boundaries, is another area mentioned in this respect.

The informant representing Russian lower middle-class, just as the Swedish informant with a similar social background, was more focussed on nature and vegetation in the environment. The housing conditions of the family were naturally determined by money, but there was no need to point this out. The immediate environment, which he also described as the safest one, was the backyard. Flats were small and modest. Families frequently moved from one flat to another. On the whole, moving flats was a very common feature in Vyborg, both for the upper class and lower middle class. Very few families used their own flats.

> And it was a very pleasant and peaceful place. Our part of the shore was close by, and a little house. In our backyard, there was a large garden, where there were apple trees and bushes [...] Small ... the last one where we lived had two small rooms and a little kitchen, and cold water. The closet was in the yard. (SLS 1881, 2000:24–25, male b. 1922.)

For the informant, the streets were off limits as a playground. Children playing in the street were considered "street children" by his parents. Besides this, it was not easy for him as a poor Russian-speaker always to have to defend his Russian background.

The *Finnish-speaker* representing the upper class lived just outside Vyborg, in Vekrotniemi, a circumstance owing to her father's profession. He was a man of good social position, and consequently, the family had an elegant residence. The informant was familiar with the whole of Vyborg. Her description of her childhood neighbourhood is dominated by the immediate environment, starting with their own yard, then the closest blocks, situated in an area with wooden houses. Later on, the area which she covers, is extended to the town centre, as she was enrolled in the secondary school for girls. Walking up and down the Torkkeli Esplanade and skating on the ice of Salakkalahti bay was an important feature of the life of young people in Vyborg. In her account of the town, traditional, safe and bourgeois daily life dominates; the father, the mother, children and servants all having defined tasks.

> The house was just opposite a sawmill on the other side of the little bay. In the winter, the bay was full of logs, which by the summer were sawn up. Together with the neighbours' kids, we used to swim in that dirty water and also by the company dock. [...] In the beginning, we had only three rooms and a kitchen and the maid's room, but as the family grew and my father advanced in his career, our flat and the flat downstairs was turned into one, and we got two more rooms and another kitchen. (MV: KEL/486, female, b. 1921.)

The informant's account of her childhood does not include descriptions of monuments or historical buildings. For her, the immediate environment was of primary significance, serving as a suitable playground. By the time she was enrolled in the Vyborg Secondary School for Girls, her way to school is described as follows:

[...] I always used to pick up Maija-Liisa in the morning and then we walked together through the Market Square, Torkkeli Street, and the Punainen lähde Square to the Myllymäki Square, where our school was situated (MV:KEL/486, female, b. 1921).

The recollection of Vyborg by the Finnish-speaking lower middle-class informant is dominated by the harbour, of foreign seamen asking the way. Contact with various languages was thus part of daily life. The informant's family lived in the district of Papula, close to the railway, as the parents were employed on the railway.

No, I have very many times met foreigners, as Vyborg also was a port, there was the big Uuras harbour, and there were many foreigners in the area, who would ask about addresses and the like. And although we were only schoolboys, we managed to answer their questions. (SLS 1771, 1993:9, male b. 1916.)

His recollections include the paved streets, the big harbour, the ships and many languages, not only the languages of the seamen, but also the fact that the town was a multi-lingual one. The town was seething with life, business was flourishing and the town grew. Social life was in the main restricted to people of the same linguistic group, living in the same area.

The informant moved about in the central area of Vyborg, both in the old and new parts of town. He does not tell of monuments or places of historical interest, but rather about languages and linguistic groups and the patriotism of his parents. He did not have a long way to school: through the district of Repola, passing the Punainen lähde Square, then along Vaasa Street to the school area.

An interconnection of several places is confirmed when a given point is mentioned frequently enough. Thus, the way to school or work makes part of an important reminiscence, with one's home as the basis. However, not only the way, or the place where one lived constitutes an important reminiscence, formed by one's relation to the environment, but the places in question also refer to the social situation of the family.

## Markers of the social situation

The immediate environment includes markers which refer to the social situation of the individual. Markers of the social situation are usually revealed in life-story narratives. These invisible markers can be seen in descriptions of daily life, of school events and leisure etc., but also in the form of a slip of the tongue, a passing remark or ways of relating to speakers of other languages or to servants.

In the interviews with representatives of the Swedish-speaking group, an awareness of language and culture is shown. Since the group was small, everyone was familiar with the social background of the other individuals. The Swedish-speaking group also had its sub-groups: one either belonged to those who "counted" or one did not. In clubs and societies, there was social interaction across the language barriers, i.e. with both Finnish and Russian-speakers. Cultural life was another domain where the barriers were easy to cross.

In the Swedish-speaking upper class interview the significance of social symbols can be seen, above all, in the informant's description of the other linguistic groups. In a way, the description of the others becomes a confirmation of what the Swedish-speakers do not represent. Concerning the Finnish-speaking servants, there is a patriarchal undertone in the account, at the same time as a symbiotic-symbolic social pattern is outlined.

> They were Karelians, yes, nice people, all of them. And they would always accompany us when we went to the countryside in the summer; they came along and I don't know about working hours and that, but if there was a knock on the door, they would always go and open it. [...]. In the winter, for Christmas, my mother always went there by a horse and sleigh to distribute sweets and coffee and sugar, because you have to consider that people there were very poor. They were much poorer than us, it was so backward. So the only way of helping them was this... [...] And all the Starckjohann and Hackman families did so, trying to help them in every way. And the result was that we were very popular and dear to them and so on. And if anyone in the village died, then some member of the family had to be present at the funeral. We thought this was horrible. So if old Minna died, you had to join the procession and walk behind the loaded cart even if it was a scorching hot day – my father was very strict about that, this was the way things had to be. We children had to do our part even if we didn't always know why; my cousin, who was good at playing the violin, would walk behind the corpse as it were, and play something on the violin [...] It was a weird kind of ritual, that one. (SLS 1881, 1996:81, male b. 1920.)

> A very common sight in Vyborg was a Russian dean or priest, and when you saw one in the street, then you were supposed to spit three times. Well, that's what it was like in those days [...] Sergejeff, Schavaronkoff, Beljajeff and so on, those were fine families, but apart from them ... they symbolized the old Russian oppression. (SLS 1881, 1996:82, male b. 1920.)

Reminiscence of a lively social life at the family summer house is given as follows:

> If there was a dinner party, and the Starckjohann family was invited, the whole clan would turn up, or the Perander or Hackman family, so suddenly there could be some 50 people present, but that was no problem, there was everything imaginable [...] Well, right now I don't quite get it, but it was all produce of our own and ... the schnapps was taken in from the ice cellar, ice cold. And there was space, there was a large veranda, and there must have been crockery and cutlery and so on. (SLS 1881, 1996:81, male b. 1920.)

Among the members of the lower middle-class, the attitude towards Russian or Finnish-speakers did not diverge much from that of the upper class, but this group also shows a particular attitude towards the upper class. The interview shows that members of the lower middle class felt that they belonged to another category. There were groups of people the informant did not socialize with. The fact that the family in question did not live in the absolute centre of Vyborg, which was the home to most of the upper-class Swedes, added to the feeling of being outsiders. Also, visible attributes of wealth such as a car, servants, a summer house, or the mother not working outside the home were differentiating factors.

*lower middle class*

> I would say that the pharmacist was such a distinguished man that you could tell that the family belonged to a different world. But the children, though, were very nice and sympathetic and kind to us, to the widow's children, so to speak [...] The fact is, that after the War of Independence there was a certain distance kept between us and the Russians and such [i.e., people who were considered to be Reds]. I remember that, in Neitsytniemi, even the children living in the area of the Osuusliike co-op were regarded as Reds and we weren't supposed to have anything to do with them. And then there were the children of the non-commissioned officers, somehow they belonged to a lower caste, so you wouldn't have anything to do with them either. (SLS 1881, 1996:130, male b. 1923.)

In the interview with the Russian-speaking upper-class informant, many symbols of the social situation are revealed. He primarily emphasizes the importance of Vyborg as a commercial town, and with this as a starting-point, how Vyborg in the 1930's was dominated by the market forces. People were thinking about the future, the development of business, transports etc. This was more important than old traditions. According to the informant, families often enrolled their sons in Finnish schools, bearing in mind that the commercial language of the future would certainly be Finnish. The informant refers to these as "children of the future". Girls usually attended a Swedish school. One reason for the orientation of the Russian minority towards the Swedish-speaking group was that they could feel a deeper understanding for their Russian background in the contacts with Swedish-speakers.

> For instance, Russian was the home language of my father, of course, there is no use denying that. [...] He had his own ship importing oranges from Messina and so on. According to this work called "Efter 1809" (After 1809) he was, at the turn of the century, one of the richest men in Finland [...] ... a part of the Orthodox church, somewhat out of the way from the main church room, to the side, there was a space where we so to speak had our own section, and there were even pews there so that one could sit out of the view of the populace. (SLS 1881, 1996:113–114, male b. 1919.)

In his immediate environment, the Russian-speaking lower middle-class informant experienced constant conflicts in his contacts with members of other linguistic groups. The reason for the confrontations was his Russian origin combined with the fact that there were army barracks situated in the area where the family lived. According to the informant, his Russian origin meant that, during the whole time he spent in Vyborg, he never really felt

*The Russian element was often visible in daily life, for example, as a Russian inspired coffee set. Photo: South Karelia Museum, Lappeenranta.*

part of society. The family never became quite accepted. For instance, in the Swedish school, his classmates never invited Russians to their homes, and neither did the family get invitations anywhere, you might be called "ryssä" (Russian, derogatory term) in the street, you might have difficulties finding employment and earning a living. For a long time, many emigrants lived in the belief that they would one day be able to return to St. Petersburg and, for this reason, they did not make the effort to learn either Finnish or Swedish. Consequently, the mother of the informant, not working outside the home, did not have any closer contact with the local population and for the whole time she lived in Vyborg, she remained outside society.

> We didn't really, no, I didn't get to know the Finnish-speaking population of Neitsytniemi before moving to Helsinki. We were isolated to some extent, I suppose it was because we were Russian. But in addition to this, also there existed on the part of the Finnish population, not all of them, but many of them had this thing against Russians, especially the garrison in Neitsytniemi, where there was this building for the officers. We had to walk past it on our way to school, and we were worrying about whether we would get past it without fighting or end up in a bloody fight. [...] It is a very unpleasant thing that I remember about Vyborg. (SLS 1881, 2000: 24–25, male, b. 1922.)

The presence of the Finnish army in the suburb where the family lived made daily life difficult in the informant's childhood. In the interview, he several times returns to his childhood and the feeling of being an outsider, the lack of a social group where one felt at home, as well as the lack of friends. On the basis of the interview, the social markers point to confrontation and outsiderness.

The social markers of the Finnish-speaking upper-class account are primarily centred on social status. In this respect, the narrative is analogous to that of the Swedish and Russian-speaking informants. The housing conditions were better than those of the friends of the informant; at home she had everything she wanted, there were servants; she had a room of her own and in the summer the family moved to the summer house or went away on holiday. The informant's father bought a summer house in the mid-1930's, and before that, many a leisurely, warm summer Sunday was spent going on a picnic in the archipelago, using the motor-boat belonging to the sawmill, this being one of the benefits of the sawmill clerks. Their clothes were sewn by first-class seamstresses or were ordered specially. Children had no particular duties at home, apart from doing their school homework.

> The furnishing was better than average in those days, probably a typical home of a salaried employee. I had a room of my own. [...] In the closed environment of the sawmill, there were clear class differences in those days, and this was also the case in Vekrotniemi. The office clerks mixed with each other, and so did the works managers and the workers. My parents socialized with the director of the sawmill. [...] With regard to clothing, my father and mother did stand out in comparison with the sawmill workers. My father had a tailor make his suits, and my mother had her dresses made by a seamstress who had a distinguished clientele. (MV:KE/486, female b. 1921.)

The life of the Finnish lower middle class was simple and unpretentious. The parents worked long hours, the family had no servants and the mother took care of the housework. However, helping out with, for instance, the washing-up, was an idea completely foreign to the informant's father. In the summer, the family visited relatives living outside Vyborg. Both parents had moved to town from elsewhere, a common situation for a large part of the Finnish lower middle class. The family usually mixed with the closest neighbours, who, in this case, belonged to the same occupational group. The parents had little contact with members of other linguistic groups, but in the family concerned, the parents had chosen to enrol the girl in a Swedish-language school, while the boys went to a Finnish-language school.

> Yes, my father, according to some it was sensible thing to do... he enrolled the eldest child in a Finnish school, the second one in a Swedish one, the next one in a Finnish one, but after me, there were no more children. He wanted his family to be bilingual. [...] My father was an engine-driver. (SLS 1771, 1993:9, male b. 1916.)

The possibilities of finding employment were increased for those mastering several languages. Also, within the Finnish group, different sub-groups could be found. For instance, there was a group of young people called "kultainen nuoriso" ("golden youth"). These were usually referred to as those spending their time in cafés, talking about the "summer house" instead of the "summer cottage". According to the informant, it was evident that different linguistic groups had their particular areas of residence. Just as for the Swedish-speaking youth, the centre for this particular group meant Torkkeli Street and the Esplanade, the area where young people gathered in the evenings.

> In Vyborg there was the Torkkeli Park and at that time ... young people gathered there, and their parents, too. There were theatres, market halls during the day, of course they were open in the day time. And the cinema theatres and so on. The young people gathered around the Alvar Aalto library, in the park and the Esplanade or by the Espis restaurant at the bandstand, where there were always concerts in the spring. And the confusion of languages. [...] People talk about it a lot, the language thing, but it wasn't really obvious in everyday life. [...]. Let's say the Punainen lähde Square and around it it was all shops, and they were, say, 75 per cent Jewish and then there were the cloth and fur stores, where there would be Tatars and Russians. [...] The Germans were intellectuals. The industry, let's say the timber exports were usually in the hands of Germans. And the Swedish-speakers ... well, what should I say to that. I must say that they were, the Swedish families, they were lawyers, medical doctors, so they were of a high rank. (SLS 1771, 1993:9, male b. 1916.)

Since the Swedish-German group had lived in Vyborg for centuries, their area of residence was generally the oldest parts of town, which was also the most prestigious area. The closer one lived to the castle, the better.

> I would say that these Swedes exactly, and Germans, lived in the so-called Old Town. It was Art Nouveau buildings and ... stone buildings. (SLS 1771, 1993:9, male b. 1916.)

What is not apparent in the interview, is how this Finnish informant looked at the social position of his own linguistic group. But he associated the oldest parts of town with Swedish and German-speakers, whom he also regarded as the local elite. Jews and Tatars traded in textiles and furs. In his daily life, he did not have much contact with members of the other linguistic groups. With one's schoolmates, one could meet Swedish-speaking girls at the school dances and have fights with Russian-speaking youths. In the interview, the informant several times returns to the class differences, which he comments on both consciously and unconsciously. According to him, Vyborg was to a great extent "a town of different groups".

## Geographic position

Just as each city regards its geographic position as important on the basis of some historically or socially important period, Vyborg also had its own important position. In memoir literature related to Vyborg, the following sorts of descriptions of the town can be found: "the last outpost to the East", "the border fortress, the blood-stained land, well acquainted with the difficult

*The Vyborg Castle, cross-section drawn by architect Jac Ahrenberg in 1885. Photo: Timo Syrjänen 1993, National Board of Antiquities, Helsinki.*

art of suffering". However, images of the opposite also occur: "The Riviera of Finland, the town of memories and hopes, the town that had the keys to freedom". Vyborgian memoir literature is generous when it comes to the town's attributes. Naturally, the geographical position plays a different role for the respective linguistic groups; for example, the proximity to Russia had another dimension for those who had lived in the town for several generations, as opposed to those who were new in town, or for those who had recently emigrated from Russia. It is justified to talk about different ways of relating to the town, depending on the linguistic group in question.

According to the interviews, the Swedish-speaking group shows a clear, intimate "historical" relation to the town. On one hand, members of this group had lived in town for more than one or two generations, and on the other hand, most of those belonging to this group lived in the oldest parts of town. This is particularly evident in the upper-class interview. Here, the town takes the form of the informant's family tree. He also focuses on important historical buildings, monuments and areas. The closeness to water is given prominence in the section of the interview where he tells about the school summer holidays and life at the summer house. Also, cultural life flourished as a result of the contacts with Sweden, Germany and St. Petersburg, for instance, as musicians, prior to the year 1917, passed through town on their way to or from St. Petersburg.

214

> As for the music, the initiative to the music was of course Russian, Jewish, or German, but it was gradually taken over by the rest [of the population]. [...] But the first ones were the St. Petersburg generation, who dominated cultural life and made an outstanding contribution in this field. It is evident that, take families as Hoving and Clouburg and such, of course they brought a great deal of cultural influences from Sweden, and the Germans did the same from there [Germany], but without the contribution of the Germans, Vyborg would never have become, so to speak; there was an incredibly splendid German contribution to the development of cultural and commercial life in Vyborg and so on. (SLS 1881, 1996:82, male b. 1920.)

The geographical position was noticeable in the strong presence of the army in everyday life. Vyborg was also a garrison town. There were army buildings in the districts of Neitsytniemi and Salakkalahti. Soldiers could be seen all over town and they were a natural part of daily life.

> There were parades on the day called Freedom day, and sometimes on the 29th of April when Vyborg was liberated, but the real parade was held on the 16th of May. And then, Mannerheim was often present and gave a speech and had a reception. [...] On the whole, the army made its mark on the town, as there was the garrison. There was order and discipline, and that also gave us a sense of security, there were several regiments and special troops in town. (SLS 1881, 1996:82, male b. 1920.)

The informant mentions the security that the army provided, and hints that having Russia next door always caused a certain feeling of insecurity. The Swedish-speaking lower middle-class informant had similar experiences in this respect. The army inspired a feeling of security, it upheld law and order, and took care that the town always looked tidy. This informant also mentions that the proximity to Russia was experienced as slightly threatening, but on the other hand, this very proximity also signified "a window that opened towards Europe". In saying so, he is referring to the old, genuine Russian emigrants, not the refugees who had arrived around and after the year 1917. One did not mix with Russian-speakers and judging from the interview, in the daily life of the informant, there was no contact with anything Russian.

In the interview with the upper-class Russian informant, the geographical position of Vyborg is mentioned as significant, as it is close to St. Petersburg, the short distance having brought many advantages. Here, the proximity is not seen as a factor contributing to insecurity, but instead contributing to the multicultural element in daily life. He emphasizes the contacts to St. Petersburg at an earlier stage in the history of the town, and points out that there was a multitude of contacts at several levels.

> Of course, they also met in St. Petersburg. The Vyborg gentlemen used to go to St. Petersburg to have a good time. You must bear in mind that St. Petersburg was only two hours' distance from Vyborg by train. (SLS 1881, 1996: 113, male b. 1919.)

The Russian origin of his family he mentions only briefly, using the following words:

215

> ... the whole family was then considered to be – as was written in [the magazine] *Suomen Kuvalehti – hyvin suomenmielinen* [very Finnish-minded] (SLS 1881, 1996: 113, male b. 1919).

With regard to culture, the Vyborg area was characterized by an unusual multiformity. Karelian peasant culture, and a manor house culture, unique in this eastern Finnish context, lived side by side. The development of communications and transport, the railway and the boat traffic, had a very stimulating effect on the building of summer houses, and the surroundings of Vyborg developed into a well-functioning holiday zone for the St. Petersburgers (Jaatinen 1996, 14, 19).

The parents of the informant representing Russian lower middle-class for a long time cherished the hope of returning to Russia. During the early days in Finland, the family obtained cash by selling off the mother's jewellery, piece by piece, since it was very hard for poor Russian-speakers to find employment in Vyborg.

> They had a summer house here in Kuolemajärvi, my mother's parents, and they had some 30 hectares of land. And they arrived at the time of the rebellion, just as they had done before, when there were disturbances in St. Petersburg. They would go there and wait for things to calm down and then return. But this time the return never happened. (SLS 1881, 2000:24–25, male b. 1922.)

In this case, the geographical position of the town meant that Vyborg and its surroundings were looked upon by the informant's parents as a recreational area where the summers were spent. The short distance to Russia was not seen as a threat, as in the case of the Swedish-speakers, but rather as a circumstance which in earlier days had provided intensive contact between Vyborg and St. Petersburg.

The way the Finnish-speaking informants related to the geographical position of Vyborg was, for the main part, connected to daily life. It was common that someone in the family had moved to the "Emperor's City" in order to earn a living and this added to the familiarity of St. Petersburg. Russian culture was not experienced as frightening. In their accounts of Vyborg, nothing special is mentioned in this respect, besides the matter-of-fact statement that the distance to Russia was short, and for this reason, there were Russian influences to be found in their everyday life. For instance, one might have pascha at Easter. In addition, there were the bells of the Orthodox church, and their manner of ringing at Easter is mentioned as part of the character of the town. Even if the interviews contain nothing particular in their relation to Russia and Russian-speakers, the accounts of the Russian-speakers tell of a higher degree of suspicion and malevolence on part of the Finnish-speaking compared to the Swedish-speaking population. Such a negative attitude towards Russian-speakers would incorporate a restrained attitude towards Russia as well.

## *Three ways of looking at Vyborg today*

At the beginning of this article, I established that my intention was to present the relationship to the town of four, or in practice, three linguistic groups, using the concepts of time, place and space. As my theoretical starting-point, I took Helge Gerndt's symbolically significant patterns of action, in order to try to explore where the members of the linguistic groups moved, how they lived, how they related to the town, what their daily life looked like and how they looked on the geographical position of the town. Local identity is constructed around social integration and activities. In daily life, the individual constructs different fields of activity in the town. He or she gets to know other people, and thus, local identity is based both on relations to inhabitants and to the environment. The urban experience may be considered as an emotionally tinged spatial experience, which means that the informants' experiences of old Vyborg will also colour their attitude to the town where they are living today. The local identity of today does not only depend on social integration and activities in the present, but the maintenance and reproduction of one's "feeling for one's native place" which is also related to the past (Gunnermark 1998, 304).

The informants' recollections of Vyborg are related to their childhood experiences. In the interviews, there is a clear variation in the "feeling for one's native place" the informants show towards Vyborg. For some, it is stronger than for others. If one has a feeling of this kind, this implies that one also has a local identity which is based on one's town of origin. The local identity means that one has assigned a certain significance to the place and the space. Which, then, are the symbols and symbolic patterns of action which show that a local identity would be stronger for some linguistic groups than others?

For the Swedish-speaking informants, the memory of Vyborg was a beautiful and dear one, but at the same time, they were aware of the fact that the town was lost.

> Well, it is a beautiful memory, which can never be brought back to life. It is something which ... like many other cities in history which have existed and had their heyday and disappeared and can never return. (SLS 1881, 1996:83, male b. 1920.)

Vyborg presents a rosy picture which has disappeared. Even so, this informant did not experience his childhood as a rosy picture, but refers to it in very respectful terms. For him, it had been easy to appropriate the town and create a local identity. The most recurrent points in the interview were marked by continuous, historical ties. Here, we can see a *historical* consciousness, and in the accounts of everyday life in Vyborg, it is more evident here than in other interviews, how easy it was for the informant to see his place in the town as his family had lived there for several generations, thereby creating a natural position for themselves. The feeling of *insiderness* partly stemmed from the fact that he belonged to "those who counted", through family ties and a naturally higher position in relation to the other linguistic groups.

217

*[handwritten margin note at top: — but how do the wealthy of the world's buying Van. dvtn, condos feel inside even if they are central?]*

Still after fifty years, the function of the Vyborgian societies is partly to maintain a Vyborgian "feeling for one's native place", but certainly also to provide the Vyborgers with a possibility of a "Vyborgian dimension" in today's world. Adapting to a new town of residence was not easy. The sense of community and the feeling of solidarity in daily life was suddenly gone, and now, the class differences became much clearer. For the informants, it was a shocking new world.

The elements in the interview with the representative of Swedish-speaking lower middle-class present a reverse picture. The family had no historical ties to the town – his parents were the first generation to live there. For this reason, it was not easy, in retrospect, to see their place in the town. The streets and the buildings in his own neighbourhood were not the asphalted yards of the naturally more important parts of town, but they represented the green and leafy suburban area. In his childhood, he experienced social *outsiderness*, a recurring feature in the interview. Still, today he finds Vyborg an interesting place, and he likes visiting the town. In the interview, we can clearly see his need to maintain contacts with other former Vyborgers. The identity of the informant is strongly Vyborgian, and it has been recreated and consolidated through his activity in today's Vyborg-related societies. His local identity is not cemented through a historical dimension, but through the linguistic group he belonged to.

*[handwritten margin note: Swedish lower middle class outsiders (suburban)]*

The rich Russian upper class member definitely saw himself as part of the town. Here, strong historical ties are clearly visible in the interview. The family had lived in the town for some generations and had definitely created a natural position for themselves. Their existence in town could not be questioned. In the sections of the interview concerning streets and buildings, development is a recurring theme. The city would expand, enterprises were to be established, blocks of flats to be built. Similarly, a self-confidence was shown with regard to their social situation and daily life. The geographical position, in turn, provided opportunities. The territorial proximity to Russia was not seen as threatening, but the informant did not, on the other hand, express any feeling of solidarity with Russia. Instead, he stressed the Finnish-mindedness of the family. His adaptation to his new town of residence was painless: "you had your wallet, of course". It appears from the interview that the informant is a Vyborgian, he has a natural local identity, but he takes no interest in the activities of the societies, even if he maintains occasional contacts with other Vyborgers. The city is a thing of the past, but it is still present today.

For the Russian lower middle-class informant, the situation was a completely different one. Here, clear reference to elements as *outsiderness, alienation* and *confrontation* is discernible. For him, it is not the asphalted street that is important, but the closeness to nature. The informant was not oriented towards the centre, but towards the periphery. The Russian background of the informant and his family was often the cause of alienation and confrontation with others. Particularly problematic was his relationship to the Finnish army. Here, the situation is reversed. For members of other linguistic groups, the military presence stood for law and order and the proximity to *get Vyborg history*

Russia, a potential threat. For the group of less well off Russian-speakers, the presence of the army in the neighbourhood signified a threat.

For this informant, Vyborg is today a foreign town. In the interview, it is possible to detect partly a bitterness related to his Russian background and its implications in daily life, but partly also, a gentle regret and a kind of feeling that the outcome of the war was justified. He has no local Vyborgian identity, but his identity is closely tied to his present location. For the informant, it was a relief to be able to settle in a new town where no one knew about his Russian background: no daily confrontation, no derogatory nicknames, no feeling of being an outsider. The informant has no contact with Vyborgian societies or Vyborgers. The informant's family was never integrated into the town, and the built environment was of no significance to him. The informant began the construction of his local identity in his new location.

In the Finnish upper-class environment, we find reference to *insiderness*, *development* and *peripheral environment*. The feeling of being an insider and the emphasis on development is primarily present in relation to the social situation. The informant's father was in a managerial position and enjoyed various benefits. The informant emphasizes development, as her father was employed in the timber and wood industry, which was the industry of the future in 1930's Vyborg. The peripheral milieu is visible in the account of the suburb where the family lived. In the narrative, it appears as a town within the town, with a natural hierarchy, with the family at the top. In the interview, no historical ties appear; they had no deep family roots in town. The geographical position primarily meant that Russian traditions had been incorporated into their daily life, for example eating pascha (a traditional dish) at Easter, but for most Finnish-speakers, speakers of Russian were like a red cloth. One did not mix with them.

The few high points the informant mentions in her life after the evacuation are also related to Vyborg. The informant likes wandering about in her memories of Vyborg, which was a safe and good place to be. The prosperity of the family, the home, the yard, the streets all contributed to the construction of her Vyborgian identity. Through her father's managerial position, the family had strong ties to the social environment and a natural place among the local population. She re-experiences and recreates her Vyborgian identity over and over again, by answering Vyborg-related questionnaires of different kinds, which allows her to return to Vyborg. Since the evacuation, she has lived in quite a number of locations, but she has not been able to feel quite at home in any of them. She has experienced disappointment on numerable occasions, while the high points have been few; the best thing she can think of is to wander about in her reminiscence of Vyborg.

The image of Vyborg of the representative of the Finnish-speaking lower middle class is focussed on the harbour, exports and contacts with the sailors. Here, quite a different picture of 1930's Vyborg emerges. It is not a cosmopolitan one, but rather one of a town in a state of development and expansion. *Historical* ties are missing. The family did not have the possibility of socializing in the right circles. For this reason, we can see a certain outsiderness in relation to the other linguistic groups. The social situation implicated a great deal of contact with neighbours, a day-to-day life dominated by work, and on the weekends, visits to or by relatives living outside town. Some Russian traditions were part of the family's daily life, but they did not have social contacts across the language barrier. One was aware of the other linguistic groups; one of the informant's sisters attended a Swedish-language school, but one did not mix with Swedish-speakers. However, the informant mentions Torkkeli Street as an important place and part of daily life.

> It was really, if you compare to other towns, it was so alive. And it was open and spontaneous. And in those days there was no television or any pastimes like that. People spent time outdoors both during the day and in the evening. And that is just why it was such a lively place. And, well, people would regularly, I mean school youth and their parents, too, they would always go for an evening walk. [...] Well, I have to give the town the highest marks possible in comparison with other Finnish towns I have seen. Of course my feelings about the place are a bit romantic, but I don't feel melancholic about it. (SLS 1771, 1993:9, male b. 1916.)

The informant misses not only the town, but also the epoch with its urban life style, which is typically associated with Vyborg. Here, we can see both a social and an architectural dimension, both being of fundamental importance for the local identity of the informant. In this case, however, there was no need to revitalize the identity concept. The informant's adaptation to his new location was dominated by his work, and his contacts with other former Vyborgers had been sporadic. The informant had a local Vyborgian identity, but whether it was reflected in his identity today was not made clear.

There are no obvious differences in the way the members of the various linguistic groups moved in Vyborg. Rather, we must assume that certain groups had closer ties to certain areas. Swedish- and Finnish-speakers felt that the whole town was their natural territory, and so did the upper-class Russian-speaking informant. Only the less well-to-do Russian-speaker tried to avoid confrontations. One's appropriation of the town was related to frequent visits to a certain area, but, for example, for the Swedish-speaking upper class, the historical dimension played an additional role here.

In most cases, the informants had not experienced any problems adapting to their new locations after the war. A willingness to preserve a Vyborgian sense of community can be reflected in the informants' active participation in various association activities today, and also in the way they reminisce about and look upon Vyborg today.

The significance of space in relation to historical ties is reflected in different ways in the interviews. In the case of the Swedish-speakers, it is visible in relation to family and the natural position of the linguistic group in town; for the Russian-speakers, in the form of outsiderness but also as having a sharing role, for example, with regard to cultural elements. In the case of the Finnish-speakers, we see growth and expansion, a Finnish town developing. The significance of place reflects one's own experience of the town. For Swedish- and Finnish-speakers, the place was strongly present through the memories they carried with them, while for the Russian-speakers, the place was a thing of the past. In connection with this, we must consider time in relation to the town. Time had different dimension for the informants. For one, Vyborg was a thing of the past, for others, very much present through other Vyborgers, but also through one of the countless Vyborgian societies active today.

To summarize, not only do the informants miss Vyborg, but also the epoch immediately preceding the war. They miss the buildings and mourn the dilapidation of them. The sense of security often associated with the town is a projection of their own childhood in the town; the early adult life of the informants was, after all, characterized by war and chaos. The various elements through which the informants have appropriated the town in their memories have, above all, a strong historical dimension, but here we also find the contrasting pairs insiderness versus outsiderness and chaos versus order. In order to assert oneself in Vyborg, one above all needed to have family roots and to belong to the right linguistic group. However, there is more to Vyborgian local identity than this; it is also based on the environment and the social integration into the town of the family in question.

## NOTES

1) The critical researcher must here point out that the time that had passed since the informants had left Vyborg, as well as the age of the informants - between 70 and 90 - made it difficult for them to express their spatial experience of Vyborg and define it verbally. I have not been able to pose additional questions or carry out additional interviews, and in order to clarify life patterns and ways of life, I have had to use other than my primary material to some extent. Also, it was sometimes difficult to determine whether the memory of childhood was of an individual or collective nature. Where can one draw a line in this respect, and to what extent will more distant and closer events merge in one's memory?

## SOURCES AND BIBLIOGRAPHY

### Questionnaires

The questionnaire "Elämänkerrat" [Life Stories] of the Finnish National Board of Antiquities (MV:KEL).
Svenska litteratursällskapets i Finland Folkkulturarkiv (SLS), SLS 1881 "Wiborgsliv och wiborgaröden" [Lives and fates in Vyborg] (band 1996:50–60, 81–115,127–134; 1997:1–11, 69–70; 2000: 24–25).

### Literature

Åström, Anna-Maria 2001. Språk, klass och kultur i småstaden [Language, class and culture in small towns]. In Anna-Maria Åström, Bo Lönnqvist & Yrsa Lindqvist (eds.): *Gränsfolkets barn – Finlandssvensk marginalitet och självhävdelse i kulturanalytiskt perspektiv* [The children of the border people. Finland-Swedish marginality and self-assertion in a cultural analytical perspective]. Folklivsstudier 21. Helsingfors: Svenska litteratursällskapet i Finland, 100–141.
Bruck, Ulla 1998. *Identity, local community and local identity.* In Lauri Honko (ed.): *Tradition and cultural identity.* NIF publ. 20. Turku: Nordic institute of folklore, 77–92.

221

Ehn, Billy & Löfgren, Orvar 1982. *Kulturanalys: Ett etnologiskt perspektiv* [Cultural analysis. An ethnological perspective]. Lund: Liber.

Gerndt, Helge 1985. *Grosstadtsvolkskunde – Möglichkeiten und probleme Grosstadt. Aspekte empirischer Kulturforschung.* 24. Deutscher Volkskunde-kongress in Berlin vom 26. bis 30. September 1983. Herausgeben von T. Kohlmann und H. Bausinger. Berlin.

Gunnemark, Kerstin 1998. *Hembygd i storstan: Om vardagslivets praktik och lokala identitetens premisser* [Native place in a big city. On the practices of everyday life and prerequisites of local identity]. Göteborg: Göteborgs Universitet.

Hoving, Victor 1960. *I gamla Wiborg taltes fyra språk* [In old Vyborg four languages were spoken]. Helsingfors: Söderströms.

Jaatinen, Stig 1996. *Elysium wiburgense, villabebyggelsen och villakulturen kring Vyborg* [Elysium Wiburgense. The villas and the villa culture around Vyborg]. Helsingfors: Ekenäs Tryckeri Ab.

Lloyd, P.C. 1974. Ethnicity and the structure of Inequality in a Nigerian Town in the mid-1950's. In A. Cohen (ed.): *Urban ethnicity.* London: Tavistock Publications.

Neuvonen, Petri 1994. *Viipurin historiallinen keskusta: rakennusperinnön nykytila* [The historical centre of Vyborg. The present state of the architectural heritage]. Helsinki: Suomen Historiallinen Seura.

Ojankoski, Teija 1998. *Oikea pieni Kaupunki. Maantieteen ja asukkaiden näkökulma suomalaiseen pikkukapunkiin* [A real small town. Perspectives of geography and of the inhabitants in a Finnish small town]. Turku: Turun yliopiston julkaisuja. Scripta lingua Fennica 147.

*Suomen virallinen tilasto* [Official Finnish statistics], SVT VI:71.

*Viipurin kaupungin historia* 1981. Osa IV:2. Vuodet 1840–1917 [The history of Vyborg, IV part 2. The years 1840–1917]. Helsinki: Torkkelin säätiö.

*Viipurin kaupungin historia* 1978. Osa V. Vuodet 1917–1944. [The history of Vyborg, V. The years 1917–1944]. Helsinki: Torkkelin säätiö.

JORMA KIVISTÖ

# Four Voices on Helsinki

Urban Space at the Turn of the Millennium.[1]

A ttitudes towards urban space have been changing in the centres of larger Finnish cities over the last few decades. The number of residents in the city centres diminishes as commercial activity takes control of the increasingly expensive buildings. A similar process has taken place in big cities elsewhere in the world, where the centres attract businesses despite the rising level of rents and price of land. This change has been taking place all over Europe, and in Finland the fastest and greatest change has occurred in Helsinki.

The meanings ascribed to the city centre by people of different ages vary greatly. New inhabitants, those born in the city and those moving into it, mostly live in the suburban areas and usually get to know the centre through work or leisure activities. The older generation also retain many buildings and spaces in their memories if they have lived close to the centre as children.

There are about 50 000 workplaces in Helsinki city centre: department stores and commercial and administrative institutions are situated there. However, a majority of the city dwellers do not travel to the city centre very frequently. Nevertheless, this central area is significant for the identity of the approximately 550 000 inhabitants of the capital, even if they personally do not live or work in the city centre. A majority of the sights and the most photographed buildings of Helsinki are situated in this area. The visual image which tends to characterise Helsinki consists, to a large extent, of the buildings, streets, squares and parks of the centre. Various happenings, particularly the numerous cultural events organised in the centre during the last few years, have greatly influenced the image of the city. The "spirit" of the city of Helsinki is located here and therefore the area is of great symbolic value. On names of the places in this article see maps on pages 12 and 22.

## The zones of Helsinki

There are about 62 700 inhabitants in the centre of Helsinki (in the Helsinginniemi and Vironniemi areas, that is, south of the Hesperianpuisto park, the Töölönlahti bay and the Pitkäsilta bridge). This is a relatively large number

223

*The Esplanade has been renovated in the style of European boulevards. The sidewalk is heated during the winter to keep away the ice and snow of the Finnish winter. Here you can find embassies, expensive shops, a hotel, cafés and resplendent architecture. Photo: Jorma Kivistö.*

in a small area. Looking more closely at this central area of Helsinki, however, there is a relatively extensive district where fewer than one thousand people live. In the 1950's, this same area had a population almost ten times larger than today. The former residential buildings have either been converted into business premises or demolished and rebuilt according to the needs of commercial life.[2]

224

The inner city area around this epicentre is, for its part, much more densely populated. However, the demography of the population in this area is different from what it used to be. The majority of the present inhabitants live alone in flats within old buildings and there are very few families with small children. Because of the rise in the prices of flats and rents, the areas of, for example, Kamppi and Punavuori have turned into residential areas of much wealthier inhabitants than before.

Because of their proximity to the city centre, there are also lively concentrations of shops, cafés and restaurants in these inner city areas. Similarly, such areas generally get quieter the further away from the centre they are. For example, on the very outskirts of the inner city there are fewer business premises and these tranquil areas already have a slightly suburban feel to them.

Outside the inner city there are old suburbs and newer residential areas, which have an increasingly independent existence as the distance and time of travel to the centre increases. The inhabitants of these areas have increasingly begun to take care of their everyday errands in their own suburban centres, such as Itäkeskus, Malmi, Kannelmäki and Vuosaari.

The significance of the suburbs for the inhabitants themselves has emerged to a large extent during recent years. The residents, particularly in suburbs built a few decades ago have started to search for the roots of their own lives in the everyday existence and history of their residential area. The revival of district associations and the activities of inhabitants for the renovation and upkeep of their own areas are indications of this trend. The city authorities have supported this development through their own activities.

In a case where the city centre is part of somebody's everyday life today, it is so usually through work. However, the central public space and its buildings are still a strong unifying factor for the city. This has been evident in the carrying through of most of the plans concerning public space in the centre.

## Factors influencing spatial change

Changes in urban space continue to happen despite periods of financial prosperity or depression. Streets and houses are repaired and at the same time smaller or larger alterations are made to them. And if active changes of the physical environment are not carried out, change will still happen through dilapidation and ageing.

Various consumption trends and fashions change the cityscape in many ways. Only shops that base their business on successful trendy ideas can afford to remain in the key locations in the centre. Information technology also changes the use of space at a continuously increasing pace. The queues to cash machines grow and new kinds of Internet café look for the keys to success.

The growth and congestion of the city centre have forced planners to search for new development solutions. New underground tunnels with business premises and car parks are still being excavated. An extension of the metro westward is being planned and traffic jams are to be reduced by the introduction of underground car tunnels. Building activity has been facilitated by companies' increased willingness to invest during the period of financial growth.

Increased business activities have also provided money for cultural activities, which are now looked at from a more financial perspective than before. It was convenient to combine the renovation of public buildings in the centre and the organisation of numerous cultural events with Helsinki being one of the Capitals of Culture 2000 and in recognition of the 450th anniversary of the city. However, this phenomenon is also explained by the emergence of companies as sponsors for cultural happenings in order to raise their profile.

## Urban space from the perspective of individuals

How, then, does an ordinary inhabitant of Helsinki experience his or her city and what is important for him or her in the city? In early 1998 a questionnaire entitled "What Helsinki means to me" was sent to the residents of Helsinki. This project was headed by Anna-Maria Åström and supported by the Helsinki City Information Centre. It constitutes the fourth part of a larger project which collects material mapping the experiences of the city dwellers. The questionnaire attracted a large number of responses. In this article, I will analyse four of these inhabitants' perceptions of 20th century Helsinki.

The respondents are separate individuals with their own personal backgrounds, and it is, naturally, impossible to make any scientifically tenable generalisations on the basis of only four answers. Nevertheless, it is plausible that individual opinions and values reflect common perceptions. My aim, however, is rather to find and present possible ways of experiencing Helsinki and, on the basis of these, find some new perspectives against the background of what we know has taken place in the city.[3]

Heikki, who spent his childhood in the 1920's in Wood-Pasila and Alppila in the inner city of Helsinki, represents pensioners. As an adult, he has lived outside or on the outskirts of the inner city, but has moved a lot in the centre because of his studies and work. Pentti, born in the 1930's, lived in the centre until he moved to the suburb Kannelmäki at the end of the 1960's.

Jaana was born in the beginning of the 1970's and moved to Helsinki in the 1990's. She works in a shop close to the Hakaniementori market square. Helena, a secretary in her 40's, has lived in Töölö all her life.

## Helsinki and the identity of its inhabitants

The inhabitants' views on Helsinki and its places are largely influenced by how long they have lived in the city. The respondents born in Helsinki think that in order to qualify as a real *stadilainen* (Helsinki dweller), one must have been born in the city. For them, a Helsinki-identity is something that is moulded by living in the city. Jaana, who has moved to Helsinki from elsewhere, places this assumption in a new light. She writes: "a *stadilainen* is a fifth generation inhabitant of Helsinki, a good-for-nothing drunk, who is rarely to be seen elsewhere in Finland".

However, for her a *stadilainen* is also a well-educated, active person who has moved to Helsinki from another part of Finland, and finds his or her way to the headquarters of organisations better than many natives of Helsinki. "Pull yourself together *stadilainen*, otherwise the city will be taken over by winners from the provinces." This actually seems to have happened already. Jaana sees Helsinki as offering a wide range of opportunities, even if life as such is much the same as anywhere in Finland: school, work, daily life of families with children, young people's pastimes and life of old people.

In the opinion of the older respondents, Heikki and Pentti, the so-called incorporated areas or suburbs are not part of the real Helsinki, even if Pentti has lived in Kannelmäki for thirty years. Jaana and Helena, who live in the inner city, also naturally regard Helsinki from an inner city perspective.

All respondents have similar images of the social differences between the various districts of Helsinki. Eira, Kruunuhaka, Kulosaari, Munkkiniemi, Lehtisaari and Kuusisaari are mentioned as distinctively wealthy areas. Jaana and Helena characterise the Kallio-Vallila-Alppila area as poor, and they think likewise of the indistinguishable suburbs. However, their attitudes to this area differ from each other. Helena thinks the Kallio-Pasila area is "shabby" and that "the backyards and side streets are found in the suburbs and Hakaniemi". Jaana, for her part, sees the areas in Kallio as favourite places of the poor, even if she herself shuns the cheap bars and cafés there.

## The pros and cons of Helsinki

Informants in different age groups perceive the city in different ways, even if their favourite places might be the same. The younger the respondent is, the more he or she emphasizes functional and social aspects. The noise, fumes and danger of traffic are negative features most commonly mentioned.

For the oldest respondent, Heikki, who is over 70 years, the best features of Helsinki are the Esplanade and the Boulevard, in the vicinity of which he worked for several decades, and the old buildings on Katajanokka. He describes the building of the company Enso-Gutzeit and the Kiasma Museum of Modern Art as "jarring sounds" in their location in the centre. Other positive features, on the other hand, include the shore of the Kaivopuisto park and the maritime character of Helsinki. For Heikki, the disturbing behaviour of young people in the city centre and some suburbs is a negative aspect of Helsinki.

The most important elements of the city for Pentti, who is ten years younger, are the old architecture and statues representing historic persons, which remind him of past decades and many people, as well as the Ulrika Eleonora Snow Church. On the other hand, the covered markets, the market squares, events and the sea are also important for him. The smell of the sea, of rugs being washed at the shore, the starry sky, walking on the ice and the view of

227

*The sea plays an active role in peoples minds. Travel abroad on the large ferries that leave from the city centre, near the Market Square, is a popular means of escape. Smaller boats run local trips to the islands from many small ports around Helsinki. Photo: Jorma Kivistö.*

the city from the sea are always pleasant experiences. Even if Pentti lives in a suburb, he weekly attends events in the inner city. According to Pentti, the most negative aspect of the centre is the transformation of former residential houses into offices. He thinks there should also be life in the centre in the evenings and during weekends.

Apart from her own well-known district, Helena, who lives in Töölö, finds the same kinds of things important: buildings, markets, cafés, the sea, the shores and the southern parts of the city. However, she emphasizes these more for their effect on the overall atmosphere of the city: "everything that creates ambiance, joy and comfort in life". As the most negative feature of the city, in addition to the traffic fumes and the street dust, Helena mentions the feeling of fear when moving in dark parks, side streets and "certain districts". People and the centre, on the other hand, create a feeling of security.

Jaana, who is under 30 years old, looks at Helsinki primarily from the viewpoint of activities and opportunities. For her, the best feature of the city is that one can never be bored here: every day brings the opportunity to en-counter something new. As important places, Jaana mentions the Kaivopuisto park, the Senaatintori square and the islands close to the city suitable for outdoor activities. These are all mentioned as settings for various activities. Kaivopuisto is perfect for a relaxing summer day in the park rollerblading, having a picnic or playing chess. Jaana thinks of the steps of the Cathedral in Senaatintori as "the living room of the inhabitants of Helsinki". The city is full of leisure activities: samba carnivals, symphony concerts and ice-hockey matches. The only negative side that Jaana mentions is the disturbance caused by drunks in Hakaniemi and Kurvi.

## Symbols of Helsinki

The respondents clearly separate between what they regard as their favourite places and what they think of as symbols of the city. Furthermore, the symbols are looked at from various angles. The choices of Heikki all, except for the Parliament House, emphasize art and culture. The buildings he mentions include the Kiasma Museum of Modern Art, the Art House, the Hakasalmi Villa, the Finlandia House, the Opera and the National Museum. In addition, he supposes some regard the statues Havis Amanda and Three Smiths as well as the Sibelius Monument as symbols of the city. However, Heikki considers the slang of the city, *stadin slangi*, as the most important symbol of Helsinki.

In addition to the buildings along the Mannerheimintie street, Pentti thinks the best symbol for Helsinki is the view of the city from the sea: the magnificent buildings and the church towers are accentuated and the lights reflected in the water. In Jaana's opinion, the most important symbols of Helsinki are the railway station, the Suurkirkko Church and the Uspensky Cathedral, but also the Kiasma Museum, the Parliament House as well as the Stadium and its tower. The city is also given its special character by the sea and the embassies, and in Hakaniemi-Kallio by the betting shops and the beer cafés.

## What should be changed?

The respondents are relatively satisfied with Helsinki. The city feels human, there is good public transport, cultural activities and a functioning system of social services. Nevertheless, the oldest of the informants, Heikki, and Jaana, the youngest, offered a few suggestions on how the city could be improved. In Heikki's opinion, the administration and business activities could be spread on a wider area outside the centre of the city. Aggressive commercialism, traffic, graffiti and the increasing drug abuse among young people are things that he would like to remove from Helsinki.

Jaana, the youngest informant, thinks Helsinki needs more trendy intensity. She is also bothered by the uniformity and boring character of the suburbs and metro stations. New areas should be built in a mixture of styles, with both detached houses and blocks of flats, basement shops and shopping centres. Young and old people should live side by side and the activities of the inhabitants and the areas should receive support. In Jaana's opinion, the problems of young people are caused by the fact that they spend too much time only with people of their own age. Schools should have more co-operation with employers, old people's homes and various communities.

## Notions of the city's significance as based on personal experiences

Above, I have mostly related the feelings of the older inhabitants of Helsinki towards their city. In these, reminiscences of lived life and the past are clearly

229

accentuated when moving around the city. Particularly in the minds of those who have moved away from the inner city, their mental map of Helsinki is strongly based on a time when they themselves lived in the inner city. When they were young, there were not yet any suburbs, and therefore the areas outside the inner city are not perceived as part of Helsinki.

Jaana's answer supports the idea that the significance of urban space is built on one's own experiences and activities. There are hardly any inhabitants left in the city centre, least of all children or young people, therefore their experiences and the significance they ascribe urban space take a different form. The residents of the suburbs, particularly young people, experience the centre only through short visits. Their everyday life happens in their own residential area and through their hobbies.

Nevertheless, the centre of Helsinki is of great significance also for those resident outside the inner city. The centre is full of places that symbolize a Helsinki-identity also for those who have never lived there. Helsinki is explicitly described through the symbols of the city, buildings that are frequently photographed. The buildings in the centre constantly figure in the press and the planning of the centre give rise to the most serious controversies in public debate.

## Old values crumble

One might also ask whether the position of the objects characterised as symbols of Helsinki and the image maintained of these correspond to reality. A clear liberation of the use of the city's public spaces is taking place. The solemn centre of the city's administrative life, the Senaatintori Square, was adopted for new kinds of uses during the 1990's. For example, rock concerts, skateboard competitions and various art installations have been new kinds of events in this hitherto sombre and dignified environment.

Carnival culture arrived in Helsinki on a larger scale, too, in the course of the 1990's. The Night of the Arts and several other arts happenings have incorporated streets and buildings as part of the works of artists. For example, Mediterranean landscapes have been projected onto the Cathedral and its steps have been covered by coats bought in flea markets. A taste of popular festival but also of international trends have been conveyed by the concerts of world famous stars at the Stadium.

The Helsinki Festival Weeks have also succeeded in breaking conventional notions and ways of experiencing the city. In addition, the Festival's party tent by the Töölönlahti bay has introduced a debate about what kinds of happenings can be organised in the city and at what time of day. In any case, these kinds of cultural events have come to be increasingly important also for ordinary inhabitants of Helsinki resident outside the inner city.

The city dwellers have furthermore displayed interest and power of initiative in taking over public spaces for their own use. The former railway warehouses by the Töölönlahti bay became a kind of symbol for citizens' activities when there was a threat and later a decision to demolish the warehouses to make way for the new Music House. The background for this project is to be found in the overall planning of the Töölönlahti area and agreements between the city and the state on the use of land in the area. The warehouses have developed into a popular flea market and meeting-place and venue for various associations and groups. The inhabitants of Helsinki obviously need their own unofficial meeting-places in the centre to provide them with experiences in the city.

## Everyday public spaces – traffic and shopping centres

A common perception is that the metro conveys an urban lifestyle outside the city centre. However, the influence also moves in the opposite direction. As suburbs were built and most people came to own cars, the large shopping centres and markets in the suburbs began to compete with the department stores and smaller shops in the centre. The advertisement of the Itäkeskus shopping centre "always warm, no flies" epitomizes the philosophy the shopping centres offer people hunting for Christmas gifts in the sleet and the biting wind. Space has become shared, but, on the other hand, it does not belong to anybody. To a great extent, newly built, covered space is semi-public and covertly presupposes shopping.

This same 'shopping centre' phenomenon has increased the number of covered and underground spaces in the centre of Helsinki. In fact, it is already possible to move underground through most of the city centre. The centre might now feel very familiar to those who are used to moving in the large shopping centres in the suburbs and the metro, as these places have come to strongly resemble each other.

The aim during the last few years has been to make the centre more pedestrian-friendly. Parts of some streets are even heated in the winter so that they will remain free from snow and ice throughout the season. However, the creation of a more extensive pedestrian area would require the removal of cars from the city centre. Underground car parks have already been built at the Elielinaukio Square and the Kluuvi area, but the actual threshold for creating a pedestrian centre is the realisation of an east-west tunnel for traffic underneath the city centre.

## Solution: combination of old and new

By building the Kiasma Museum of Modern Art next to the equestrian statue of Marshal Mannerheim, even the authorities have demonstrated that not all old values are sacred. Yet, the result is a compromise: the statue was not moved elsewhere, as was suggested, and a window was added to the museum through which the statue is more visible.

During the years 1998–99 the Lasipalatsi (Glass Palace), Kinopalatsi (Cinema Palace) and Tennispalatsi (Tennis Palace) buildings were renovated or rebuilt. The project for the restoration of the copy of the Kämp Hotel strove

*Half of the centre's buildings are older architecture. Strong feelings about these buildings have made authorities protect them. The Glass Palace was restored in the late 1990's by the City of Helsinki and now serves as a centre for modern media. It houses a movie theatre (Bio Rex), television broadcast studios, internet library and media café. Photo: Jorma Kivistö.*

for the same retro mood. There is a wish in architectural developments to partly return to the past by restoring old buildings to their former – and probably grander than the original – glory. However, inside the exterior modelled on the old styles a lot of new features are built.

Television networks broadcast live images from the very heart of the city, in the studio on street level in the restored Lasipalatsi. They seek more "street credibility" for their broadcasts by looking for the latest trends in the most central place in Finland, and simultaneously, they create a profile, starting from their logotypes, adapted to the functionalism of the 1930's and 1950's. This same compromise – perhaps a successful one – is typical for Lasipalatsi as a whole. The activities in the building owned by the city focus on the production and development of services for the field of media.

A similar combination of new and old is attempted in Kinopalatsi and Tennispalatsi, here applied to more commercial aims. Both house cinemas showing new trendy films. Kinopalatsi merges its modern style with a name chosen from the 1950's golden age of the Finnish film industry (Kinopalatsi was one of Finland's most famous – now demolished – cinema theatres). Tennispalatsi, representing the style of functionalism, but totally rebuilt inside, offers its visitors not only cinema, but also restaurants and two museums. Another new covered shopping centre was built adjacent to the renewed Hotel Kämp, which rides on the image of the legendary hotel.

The restoration of old buildings also pleases the eye of old inhabitants of Helsinki. However, the activities in these buildings, for their part, are aimed at a younger audience. New residents of Helsinki, those who have spent their childhood outside the centre and those who have moved here from elsewhere, experience the centre differently from those who have at some point lived in the centre and hold memories from there connected to their own daily lives.

Nevertheless, the centre is also important for many new inhabitants. Most people move several times within the Helsinki region during their lifetime. Identification with Helsinki also through the city centre helps in adjusting to a new district or residential area.

For the older generations, the images of the centre are largely built on memories of the times when this area was their physical living environment. The younger generations increasingly obtain their own experiences of the centre through leisure activities. The quality of these experiences is being threatened by the centre developing into a faceless space serving narrow-minded commercial interests, or, on the other hand, into an externally beautiful city of façades, used for the marketing of the city and country abroad.

Helsinki has also begun to develop a profile as a city of culture that offers a multitude of experiences. However, apart from supporting high culture,

*The Citykäytävä is an old passage connecting the Railway Station to the city centre. It is inside a block that has both protected old architecture and modern architecture, such as the much hated "Makkaratalo" (built 1967). Photo: Jorma Kivistö.*

cities should also be able to provide space and premises for spontaneous public activities, voluntary work and alternative cultures. Somehow a means should be found for fighting the pricing principles of the value of land in the city centre and for an experience of pluralistic urban spaces.

Recently, a possible renewal of what has been called the ugliest building in Helsinki, the so-called Makkaratalo (the Sausage House) has been discussed. This has brought to the fore the wish of many inhabitants to keep the exterior of the building intact. They already perceive of the building as being part of their own world of experience. The everyday experiences are significant.

In order to increase the opportunity for a variety of experiences, spaces offering diverse activities should be provided. These create new ways of experiencing the city in everyday life. Through everyday experiences, also new inhabitants grow attached to their living environment.

## NOTES

[1] Part of this article has previously been published in the article "Kompromissiin päättyvä vuosisata – kaupunkitilan muuttuvat merkitykset" [A century ending in compromise – the changing meanings of urban space] in Keskinen Vesa (ed.), 1999 *Lama.nousu@hel.fi*, pp 63–72. Helsingin kaupungin tietokeskus.

[2] This sparsely populated area is limited in the north by the Töölönlahti bay and the Pitkäsilta bridge; in the east by the Suurkirkko church, the Senaatintori square and the Market Square; in the south by the covered market, the Kasarmintori square and the Erottaja crossing; in the west by the Vanha kirkko church, the bus station and the Parliament House.

[3] The names of the respondents have been changed.

## SOURCES AND BIBLIOGRAPHY

### Questionnaire

Questionnaire 1998 "Mitä Helsinki merkitsee minulle" [What Helsinki means to me].

### Literature

Astikainen, Riitta, Heiskanen, Riitta & Kaikkonen, Raija (eds.): 1997. *Elämää lähiössä* [Life in the suburbs]. Helsinki: Helsingin Sanomat.

Åström, Anna-Maria, Olsson, Pia & Kivistö, Jorma (eds.): 1998. *Elämää kaupungissa. Muistikuvia asumisesta Helsingin keskustassa* [Life in the city. Recollections of living in the centre of Helsinki]. Helsinki: Helsingin kaupunginmuseo.

Cantell, Timo 1998. *Yleisfestivaalien yleisöt* [The audiences of general festivals]. Tilastotietoa taiteesta nro 19. Helsinki: Taiteen keskustoimikunta.

Kivistö, Jorma 1999. Kompromissiin päättyvä vuosisata – kaupunkitilan muuttuvat merkitykset [A century ending in compromise – the changing meanings of urban space]. In Keskinen, Vesa (ed.): *Lama.nousu@hel.fi* [Depression.upswing@hel.fi]. Helsinki: Helsingin kaupungin tietokeskus.

TIINA-RIITTA LAPPI

# Nature in the City

## Remembrances and Modern Practices

In any discussion of the city and research into urban phenomena, our attention is often directed towards specifically urban cultural forms, urban
lifestyles; and when the urban environment is invoked, it is usually the built
environment that is in focus. The city is defined in opposition to the countryside and culture is that which is not nature. It is in this way that our thinking
– and thus also our research – often seems to be governed by dichotomies,
where the opposing poles of each dichotomy – in this case either the city
and the country, or culture and nature – are perceived as mutually exclusive
concepts. However, it is a consequence of the relatively late urbanisation of
Finland that here the countryside has for a long time been considered to be
the natural habitat for human beings, while the city has been regarded as an
"unnatural" one. Furthermore, in this context, the concept of 'unnatural' can be
understood to refer to two different qualities pertaining to the urban environment – the idea that it is an unsuitable place for humans and that it is a place
lacking nature, or perhaps rather as being above, or outside of, nature.

The modern city is, to a large extent then, based on the idea of a juxtaposition of nature and culture. The perception of cities as the highest achievement
of culture and development has affirmed the idea of the city emerging from a
process of taming and suppressing nature by imposing the conditions of culture upon it. As a result of this suppression, any nature which does exist in the
city has in a sense been made invisible and meaningless. In the juxtaposition
of nature against culture, the city has emerged as a place almost exclusively
of culture; consequently, nature has been equated with the countryside. In
this article, I will discuss the relation between nature and the built environment in the city, both from the viewpoint of the inhabitants' everyday lives
and life styles, and from that of city planning. My examination is not based
upon a juxtaposition of nature and culture, but primarily upon what characterises perceptions of the relation between nature and the built environment
amongst town dwellers and how these perceptions, for their part, construct,
on the one hand, the lived space of the town dwellers and, on the other, the
presented space of city planning.

> One big plus is that nature is close by here. I mean, we don't have to do
> anything but walk across the street to the schoolyard and then we can

235

go skiing from there. And the beach is only a couple of hundred metres from here, although we are still so close to town that one can cycle or walk there: no need to take the car. (Female, b. 1968.)

## Nature in the town dwellers' memories, experiences and daily lives

The attention of ethnological urban research has primarily been directed towards the cultural and social aspects of urban life. The inhabitants' relation to nature in the city has hardly ever been problematised, since nature is not regarded as belonging to an urban lifestyle. However, nature is so strongly present in Finnish cities and towns that it cannot be disregarded. Urban nature is a significant part of their environment and thus it is also significant for the ways in which the inhabitants experience their city and its various places, as well as for the meanings they attach to these. Here nature is part of the urban experience.

The experience of nature is part of an individual's relation to a place, their life in the place and their sense of location. "Where I am" is connected to "what I am". Nature is talked about through the expression of experiences, feelings, memories, values and functionality. Nature as it is experienced has concrete physical manifestations, such as a certain area such as a beach or sea view. Nature is realised in action through bodily experience, sensual experience: outdoor activities, boating and trekking. Nature can acquire considerable symbolic significance, even if it is only as an object of sight, such as the view from a window. Nature is also connected to spatial and temporal experiences, such as the changes of season and of the time of day. (Vilkuna 1997, 174.)

## "The forest"

We were in this place: there were cliffs and then further up there were more cliffs and when that school wasn't there, in the forest there where these big rocks on which we played a lot. So they were a very popular sort of playground, especially for girls, and sometimes, there, at the entrance to our sauna we played, and there on the steps, but often we sought out 'natural' playgrounds. There was also a beach there, we went right down there, it was called the Pysäkki beach. At that time there was a washing place at the beach. There was a big rock and around that rock there were large pots. They were there for general use: we didn't have one of our own, so we borrowed one of those. Everybody got a turn with a pot. We did the washing right there in these large pots and we rinsed the washing in the lake – the water of the lake was clean. And then there was Nurkkala the fisherman, who worked at the Schauman factory. He lived further up, on the other side of the road, but he often came down. Once I remember, I was doing the washing with Mum and we brought it back home to dry. But while we were washing, he came around, it was around five when he had come home from work and he said, now ladies come buy bream: his boat was packed with bream. He had caught some enormous bream in

236

the Jyväsjärvi lake. We also bought some and then we salted and boiled and fried the fish. (Female, b. 1929.)

Here is a town dweller's narrative which includes a description of her important childhood places in the Halssila district in Jyväskylä. The narrator reminisces about various activities in her local environment, but this is also quite an extensive description of the varieties of natural environment extant in the town at that time. The natural environments were important because of the activities connected to them, but they also display the significance of nature as part of the urban experience and the urban lifestyle of the period. Nature and the built environment were intertwined so that each formed an important part of the everyday lives of the town dwellers. Jyväskylä as a town has changed considerably since the period described above. The urban lifestyle and the inhabitants' relationship to places in the town have also changed. However, their relationship to nature is still a significant part of the town dwellers' environmental relation.

Interviewer: How do you feel about this as an environment for a child? Does the child find the kinds of thing here that she will still remember as an adult?
Informant: Well my immediate answer is that as a rule, no. There are a couple of parks, but that's not very much. They aren't really experiences. They're part of everyday life, but they don't provide that kind of experience. For example we realised that there is a bit of forest around here, and that's the kind of thing which does. We realised this when Sylvia wasn't even one year old, when we took her to the forest for the first time. She shouted for joy, it was so different. So the thing is that the forest is a special experience, but there isn't that much else here. Of course, there's the Äijälä place not too far from here. We went there in May and there were some animals there and it was like an old farmyard environment. That's like the kind of place I would like to be able to offer. The kind of place where there are things to look at and experience. And there aren't that many of these kinds of places. But one should seek them out.
Interviewer: Would you like to add any other place that you've come to think of?
Informant: At least one thing about Kuokkala, now that this shoreline is being developed, this Ainola shore area, so… I don't know exactly about the plans, what they are, but blocks of flats seem to have been built very quickly. I think it would be nice if they reserved some area there as a recreational space, that they would landscape properly as they are building, and include a recreational area, too. I mean some sort of park and a good bit of forest could be left, too. So that there would be something to offer the kids. Something that oneself had as a kid, that thing of being able to just go into the forest and have adventures and things like that… It was still so different at that time, one could find places to play and… Now most of the playgrounds are in the centre and they are like urban parks. They are parks, but the park consists of climbing frames and that kind of thing, there isn't anything natural – there could be just paths and the like. But it could still be a built area. There could also be some animals for example, but then the problem is how that would be arranged, how they'd be looked after and so on. So that's the kind of thing needed here.

237

> For example, as an environment the Korpela area is such that we often go walking there, since there are the kinds of thing to be found that can't be found here in the centre. It always feels like a release into something totally different. I go there a lot: when we go out we often walk there. (Female, b. 1964.)

The narrator's references to nature show, above all, the significance of nature as a shared world of experience for adults and children. In the rapidly changing town, the natural environment may function as a frame of reference for shared experiences, which feels less remote than the rest of the experiential world surrounding the child, since this differs from the childhood of the parent. "The forest" represents continuity and permanence. Another perspective is that the built urban environment is no longer necessarily experienced as so exciting and surprising as it perhaps was before. The town has become the arena for everyday rush and routine and therefore the town dwellers seek experiences and breaks from their daily routines in nature. Defenders of the town and urban lifestyle usually pay less attention to the fact that the town, to a large extent, is also a place of various compulsions and limitations. However, nature in town offers the inhabitants an environment the use of which is not defined as strictly as that of most other urban environments. In nature, the town dwellers can be relatively free or at least momentarily experience a feeling of freedom, as the use and experience of space is not externally defined.

At the level of people's experiences, nature can function both as a spatial and as a temporal marker. Nature as a concept separates grey from green, but, at the same time, it can function as a signifier in the relation between new and old. Nature can signify both presence and absence, that which is already lost, time and space. It can be a place to return or escape to; a place where people seek something pure and authentic. Resorting to nature can also be an acting out of a need to recover the past. It can be the focus of a desire to symbolically reach a space and time of purity that has never even existed in reality – a time before history and culture. The desire or need to be in nature is, in this sense, as much an expression of detaching oneself from a certain time as from a certain place. (Soper 1995, 187–188.)

> That clump of trees over there, that's where the older ones have their playground. Our son too has built there, in the old days, when there were more remnants from the building sites lying around: they built tree-houses and all kinds of thing there. This clump here, this nearer one. There should really be more of these, they should be left and not cut down. And take this one for example: this one is completely bare. If those trees were a little bit closer together, the area would be much nicer than those artificial parks. (Female, b. 1949.)

This narrator, as did the previous one, reflects on the significance of "real" urban nature, that is, planned nature, and of nature which exists outside the planned areas. Both narrators also emphasize the opportunities which are uniquely offered by the natural environment, and which are lacking in constructed parks and playgrounds. Within planning, parks usually belong to

238

the category "nature in town", but the town dwellers interviewed here rather perceive of them as built environments than natural ones. Only areas that are "left outside" planning are seen as part of the natural environment. From the viewpoint of the inhabitants' relation to nature, the built and cultivated parks belong to a different category to that of the areas of natural environment within the town. These two are also different environments from a functional and experiential perspective, which are not mutually exclusive, but different dimensions of people's relation to their environment.

From the town dwellers' point of view, the spatial significance of the parks is connected not only to their closeness to nature, but also to their functional character. Parks are not regarded as actual natural environments, but rather their importance consists in the way they effect a smooth intertwining of nature, built environment and social activity. In Jyväskylä, this has recently emerged strongly in the debate concerning the plans to change two different parks. The plans to move the Mäki-Matti Family Park to make way for a new school building were abandoned because of the town dwellers' resistance to the project (Korkiakangas, in this book p. 161). Work to change and renovate the Kirkkopuisto (Church Park) in the very centre of town was started in the autumn 2000. The renovations were described in the newspaper *Keskisuoma-lainen* (16.2.2000) as follows:

> The side of the Kirkkopuisto facing Vapaudenkatu will be developed into a more formal side of the park, as it is bordered by important public buildings of Jyväskylä, such as the Town Hall and the Civic Theatre. A small multi-purpose square will be built in the corner of Vapaudenkatu and Kilpisenkatu and on the Kilpisenkatu side a foliage-covered area will be created for cultural events organised by, for example, the future Centre for Music and the Arts. - - The aim is to achieve a harmonious and elegant solution comprising the area of the whole block. Apart from the park, the façades of the surrounding buildings and the parish church itself will also be illuminated. Soft light will also be directed onto trees, statues and benches. A water-and-light statue will be constructed in the park to create a separate theme.

Before work in the park was started, the town dwellers were given the opportunity to put forward their opinions in, for example, a notebook placed in the reception hall of the Art Museum. Strong opinions concerning the preservation of the valuable trees of the park and the general character of the Kirkkopuisto were voiced. Most of those who commented on the project think of the Kirkkopuisto as, above all, an important cultural environment, which is grounded in a balanced interaction between nature and the built environment. The Kirkkopuisto is hoped to provide a counter-force to the commercialism of the pedestrian thoroughfare starting from the corner of the park, and to remind the inhabitants of the town's temporal layers and continuity in the centre, which has undergone quite dramatic changes during the last decade. The following three quotes are examples of comments offered on the park project by town dwellers:

The exoticism of the town of Jyväskylä is based on the authenticity of its environment. On the university campus, old and new buildings stand harmoniously, surrounded by an untempered nature. Shopping areas have already occupied the centre of the town. Hopefully the spirit of the Kirkkopuisto will not be buried under this invasive materialism. Naturally, the old park must be renovated and its appearance freshened by new plantations, but obstructive and superfluous water features could be dropped: we already have our Aino and Minna (statues in the Kirkkopuisto).

Having lived in Jyväskylä for most of my life, I sincerely hope that the use of sense and sensibility would not be forbidden even in connection with so called renewals. The best feature of this rural university town is the respect for its proportions and its original natural growth. The Old Church of Jyväskylä, its old trees, the charming, unpretentious atmosphere of the park, all this should absolutely be preserved, if not for its spiritual, at least for its material values; tourists do not seek Disneylands in this part of the world, on the contrary. Leave the Kirkkopuisto in peace, instead, the town could be opened towards Puistokatu, using coloured lights and fountains, if that is absolutely necessary. Today, the pedestrian thoroughfare is a dead-end which needs opening up onto the Market Square and the Central Station: meanwhile the Kirkkopuisto is already alive and breathing. It seems to be difficult to admit the value and beauty of things old and original when they are close by, while people travel to foreign lands and cities to admire such things. So we should beware of strained, superficial trends that are forced on us in the name of renewal.

I think the surroundings of the dignified and beautiful church should not be changed this radically. The area around the church is planned to be a kind of market place with a mixture providing something for everybody. It is not an unreasonable wish that there be at least one real park in Jyväskylä. There is enough concrete on the shore of the Jyväsjärvi lake for those who want that. There are never too many trees in a town. Trees are the lungs of a town. Decision-makers, look at the stunning colours of the leaves in autumn! The old cultural heritage of Jyväskylä should be valued and the Kirkkopuisto renewed using moderate changes. We already have the Lounaispuisto park and the pedestrian thoroughfare with its restaurant terraces. The environment of the dignified church is not suitable for nightly noise, smells and untidiness which will undoubtedly increase if the character of the park is changed.

The inhabitants' relationship to nature and that of the planners appear very differently in town. From the perspective of planning, real urban nature is defined as built and cultivated nature, which has been appropriated and aestheticised by planning and tending (Vilkuna 1997, 171). The town dwellers' relation to nature is directed both towards this urban nature, defined by the planners as "real", and towards the urban nature, which from the planning viewpoint does not exist. When I refer to nature invisible to the planners, I mean the nature in town that has not been appropriated by planning. The area in Jyväskylä, where the centre of the district of Kuokkala was later built, can be instanced as an example of invisible nature or environment, which is thus meaningless, in terms of planning. In his book on Finnish urban architecture,

Jukka Turtiainen (1990, 52) describes Kuokkala as the centre of a district to be built "on empty terrain". From the perspective of planning, unbuilt terrain is empty, that is, void of meaning, until it is signified by building.

The town dwellers' expressed need to experience nature in town might also be an indication of the fact that their relation to the wider, free nature outside of town has been weakened or broken. The nature in town is familiar and safe; moving there does not require any specific skills or knowledge, in contrast to travelling, for example, to the wilderness or other large forest areas. The relationship of many town dwellers to nature has, in this respect, been urbanized. Nature in town is neither threatening nor alarming, since it is situated "inside" as opposed to the nature outside of town.

## The suburb – life on the border between nature and culture?

Suburbs are not perceived as proper urban spaces, since nature is strongly present in them, despite massive building, and they are often situated in the middle of a forest and in this way separated from the city itself. Thus, suburbs are a kind of border zone between city and nature. This border character is a feature of suburbs both from the point of view of city planning and in people's experience. Many studies have shown that the inhabitants of suburbs regard themselves as city dwellers, but emphasize the importance of the surrounding nature in their environment. The suburb is situated on the border between city and country spatially, but it is also a border zone in terms of its culture, which can be described using both natural and urban metaphors (Roivainen 1999, 196–197). In her doctoral thesis, Irene Roivainen interprets the suburb as a place situated not only on the outskirts of the city, but also on the outskirts of culture. It is not easy to classify the suburb according to those basic dichotomous categories which are particularly used within public discourse when describing reality. As a spatial phenomenon, the suburb disturbs a reality which is organised around binary oppositions. In the suburb, forests and fields are interspersed with an urban built environment. This relativizes and challenges cultural worlds which demand clear borders (Roivainen 1999, 200).

The definition of the suburb as a border zone between nature and culture, or between the country and the city, shows, above all, the desire on the part of both architects and planners to define what is "proper" urban culture and where this is spatially situated in the city (cf. Karvinen 1997, 150). This kind of definition ignores the significance of the city dwellers' own experiences. Urban culture is defined from a viewpoint which is wider than that of the inhabitants. For the city dwellers, their relation to nature and their relation to the built environment are both part of their relation to the environment, and not mutually exclusive or in opposition to each other. An outsider often finds it difficult to understand how a suburb consisting of huge boring concrete boxes can be characterised as a cosy living environment. However, outsiders usually form their view of a suburb through its visual appearance, while the inhabitants' relation to their own local environment is considerably more diverse. The significance of the natural environment might be particularly important in areas where the built environment is relatively monotonous. Nature offers suburban inhabitants access to experiences that they use to compensate the limitations of the built environment and possibilities of social interaction.

> As I just said, perhaps these houses here are a bit too close to each other, these yards and others are left so small, but of course this has again been decided by these outside considerations. But what I think is good here, is that one can go out into nature so easily. Even if this [Kuokkala] centre is so cramped, there are actually good routes in all directions into nature. There are lakes there and forest and so on, and that's like, if one feels restless one has to go there. (Male, b. 1928.)

Tage Wiklund (1995, 145), who considers the character of the Nordic city, does not perceive the city and the countryside as opposing categories, but understands them as standing in a dialectic relation to each other. Nordic suburbs and housing estates do not, in his view, externally differ very much from those in Southern Europe, but there is a decisive "invisible" difference between these. The suburbs in Southern Europe are of an expressly urban character. The Nordic suburbs, however, turn their backs on urban culture, artificial landscape and take on the identity of "suburbs of nature," looking out towards the natural landscape. As with Irene Roivainen, Tage Wiklund's view acknowledges the position of the suburb as being in a border zone, but he characterises housing areas according to whether they are more city or country oriented. However, suburban housing areas could also be studied as offering a distinctive way of living and being in the city. In that case, it might not be significant to ponder whether suburbs represent the country in the city or the city in the country, but what kind of urbanity is lived in the suburbs. Perhaps the distinctive character of suburban life could be found in that the lifestyle and identity of the suburbs is defined by the layering and intertwining of nature and city.

> When somebody asks me where I live, I say in Pupuhuhta. "Oh horrible, in Pupuhuhta, how can you?" And I say that's no problem, I can really live there very well and it's the most wonderful place to live. There's forest, nature, playgrounds for the kids, parks, schools, day-care. What else can we ask for? There's a shop, there are kiosks. Well, some like it that there's even a pub. - -There are family parks. What a wonderful environment for families with children to live in and now that they've done these renovations, improved the parks and the pathways and other things, and the houses have been renovated, too, so it's really nice. (Female, b. 1951.)

## The shores in town

In Jyväskylä, the building on the shores of the lake Jyväsjärvi has been debated – even, at times, heatedly. The shoreline leading to the town has been developed and moulded ever since the town was founded, but the opposite shore was left more or less in its natural state until the building of the new district Kuokkala was started there in the 1980's. The industrial estate situated on Lutakko Point since the beginning of the 20th century, moved in the 1990's and thus the area was available to be used for other purposes. The present building development on the shores of Jyväsjärvi is part of a trend to renew the town, which Jussi Jauhiainen (1995, 51–52) calls the phase of re-evaluating the inner town. A central aspect of this phase is the re-evaluation of the concept of urban space, which is a consequence of the increasing competition between towns and the growth of the information sector following the decline of industrial production. A re-evaluation of urban space has taken place particularly along the shore areas and on the former industrial sites. In the competition between towns, the creation of a positive image has become a central advantage, and this new image has been built by creating a new connection to the physical environment, particularly to former industrial sites and wastelands on the shores of the lake.

> Of course, it [Jyväskylä] was a small town, but extremely beautiful particularly when seen from the shore, there was the wonderful Rantapuisto park and in the park there was the restaurant. During all of my schooldays, Rantapuisto was this wonderful place, in the way that it represented something, something of times past. At some point there has even been a kind of spa there. It was very beautiful what with the whole boat pier and everything, and on the left there were these motorboats, and we too bought a motor and used it. So the whole of that shore, it was kind of very much alive and closely connected to the town. That's why I feel so sad now, when it's absolutely closed, the doors are closed to Jyväsjärvi, to the shores of Jyväsjärvi. Besides what happened there in the summer, in the winter there was a skating rink. It was there – if the jetty is here – then to the left a bit further off was the skating rink, where of course we bought skating badges and fastened on our hats and then always went out skating. (Female, b. 1913.)

For this narrator, Jyväsjärvi and its shoreline is a place connected with many important memories from her childhood and youth. The shore holds a very central position in her description of the town and life in it. The shore of Jyväsjärvi was the place for many activities and leisure and was thus closely intertwined in the everyday lives of the town dwellers. The narrator's first image of the town is connected to this shore as she arrives by boat from Lahti to take part in the entrance examination to the Girls' School. In the narrator's description, the shore emerges above all as a place for the inhabitants' activities rather than as a natural environment. Jyväsjärvi and its shores are, for the narrator, identified as an essential part of the centre of Jyväskylä. She feels that new building developments have detached the shore from its earlier connection to the rest of the town. A central individual factor changing the character of the shore was the construction of the four-lane carriage-way, the Rantaväylä, in the 1980's. Erkki Laitinen (1997, 87), in his article on the history of the road network of central Finland, notes that the Rantaväylä and its massive constructions landscape-wise have distanced and isolated

243

the centre of Jyväskylä from the Jyväsjärvi. However, according to Laitinen, the cycle and pedestrian lanes following the shore and the bridges and tunnels leading to these actually made the shores more easily accessible for the town dwellers.

In *The Book of Jyväskylä*, Anna-Maria Luukkainen (1997, 361) writes that even a lake within a city can be a real lake. According to her, however, the Jyväsjärvi should not be developed by planners into a mere pool surrounded by stone and concrete shores. The shores with extant vegetation should, whenever possible, be left in their natural state since water plants are an inseparable part of an authentic lake landscape. At the same time, they offer shelter and nutrition for the numerous other natural inhabitants of the lake. Luukkainen further notes that the contrast between nature and built environment does not conflict with the townscape of Jyväskylä, but enlivens it for the enjoyment of all town dwellers. Luukkainen focuses her exploration on the ecological features of the lake and its shores, but, in addition, she discusses the significance of the lake and its at least partly natural shores as part of the experiential world of the inhabitants. If the entire shoreline is built up, the lake is no longer a lake, but has become a pool. The landscape and image of the lake cannot be separated from its shore, since these together form the entity that we culturally understand to be a lake. When the shores change or they are appropriated by building, the image of the lake also changes. In the town dwellers' narratives, nature and the forest emerge as, above all, experiential dimensions, while the waterways and their shores are described in terms of landscape. The changing and building of the shores primarily change the landscape; they are clearly experienced as visual objects.

The shore in town is a concrete borderline between the built and the natural environment (cf. Karvinen 1990, 161), but does this border disappear when the shores are built? By moulding and building the shores of Jyväsjärvi, the lake is turned into a lake within the town: it becomes a "pool of knowledge". When the lake is appropriated by developers building on its shores, does the lake any longer form a natural environment? Has the border between the natural and the built environment disappeared? On the other hand, one might ask whether there needs to be a clear border between the natural and the built environment, or can these be successfully interlayered? The shoreline of the Jyväsjärvi, particularly that part which faces the town, has been filled out and moulded several times over more than a hundred years, a fact which is often used as an argument against those who criticise the increasingly rapid current building activity on the shoreline. If the shore has always been shaped to fulfil the needs of the growing and changing town, why could this not be done now? However, the debate on the building of the shores of Jyväsjärvi is not only concerned with building and changes in the urban environment, but also with the demarcation of the boundaries between nature and urbanity.

## On the relation between nature and urbanity

Nature is significant for town planning and associated decision-making, even if it is seldom problematised or otherwise made visible. Geographical and natural conditions have influenced the historical development of every town. Nature, for its part, has defined the development opportunities of each town. In addition, during various periods, different views on the relationship between the built environment and nature have governed urban building and the direction of the development of a town. For example, in the general plan for Jyväskylä made in 1968, "housing is placed on the shores of the waterways in urban strips, in order to maintain direct access to, on the one hand, the waterways of lake Päijänne and the river Tourujoki, and, on the other, to unspoilt nature".

The 1968 general plan reflects the influence of the garden city ideology on the definition of the inhabitants' relation to nature. The aim is to guarantee the residents an easy way out of the densely built areas and into the peace of nature (Päivänen 1996, 30). The connection to nature is also seen as relating to the increased leisure opportunities of the town dwellers and therefore special attention is paid to making nature accessible in the urban structure. The presentation of the general plan notes that the most common forms of leisure activity are outdoor ones that do not require any special skills or equipment – such as walking, swimming, trekking and skiing. Therefore, to meet the interests of the majority of the population, the main focus should be on the location and quality of areas that provide a setting for these simple forms of outdoor activity. Attention is also paid to the value of the natural landscape. The town dwellers' wish for access to nature and an experience of the landscape actively influences the development of the townscape. According to the presentation, the objective should be to preserve whole landscapes as natural scenic areas (Jyväskylä General Plan 1968, 28, 82–83). The primary aim of Nordic town planning at the time of the plan, to serve democratic humans in a democratic society (cf. Ilmonen 1997, 57), emerges also when the plan is studied from the perspective of the inhabitants' relation to nature. Contact with nature and as easy an access to nature as possible is understood as the inalienable right of all town dwellers.

In today's town, the relation of planning to nature appears quite differently. The emphasis on the urban character of the town also influences how nature in the town is understood. The urban relation to nature is perceived as pertaining only to nature that has been defined as urban nature from the perspective of planning: which is to say it has been aestheticised and appropriated through planning. Appropriation defines who the assumed and welcome users of these places, for example parks, are, and how these areas should be used. From the viewpoint of planning, areas in town that are in their natural state are only potential building sites, meaningless until signified through planning and building. When developing the town, various areas, places, spaces and building are ascribed meanings and from the perspective of planning these always exist for a certain purpose. Nature is not defined in this sense and thus it does not belong to the same category as the rest of the urban environment. Nature escapes planning since it cannot be defined and signified in the same way as the built urban environment. It is not appropriated and controlled by planning.

The significance of urban nature might be emphasized in, for example, the marketing of a certain housing area. The Kuokkala district in Jyväskylä was marketed as a town of the future: close to nature, surrounded by forests and lakes, comprising spaciously built houses, workplaces and services located in the midst of nature, but closely connected to the central town (Brochure on Kuokkala 1.10.1987). When the inhabitants later oppose additional building on some of the district's natural areas, this perspective on the significance of nature is no longer regarded as important.

> Of course, that is, if you topicalise it, it seems as if like they talk about it: when she comes in and the talk turns to nature, she at once raises her hand. Some niggler again. They have kind of a negative attitude at once. Not everything is as negative though. When you really think about it a lot of money has been invested in these large recreational areas here. When projects come up in which they used to try and improve these places too, the blunders that have been made here. Why make them again? (Female, b. 1951.)

Defenders of the natural environment are alleged not to understand what constitutes a real town. Nature in town seems to be an extremely ambivalent phenomenon. It is present everywhere, but its existence and significance is still difficult to grasp or define clearly. Nature in town does not seem to have any value in itself: its meaning (or meaninglessness) is always defined in relation to something else.

As the ideal of social equality, which earlier governed the development of towns, has been relegated to the background in planning, the perception of the town dwellers' equal right to nature has also changed. For example, areas on the lakeshores which have been open to all inhabitants are increasingly planned to be turned into areas for private housing. "Dream plots for the wealthy" was the headline of an article in the newspaper *Suur-Jyväskylän lehti* (14.6.2000) about the planned building on lakeshore plots. According to the article, there is a plan to build "a Viitaniemi for this millennium, an abode for modern living" in Haukanniemi on the lake Tuomiojärvi. Earlier, the town council had decided that the area would be planned as a public park and recreational area for the inhabitants. The explanation for the changed plans is the wish to attract good taxpayers to the town by offering them the opportunity to high-quality living by a lake close to the town centre. The elite is attracted to the town by offering them housing opportunities close to nature, while, at the same time, suburban inhabitants are accused of a lack of understanding when they defend the nature and recreational areas surrounding their housing estate.

Both building on the shores and the additional building planned in existing housing areas are expressions of the prevailing ideal of a densely built townscape. This ideal can be seen as part of ecological modernisation, a concept that refers to a change in the relation between humans and nature, which is taking place throughout society. While earlier phases of development in society were governed primarily by economic and social issues, there are now signs that the relation between human beings and nature is emerging as the central defining factor in the new developmental phase (Kortelainen & Vartiainen 2000, 10). In town planning, concentrated building is regarded as producing both environmental benefits and financial savings. However, within town politics and planning, ecological modernisation and the ideal of concentration as part of this have, so far, appeared more frequently in discourses and social constructions used to plan and define the outline of societies, rather than in actual practical measures taken (Kortelainen & Vartiainen 2000, 14).

The debate on concentration also reveals a connection to a wider discourse on urban politics, one which pertains to the definition of a good townscape and desirable urbanity (cf. Päivänen 1996, 25). A densely built town is regarded as a cultural expression of a "real" town and as creating a clearer and sharper distinction to the surrounding countryside. Thus the discourse on concentration is not only a matter of ecological sustainability, but also of the competition between towns, where the idea of towns as concentrations of financial and cultural attraction factors is increasingly important (cf. Päivänen 1996, 25). The politicised ideal of concentration might become a socially accepted rationalisation for many of the more tacit objectives of urban renewal (Kortelainen & Vartiainen 2000, 18). Building on the shores and additional building, that is, concentration of the urban structure, thus express the changing perception of the relation between the built and natural environment in town:

> The creation of a kind of stone town character here in central Finland, in the Lake District of Finland, is almost a kind of mission in my life. At the moment there's precisely one major city in inland Finland, and that's Tampere, and I hope that Jyväskylä will be the second one. To achieve this the town must be properly developed. It must look like a city and there must be paved streets and quays and stone shores, and of course there must be parks on the shores too. That's obvious. But I think it's totally stupid to maintain a kind of weed thicket in the middle of town. (Civil servant.)

The juxtaposition of nature and urbanity is strongly present in the thinking and work of the town planners, although these are not mutually exclusive as experiential dimensions. From the viewpoint of the inhabitants' experiences and signification, nature and urbanity are not alternatives or opposites, but both have their own positions and meanings in the lives of most town dwellers. A town of opportunities could be envisaged as one that offers opportunities for both natural and urban experiences. Riitta Nikula refers to a conviction that often emerges in debates on urbanity, namely the one that Finns are people of the forest who only move into towns when they are forced to do so. This is related to the idea that being in direct touch with the earth and nature is more important for Finns than being in contact with other people (Nikula 1990, 5). However, I find that such a juxtaposition in exploring urban identity and urban life narrows the interpretation of the town dwellers' relation to nature.

Using narratives on forests, shores and suburbs, I have explored the significance of the interaction between nature and the built environment as part

247

of an urban lifestyle. The town dwellers' narratives on nature are not only narratives about nature and its meaning, but also narratives about culture. They can certainly be perceived as narratives on culture since the intertwining and parallel existence of nature and the built environment are used to define and defend the uniqueness and identity of Jyväskylä as a town. While a visionary of the future wants the Rantaväylä of Jyväskylä to be reminiscent of the seaside boulevard in Cannes (KSML 9.4.2000), letters to the editor criticize the building on the shores of Jyväsjärvi as turning Jyväskylä into "another Helsinki":

> The concrete on the Kuokkala side of the bridge is also advancing rapidly. The shore is already becoming a competitor for the horrible coal dusty concrete hell intended for living in the Merihaka area on the Sörnäinen shore in Helsinki. During the next few years, all of the Ainolanranta area will be turned into something resembling the gloomy housing along the Mannerheimintie street [in Helsinki], where all the trees have been felled and the empty spaces filled with houses. (KSML 1.3.2000.)

As urban culture changes, urban landscapes are increasingly places for consumption, places for social activity and round-the-clock carnivals. The opportunity for public display is a defining characteristic of towns, and thus the idea of withdrawal and detachment which is typically included in discourses of nature functions as its counter-force. However, nature and the built environment are not separate, but intertwined, and together they structure the urban landscape and the town dwellers' relation to nature. The parallel existence of nature and the built environment is a matter not only of the uniqueness and identity of Jyväskylä, but also of urban culture, which is not based on a dichotomy between greenness and urbanity, but on the significance of these as different dimensions of an urban lifestyle.

## SOURCES AND BIBLIOGRAPHY

### Material

My main material for this article was the body of interviews with inhabitants of the centre of Kuokkala which I collected in Jyväskylä during 1994–1995 (20 in total), interviews collected within the Finnish Academy project *Kaupunkilaiset ja heidän paikkansa* [Town dwellers and their places] in Jyväskylä (22 in total), and feedback given at the information desk for the planning of the Kirkkopuisto park during 13.8.1999–10.1.2000 (102 entries in total).
KSML = Newspaper *Keskisuomalainen*

### Literature

Ilmonen, Mervi 1997. Pohjoismaisen kaupungin aika [The era of the Nordic Town]. In Liisa Knuuti (ed.): *Aika ja kaupunki* [Time and town]. Teknillinen korkeakoulu. Yhdyskuntasuunnittelun täydennyskoulutuskeskus. C 44. Espoo, 51–59.
Jauhiainen, Jussi S. 1995. *Kaupunkisuunnittelu, kaupunkiuudistus ja kaupunkipolitiikka. Kolme eurooppalaista esimerkkiä* [Town planning, urban renewal and urban politics].

*This paper serves some of what is needed in a closing perspective or epilogue. But only on certain themes.*

Turun yliopiston maantieteen laitoksen julkaisuja N:o 146. Turku.

Jyväskylä. *Yleiskaava 1968. Kaupunki ja maalaiskunta* [General plan 1968. Town and the rural district].

Karvinen, Marko 1997. Kaupungin ranta kulttuurisena rajana [The urban shore as a cultural border]. In Tuukka Haarni, Marko Karvinen, Hille Koskela & Sirpa Tani (eds.): *Tila, paikka ja maisema. Tutkimusretkiä uuteen maantieteeseen* [Space, place and landscape. Explorations in the New Geography]. Tampere: Vastapaino, 143–162.

*Keskisuomalainen* 16.02.2000: Kirkkopuiston kunnostus alkaa ensi elokuussa [The renovation of the Kirkkopuisto begins next August].

*Keskisuomalainen* 01.03.2000: Betonilla vuorattu Jyväsjärvi (mielipidekirjoitus) [Jyväsjärvi lined in concrete. Letter to the Editor].

*Keskisuomalainen* 09.04.2000: Jyväskylä voi pelastaa itsensä ja koko maakunnan [Jyväskylä can save itself and the whole region].

Kortelainen, Jarmo & Vartiainen, Perttu 2000. Kohti ekomodernia kaupunkiseutua? [Towards an eco-modern urban region?] In Jarmo Kortelainen (ed.): *Vihertyvä kaupunkiseutu. Suunnittelun ja hallinnan ekomoderni käänne* [Urban regions turning greener. The eco-modern turn in planning and administration]. Jyväskylä: Jyväskylän yliopisto. SoPhi 47, 9–31.

Laitinen, Erkki 1997. Reunasta reunaan – Keski-Suomen tiepiirin 50-vuotinen taival [From end to end – 50 years of the Road District of Central Finland]. In Seppo Kosonen, Tauno Rantala, Rismo Virpimaa & Inka Joensuu (eds.): *Keski-Suomen teillä. Keski-Suomen tiepiiri 50 vuotta* [On the roads of Central Finland. The Road District of Central Finland during 50 years]. Tiemuseon julkaisuja 16, 9–196.

Luukkainen, Anne-Maria 1997. Kilpailu rantaviivasta kiristyy. Jyväsjärven kasvillisuus muutostilassa [Tighter competition for the shoreline. The vegetation of the Jyväsjärvi in a state of change]. In Ilkka Nummela (ed.): *Jyväskylän kirja. Katsauksia kaupunkielämän vaiheisiin 1940-luvulta 1990-luvulle* [The book of Jyväskylä. Studies of urban life from the 1940's to the 1990's]. Jyväskylä: Jyväskylän kaupunki, 358–361.

Nikula, Riitta 1990. Hyvä luonto ja paha kaupunki [Good nature, bad town]. In J. Kautto, I. Holmila & J. Turtiainen (eds.): *Suomalaista kaupunkiarkkitehtuuria* [Finnish urban architecture]. Helsinki: Suomen rakennustaiteen museo, 5–19.

Päivänen, Jani 1996. Avara luonto, tiivis kaupunki? [Spacious nature, dense town?] *Yhteiskuntasuunnittelu* 2/96, 24–36.

Roivainen, Irene 1999. Loukoista lukaaleihin eli miten työväestö kotiutui lähiöön [From huts to flats, or how the working class settled in the suburb]. In Elina Katainen, Anu Suoranta, Kari Teräs & Johanna Valenius (eds.): *Koti kaupungin laidalla. Työväestön asumisen pitkä linja* [A home on the edge of town. Long-term trends of working-class housing]. Työväen historian ja perinteen tutkimuksen seura. Väki Voimakas 12, 187–203.

Soper, Kate 1995. *What is nature? Culture, politics and the non-human.* Oxford & Cambridge: Blackwell.

*Suur-Jyväskylän lehti* 14.06.2000: Unelmatontteja varakkaille [Dream plots for the wealthy].

Turtiainen, Jukka 1990. Suomalaisen kaupungin jälleenrakennus [The rebuilding of the Finnish town]. In J. Kautto, I. Holmila & J. Turtiainen (eds.): *Suomalaista kaupunkiarkkitehtuuria* [Finnish urban architecture]. Helsinki: Suomen rakennustaiteen museo, 49–54.

Wiklund, Tage 1995. *Det tillgjorda landskapet. En undersökning av förutsättningarna för urban kultur i Norden* [The pretentious landscape. A study of the prerequisites for urban culture in the Nordic countries]. Göteborg: Bokförlaget Korpen.

Vilkuna, Johanna 1997. Kaupungin eletyt ja institutionaaliset luonnot [Lived and institutionalised nature in towns]. In Tuukka Haarni, Marko Karvinen, Hille Koskela & Sirpa Tani (eds.): *Tila, paikka ja maisema. Tutkimusretkiä uuteen maantieteeseen* [Space, place and landscape. Explorations in the new geography]. Tampere: Vastapaino, 163–178.

Compare chapes 3 + 9 ∴ they are by the same
author + the only pieces on Nyborg.